STRATEGY IS YOUR WORDS

# Strategy Is *Your Words*

A STRATEGIST'S FIGHT FOR MEANING

## Mark *Pollard*

NEW YORK CITY

Design by Nerrida & Ben Funnell, April77 Creative www.april77.com
Editor Lauren Wilson, Glow Words www.glowwords.com
Printed in China by Asia Pacific Offset.

ISBN: 978-1-950372-00-3

Mighty Jungle
www.mightyjungle.co
More strategy writing exists at www.markpollard.net and @markpollard.

DEDICATED TO TEJA, KADEN, AND KISUN.

# Table of
## *Contents*

**INTRODUCTION: FIGHTING WORDS** . . . . . . . . . . . . . .13

**SECTION I: OPERATING WORDS** . . . . . . . . . . . . . . . .29

**CHAPTER ONE: LIFE WORDS** . . . . . . . . . . . . . . . . . .31

Meaning Is Yours to Make . . . . . . . . . . . . . . . . . . . . . . . .32

Clarity Is When You Say It Is. . . . . . . . . . . . . . . . . . . . . . .36

Truth Is Disobedient. . . . . . . . . . . . . . . . . . . . . . . . . . . . .40

Fog Is Clarity Coming . . . . . . . . . . . . . . . . . . . . . . . . . . .45

Mischief Makes for Danger . . . . . . . . . . . . . . . . . . . . . . .51

Rejection Waits to Pounce . . . . . . . . . . . . . . . . . . . . . . . .53

Impostors Belong, Too . . . . . . . . . . . . . . . . . . . . . . . . . . .57

Lone Wolf, Are You Really? . . . . . . . . . . . . . . . . . . . . . . .60

Tether Yourself to Yourself . . . . . . . . . . . . . . . . . . . . . . . .66

Practice Plays the Bass . . . . . . . . . . . . . . . . . . . . . . . . . . .70

Publishing Takes You Public. . . . . . . . . . . . . . . . . . . . . . .76

A Gang Can Keep You Safe. . . . . . . . . . . . . . . . . . . . . . . .81

**CHAPTER TWO: WORK WORDS** . . . . . . . . . . . . . . . . . . . .87

Art Is in the Margins . . . . . . . . . . . . . . . . . . . . . . . . . . . . . .88

Existence Is for Arguing . . . . . . . . . . . . . . . . . . . . . . . . . . .95

Empathy Is a Powerful Burden . . . . . . . . . . . . . . . . . . . . . .98

Feelings Are Clues . . . . . . . . . . . . . . . . . . . . . . . . . . . . . . .103

Drama Sets Your Stage . . . . . . . . . . . . . . . . . . . . . . . . . . . .107

Information Can Crush You . . . . . . . . . . . . . . . . . . . . . . . . .111

Opinions Are Everywhere . . . . . . . . . . . . . . . . . . . . . . . . . .116

Sounds Are Pleasant Surprises . . . . . . . . . . . . . . . . . . . . . .124

Selling Isn't Cheap . . . . . . . . . . . . . . . . . . . . . . . . . . . . . . .127

Monogamy Makes Words Mean . . . . . . . . . . . . . . . . . . . . .131

Writing Breaks Open Safes . . . . . . . . . . . . . . . . . . . . . . . . .134

Patience Is Long Enough . . . . . . . . . . . . . . . . . . . . . . . . . .140

Operating Words: Summary . . . . . . . . . . . . . . . . . . . . . . . .147

**SECTION II: STRATEGY WORDS** . . . . . . . . . . . . . . . . . .151

**CHAPTER THREE: IDEAS ARE FIRST & FOREVER** . . . .153

The Secret About Ideas . . . . . . . . . . . . . . . . . . . . . . . . . . .153

Ideas Live To Fight . . . . . . . . . . . . . . . . . . . . . . . . . . . . . . .156

Not All Thoughts Are Ideas . . . . . . . . . . . . . . . . . . . . . . . .162

All Ideas Cross the Line . . . . . . . . . . . . . . . . . . . . . . . . . . .165

Silent Adjectives Are Slow Deaths . . . . . . . . . . . . . . . . . . .173

Ideas Come Big and Small . . . . . . . . . . . . . . . . . . . . . . . . .177

Every Idea Has a Type . . . . . . . . . . . . . . . . . . . . . . . . . . . . .180

The Types of Ideas in Advertising . . . . . . . . . . . . . . . . . . . . .181

The Types of Ideas in Detail: A Walk-Through. . . . . . . . . . . .182

An Example: Hello Hallow—A Company In the Business
Of Fear . . . . . . . . . . . . . . . . . . . . . . . . . . . . . . . . . . . . . . . . .192

Who Gets to Have Ideas? . . . . . . . . . . . . . . . . . . . . . . . . . . . .194

The Ideas of a Strategist . . . . . . . . . . . . . . . . . . . . . . . . . . . .199

For Campaign Ideas, Specific Is a Savior . . . . . . . . . . . . . . . .203

How to Write an Idea. . . . . . . . . . . . . . . . . . . . . . . . . . . . . . .206

These Ideas Are Scary, Aren't They? . . . . . . . . . . . . . . . . . . .212

**CHAPTER FOUR: THE FOUR POINTS FRAMEWORK** . .217

A Warning About Frameworks. . . . . . . . . . . . . . . . . . . . . . . . .217

A Stroll Through The Four Points Framework. . . . . . . . . . . . .220

The New York Knicks in The Four Points Framework . . . . . . .227

Form Your Points Then Frame Them . . . . . . . . . . . . . . . . . . .233

**CHAPTER FIVE: PROBLEMS ARE WORTH HAVING** . . .237

Problems Can Do Good . . . . . . . . . . . . . . . . . . . . . . . . . . . . .237

Problem Tools. . . . . . . . . . . . . . . . . . . . . . . . . . . . . . . . . . . . .248

*Winning Happens High.* . . . . . . . . . . . . . . . . . . . . . . . . . . . . .248

*Dump-a-Problem* . . . . . . . . . . . . . . . . . . . . . . . . . . . . . . . . . .252

*SWOT* . . . . . . . . . . . . . . . . . . . . . . . . . . . . . . . . . . . . . . . . . .255

*The Problem Behind the Problem* . . . . . . . . . . . . . . . . . . . . . .259

*The 5 Whys* . . . . . . . . . . . . . . . . . . . . . . . . . . . . . . . .262

*Four Lines On A Big Piece Of Paper* . . . . . . . . . . . . . . . . . . . . .262

**CHAPTER SIX: INSIGHTS ARE SURVIVAL** . . . . . . . . . . .267

Yeah, but How Serious? . . . . . . . . . . . . . . . . . . . . . . . . . .267

The Difficulty with Insights . . . . . . . . . . . . . . . . . . . . . . .270

How Insights Work . . . . . . . . . . . . . . . . . . . . . . . . . . . .277

How Insights Happen . . . . . . . . . . . . . . . . . . . . . . . . . . .283

Questions That Fetch Insights . . . . . . . . . . . . . . . . . . . . . .288

How to Write an Insight . . . . . . . . . . . . . . . . . . . . . . . . . .292

How to Help a Workshop Write an Insight . . . . . . . . . . . . . . .294

Insights Help Us Escape Problems . . . . . . . . . . . . . . . . . . . .298

**CHAPTER SEVEN: ADVANTAGE IS YOURS TO GIVE** . . .303

Ask Your Way to the Edge . . . . . . . . . . . . . . . . . . . . . . . .303

The Pyramid of Advantage . . . . . . . . . . . . . . . . . . . . . . . .305

The Benefit Ladder . . . . . . . . . . . . . . . . . . . . . . . . . . . . .312

The Product World . . . . . . . . . . . . . . . . . . . . . . . . . . . . .316

The Decision Funnel . . . . . . . . . . . . . . . . . . . . . . . . . . . .321

Path to Purchase . . . . . . . . . . . . . . . . . . . . . . . . . . . . . .324

**CHAPTER EIGHT: STRATEGY RATS OUT PROBLEMS** . .331

Strategy Is Important but Whose Is Most Important? . . . . . . .331

A Secular Start is a Clear Start . . . . . . . . . . . . . . . . . . . . . .332

What Strategy Is Not . . . . . . . . . . . . . . . . . . . . . . . . . . . .334

How Other People Block Strategy . . . . . . . . . . . . . . . . . . . .336

How to Know When Strategy Has Happened . . . . . . . . . . . . .338

Ten Ways to Write a Strategy . . . . . . . . . . . . . . . . . . . . . . . . . .341

1. Strategy Statements . . . . . . . . . . . . . . . . . . . . . . . . . . . . . .341

2. Single-Minded Propositions. . . . . . . . . . . . . . . . . . . . . . . . .341

3. Brand Essences. . . . . . . . . . . . . . . . . . . . . . . . . . . . . . . . . .344

4. CEO Announcements. . . . . . . . . . . . . . . . . . . . . . . . . . . . . .345

5. Purpose Statements . . . . . . . . . . . . . . . . . . . . . . . . . . . . . .345

6. Vision and Mission Statements . . . . . . . . . . . . . . . . . . . . . .347

7. Strategy Stories. . . . . . . . . . . . . . . . . . . . . . . . . . . . . . . . . .349

8. Creative Briefs . . . . . . . . . . . . . . . . . . . . . . . . . . . . . . . . . .353

9. Strategy Shapes . . . . . . . . . . . . . . . . . . . . . . . . . . . . . . . . .359

10. Press Release Headlines . . . . . . . . . . . . . . . . . . . . . . . . . . .359

Communications Frameworks – A Short Word . . . . . . . . . . . .361

STRATEGY WORDS: SUMMARY . . . . . . . . . . . . . . . . . . . . .369

FINAL WORDS . . . . . . . . . . . . . . . . . . . . . . . . . . . . . . . . . . .373

WORD . . . . . . . . . . . . . . . . . . . . . . . . . . . . . . . . . . . . . . . . . .377

ABOUT THE AUTHOR . . . . . . . . . . . . . . . . . . . . . . . . . . . .379

BIBLIOGRAPHY . . . . . . . . . . . . . . . . . . . . . . . . . . . . . . . . .381

STRATEGY IS YOUR WORDS – CHEAT SHEET . . . . . . . .386

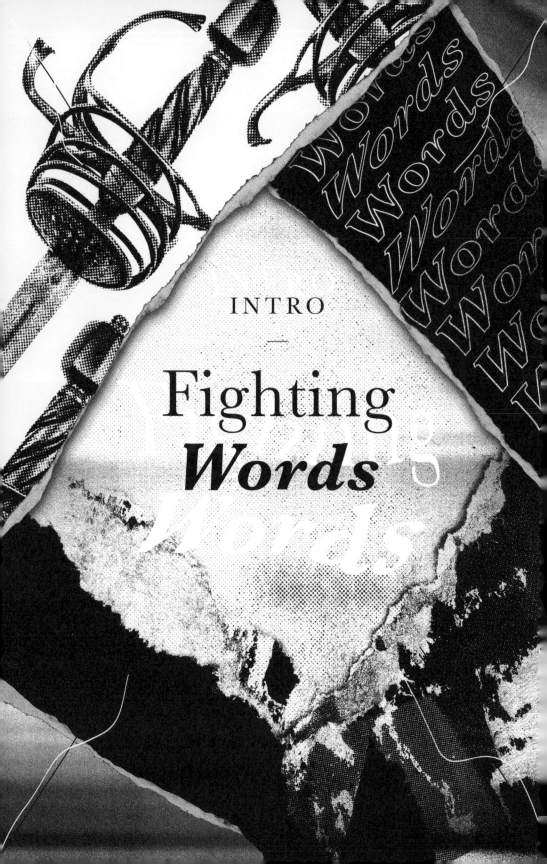

INTRO

—

# Fighting *Words*

# Fighting *Words*

T he village of Flero, Italy, once sent forth into the world a
man with the mane and mettle of Inigo Montoya. A stroll
from Brescia and a male gaze east from Milan, Flero features
on few lists. It is an enigma beyond public review because all
a review of Flero could say is this: "Once, I passed through."
A bus stop on the way to places where people race to lose
themselves, find themselves, and document themselves losing
and finding themselves, Flero's singular claim to fame is this
angelic person it made. The claim to fame is so muscular
it makes the town adequate for history – an utmost Italian
accomplishment. After all, how much history is enough history
when one shrewd way to handle the present is to let the
future dribble through and not chase after it? So, Flero's nine
thousand villagers now watch the future rush everywhere else,
while enjoying their handshake with fame and guarding the
elixir from which their man burst.

Unlike the angel from Flero, Inigo Montoya lives in fiction.
Born in William Goldman's *The Princess Bride* and raised in
Florin, Montoya is a swordsman whose broken heart beats

to avenge his father's death. He is a human rainbow with the hair of a stallion battling the world between drunken storms. But this rainbow beams only when he feels close to revenge, because revenge is how he knows himself.

Montoya's violence dances the tango. His catchphrases are the high notes of a sommelier tasting wine from ancient space grapes. His single-mindedness ravishes the loins of the soul. In *The Princess Bride*, Inigo Montoya is the mourning spirit inside everyone, yet he perseveres.

And what Inigo Montoya can do with his hands and a rapier, the man from Flero could do with his feet and a ball. The name of the man from Flero is Andrea Pirlo.

Andrea Pirlo sports a pristine carpet of beard. All beard hairs know where to stand at all times. Their rectitude is the definition of "kempt" for they are bonsai and kempt bonsai is the only bonsai. Hair the color of wet sand frames Pirlo's face. Its wisps lash and dart with every tack, turn, and twist. His sun-leathered skin is a souvenir from a lifetime in football's riskiest arenas.

Football, not fencing, is Andrea Pirlo's romance. He makes love with a football as Inigo Montoya makes love with a sword thrust to the heart. To marvel at Andrea Pirlo's passes is to watch comets and stars shoot through the night sky. If a pass streaks overhead, lovers touch lips to seal their fates. Andrea Pirlo's romance with football is a whole-body romance. But his feet make it happen. His feet can get balls places, and this skill takes him places.

From Brescia to AC Milan and Juventus, from the Olympics to the FIFA World Cup, from Italy's Serie A to the UEFA Champions League, Andrea Pirlo's ability to get the ball where it didn't know it needed to go took him where he didn't know he needed to go. After a long career in the powerhouse clubs of Italy, it took him to the fledgling football fiefdom of the United States.

On July 26, 2015, at the age of 36, Andrea Pirlo's aging feet raced him from the rich emerald grass of Europe to the temporary turf of a South Bronx baseball stadium. This move would have surprised the young Andrea Pirlo, because New York City Football Club didn't exist until 2015, Yankee Stadium isn't big enough for a full-sized soccer field, and one year earlier Pirlo was still able to place as the seventh-best football player in Europe. The UEFA Men's Player of the Year Awards were a long-haul flight from the Bronx, but the Bronx is part-Italian, so perhaps it wasn't too far from home—just far away enough for a gradual retirement. After all, Pirlo's feet were always up to something.

And then it happened. The man Flero's pride propelled into the world, who bore the nicknames "the architect," "the professor," "maestro," and "Mozart," spoke for strategy by speaking about football. And he spoke about football by speaking about football in his new and temporary abode, the United States of America, during his brief fling with Major League Soccer.

"It's a very hard league to play in. It's very physical, there's a lot of running. So there is a lot of physical work and to me, in my mind, too little play," Pirlo said.[1]

Yes, Andrea Pirlo turned 37 the week he said this, in the spring of 2016, but he wasn't airing an old athlete's chagrin. Listen again: "A lot of running … too little play." This is wisdom from the mystical bowels of Flero. And if you draw your ear close to the words—yes, closer still—you can hear the deathbed snake rattle of a strategist.

A lot of running; too little play.

Andrea Pirlo knew how to get a football where it didn't know it needed to go. This meant some of his teammates didn't know where they needed to go to greet the footballs that didn't know where they were going. *Andrea Pirlo's game was to make the football do the work; the American game was to make the player do the work.*

American players grow up in a culture that prizes running. The USA knows who can run. It knows who can't run and it watches to see who runs. If a player doesn't run, the player doesn't last. This is a survival reflex born from the dregs of the Puritan work ethic, where work thrusts believers closer to God. And in a vast and bountiful country from which many have thought they could take what they could find if they could just

---

[1] Henry Engler, "MLS making gains to bridge 'cultural void': Pirlo," Reuters, May 20, 2016, https://www.reuters.com/article/us-soccer-mls-pirlo-idUSKCN0YB23Y.

run there first—a belief that saw the trampling of the continent's native peoples and environment—running still has its uses.

Running helps us catch airplanes from the broken maze of LaGuardia Airport, keep up with Maryland crab races, flee bad first dates with white-collar fishermen in Seattle, sightsee Nashville's hot chicken in an hour, beat Los Angeles freeway traffic, gallop around Central Park in New York so we can tell the Internet later, chase venture capital funding in San Francisco while avoiding 3:00 a.m. trouble in the Tenderloin, make dramatic entrances into Miami surf even though it doesn't really surf there, dodge drunken traffic late at night in Austin, grab Black Friday discounts from a Minneapolis shopping mall without strangers treading on us, release endorphins during a stint of celibacy in rural Oregon, and enter Heaven before everyone else. Running is so American, it made the USA. In return, the USA made jogging.

These evolved uses of running are light years away from its original uses: to flee predators and to eat. Indeed, running to eat might have made us look the way we look. We used to chase animals until they collapsed. With extreme fear, stress, or exhaustion, our prey would experience "capture myopathy." Their muscles would just stop. We'd run and run and run until the animals froze. Then we'd eat the animals, unless we were vegan. All the chasing led to humans with running legs that could last for long distances. This was before farming, refined sugar, couches, traffic, office desks, and home delivery. It was also before football.

The differences between a football and an animal abound. Footballs do not have legs, brains, eyes, ears, voices, wings, arms, instincts, adrenaline, or meat. Footballs are inanimate objects. We do not *need* to chase footballs until they collapse. We don't eat footballs, even though some footballs are vegan.

But chase-to-collapse is how some people play football and how many people play business. Running is the most important activity. Having others see one run is the second most important. And, if you think about it, all this running represents the gears of capitalism: people inventing needs for others to chase. "Look, here's a ball. Go fetch. Yes, bring it back to me and I'll throw it somewhere else and you'll go fetch it for me, won't you? Of course, you will. Good dog." The US is a world leader at this. It's also a world leader at exporting this mindset. And so the world started running because running made the USA.

A lot of running; too little play.

Running is everywhere. When people think they have never attended so many meetings, received so many emails, and watched so much Tetris on organizational charts while having so little work to show, that is running. When weekly check-ins, annual reviews, and an urban sprawl of job titles do not arrive at better work, that is running. When vague marketing briefs produce vague workshops with too many people in them who are vague about why they are there, but each has to act like the boss of the room, that is running. When timesheets are a career's oxygen, profit-and-loss statements are kingdoms, and salary freezes last an ice age, that is running. When people discuss meeting agendas, meeting minutes, and email chains more than good work, that is running. When a strategy deck is one hundred slides long, ideas need twenty-five reviews by people who do not put pen to paper, and company decisions demand every human in the village, that is running. When the management team hosts offsites that lead to initiatives that lead nowhere, when the management team announces another agency repositioning in gobbledygook, and when the management team spends more time with itself than with its people, that is running.

Company hackathons with no follow-up, late nights patching together a pitch because the new business team sat on the marketing brief for two weeks, speaking about thinking at ad-tech conferences, senior people absent from a pitch changing the pitch the night before the pitch, whole agencies being ordered to brainstorm together but only the account team showing up, clients briefing agencies before they go on vacation, nearly all HR interactions, pitching to keep an abusive client—running running running.

Besides, are you even working if other people can't see you working?

Jobs are now spectator sports. That's why thinking must happen in public. That's why we are suspicious of introverts and their inner lives. That's why we need everybody together at all times even if somebody tries to take a day off.

But some running is better in the head. This running is called "strategy." Because if everyone is running, who's thinking? And what game is this? And isn't there another game we can play?

To play a game, you need a goal, rewards, rules, an
opponent, somewhere to play, and something with which to
play. Inigo Montoya knows his game. He is the only person
playing it. His goal is to avenge his father's death. Revenge
is his reward. His rules are a swordsman's honor. The man
who killed his father and scarred his face, Count Rugen,
is his opponent. A sword fight is the place, and a sword his
play object. Andrea Pirlo knew his game, too. His goal was
to win football matches. Fame and riches were his spoils.
His rules were the rules of an international football association.
A football field was the place, and a football his object.

As much as their manes mark them similar, one flaw
distinguishes Inigo Montoya from Andrea Pirlo. This flaw
is a lack of strategy.

In *The Princess Bride*, Inigo Montoya knows what game he
wants to play, but Inigo Montoya does not have a strategy.
Unable to play his game for many years because he was unable
to find Count Rugen, Inigo Montoya drinks himself into
stupors. His stupors are his soul laughing at his lack of strategy.
His stupors are his soul yelling at his brain to find new meaning.
And his tale lays bare the perils of a life that commits to a
single event of meaning before it ends. The soul knows irony
when it sees it.

Andrea Pirlo had a strategy: to make the football surprise
opponents. His tactics were to play in deep positions just in
front of his center backs, to keep the ball moving pass after pass,
to dispatch the football in stunning ways to his teammates, to
drill it at the goal from further out than expected, and to wear

his Italian locks and bonsai beard throughout. These tactics broke conventions—certainly in the US, and often in Europe as well—because the conventions were based on athleticism. The conventions were to run, dribble, blast, yell, and muscle your way to the goal. The conventions didn't include finesse, calmness, and moving the ball in rare ways. For his entire career, Andrea Pirlo's strategy dismantled opponents because his strategy understood the conventions within which his opponents and teammates operated. Where Inigo Montoya had flailed without a strategy, Andrea Pirlo had vanquished with a strategy. But strategy doesn't happen in isolation and, in New York, Pirlo's waning legs knew they were running on foreign ground.

"What I'm talking about is actually a system or culture. I don't mean that the level of technical skills are low. I just mean there is a cultural void that needs to be filled," Andrea Pirlo explained during the same interview in which he lamented the lack of play in US football. To acknowledge this void was for Pirlo to see his strategy without a home. New York is full of surprises for people who've succeeded elsewhere.

A lot of running; too little play.

When Andrea Pirlo diagnosed football in America, he also diagnosed the field of advertising and strategy. He could easily have been describing agencies, clients, and colleagues running around a football field. And among them is one strategist, hoping to Andrea Pirlo a winning strategy to the rest, but nobody knows how to receive it and people are too busy running to receive the ball anyway. And this assumes the strategist is capable of creating a strategy at all.

A culture is a set of behaviors born from a set of beliefs. Running for no reason comes from a belief that conspicuous activity makes your career happen. Conspicuous activity is a yellow Ferrari roaring in slow-moving traffic down the New Jersey turnpike. It's unnecessary activity that others can see. At first, it's confusing in the way that the husky heavy-metal men of Oslo's late-night bars resemble runway models more than broken spirits. But then it catches on. Timesheets measure it and job titles reward it.

Thinking is an inconspicuous activity. It happens in the privacy of the mind. This makes it hard to watch. It's one reason meetings exist—to weed out thinking. But, here's the trick: like businesses, meetings are not democracies. Just watch how your next meeting discusses what's normal to the group, how it attempts to reinforce hierarchy, and how it talks over any out-there thinking. Come for the ideas but stay for the mind control.

This game confuses many migrant office workers who believe they have landed in a country fond of the individual, freedom, and democracy. All this talk about how important you are and how teamwork makes dreams work flies in the face of research. Research shows top-down decisions are common in American businesses,[2] and this is despite the number of meetings businesses have (more than ever)[3] and the length of

---

[2] Erin Meyer, *The Culture Map: Breaking Through the Invisible Boundaries of Global Business*, PublicAffairs, 2014. Richard D. Lewis, *When Cultures Collide: Leading Across Culture*, Nicholas Brealey International, 2006 (Originally published 1996).

[3] Leslie A. Perlow, Constance Noonan Hadley, Eunice Eun, "Stop the Meeting Madness," *Harvard Business Review*, July-August 2017, https://hbr.org/2017/07/stop-the-meeting-madness.

time they take to reach decisions (longer than ever).[4] We believe in your opinion as long as you keep it to yourself.

If you work in a creative company, this game is even more bewildering. You plug your rebel self into an organizational chart where your job is ideas but only if someone more senior than you doesn't have ideas and then your ideas might end up as their ideas. You must share your thinking as it happens while never knowing what someone more senior than you is really thinking– if they are thinking. Your thoughts must rush into words in front of other people otherwise people won't know you're working. You see others who excel at this climbing the ladder above you. You think, "Work out loud. It's safer that way." But is the work any good? And have you forgotten what you believe in?

Beautiful creative companies build themselves on behaviors that serve the creative mind—all of the creative mind. That includes the creative mind's strengths and weaknesses, its need for quiet and for stimulation, its need for validation and its struggle to accept it, its need to create for the sake of creating and for this act to happen daily, its need for space to explore meaning, and its constant attempts to find a place in the world. A creative company does this because it believes creativity gives it and its clients an edge. Creativity needs private time, and, when ready, creativity then needs public fame.

And since words are the basic unit of meaning in human communication, creative companies demand more from words.

---

[4] *Tom Monahan, "The Hard Evidence: Business Is Slowing Down", Fortune.com, January 28, 2016, https://fortune.com/2016/01/28/business-decision-making-project-management/.*

Creative minds use words to expose truth, not hide from it. Creative minds want to free their words, not constipate them. Fierce brains abound in strategy, but too many of their public words enter a corporate-business-park dystopia. That is the cultural void Andrea Pirlo saw.

With football and revenge and glorious hair, Andrea Pirlo and Inigo Montoya achieved meaning. This is more than many of us accomplish. Pirlo achieved it with a strategy that worked on one continent but not on all. Montoya achieved it in spite of his lack of strategy. This is called luck.

Meaning can fleet; focus can drift. And running because everyone is running, especially when everyone is running off cliffs and bridges, with scissors and bayonets, with maps stuck to their faces—well, what is this?

It's not play. Play is majestic. Play knows the heart of the game. Play knows itself. Play is unafraid to create new rules, to challenge new opponents, or to adapt itself because of new challenges. Play is you, a strategist, returning to your principal object with a light heart. This object is words.

Andrea Pirlo has retired from football and now explores the meaning of the second half of his life. This is a spiritual exercise for most humans, in which we must reckon with ourselves before reckoning with death. Meanwhile, Inigo Montoya has reckoned so much with death in his lifelong quest that he will have to reckon with life—and whether he can find a strategy to stave off the drunken stupors—after avenging his father.

In the film version of *The Princess Bride*, Inigo Montoya staggers to his revenge after stumbling into Wesley's mission to free Buttercup from the terror of Prince Humperdinck. His final scuffle with Count Rugen starts with a dagger piercing his stomach as he flies into the banquet room of Humperdinck's castle.

Montoya sinks against the wall and bumps to the ground, pulling the blade from his guts. Count Rugen mocks him and prepares for his victory. But Inigo Montoya finds muscles in his elbow and parries the Count's mustached thrusts. Once. Twice. Two more times. He gathers himself and pushes off the wall, his dreams faltering in his blood-drenched vest and shirt, and he stalks the retreating Count Rugen with a new, eerie resolve.

"Hello. My name is Inigo Montoya. You killed my father. Prepare to die."

Montoya says this three more times between sword thrusts. He corners Count Rugen and tells him to offer him everything he asks for. The six-fingered man says, "Anything you want. I'll make you associate senior strategy director or executive junior head of planning. I'll give you a five-thousand-dollar bonus. I'll give you phantom equity so you think you own the company but you'll never own the company. I'll let you work all the hours in the world. I'll give you a corner office, though not mine. I'll send you to Cannes. Do you want a summer intern? How about extra legroom for your swords? You can fly to meetings in business class from now on." Then he sneak attacks. But Inigo Montoya catches his arm. And as Montoya slashes a fatal stab into Rugen, he whispers, "I want my craft back, you son of a bitch."

Enough running. It's time to play.

YOUR MISSION:
PLAY
MORE THAN YOU
RUN

@MARKPOLLARD

# SECTION I

—

# Operating *Words*

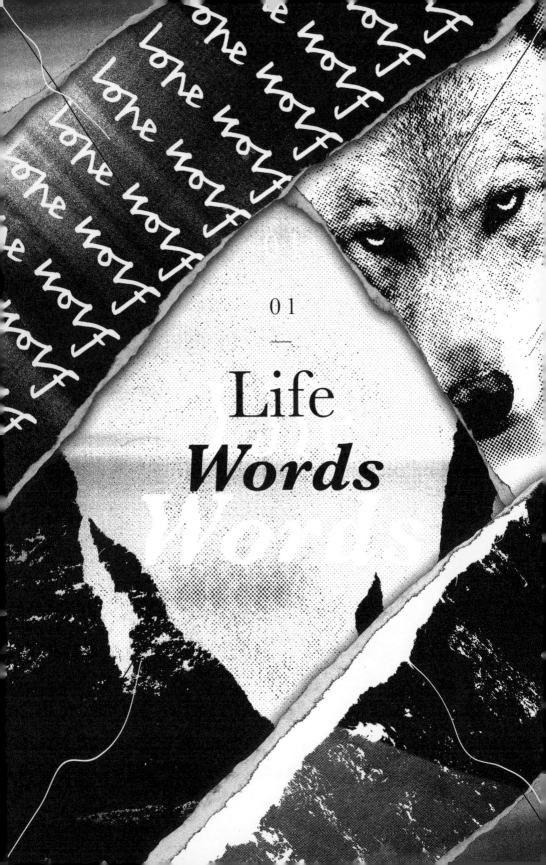

01
—
# Life
## *Words*

# CHAPTER ONE

# Life *Words*

I f you live a strategy life, you live in a constant rummage
for meaning. Your cravings for clarity hurtle you in every
direction. You pause only to glare truth in the face. Truth is
dangerous when it glares back, and there is always more truth
to find, and so your strategy life is restless. In a hushed frenzy,
you lurch between knowing, wanting to know, not knowing
what you need to know, and worrying you'll never know
enough. You're a maniac for meaning, but your binges turn
to driftwood as listless phases tempt you from your quest. A
career high falls to Earth and you lay fetal next to it and spoon.
A frosty fog drapes itself on you, and you await the next frenzy.

Truth-hunting makes your strategy life a life of mischief.
Societies prefer obedience rather than mischief, so you'll run
into rejection like a seagull flying into a sky-sized pane of glass
as it tries to snatch the world's finest fish and chips from a
deep-ocean trawler in a shallow harbor. Every day. Into glass.
That crispy batter. Over years, this lust for mischief can turn
on you. What am I even doing here? Am I the only one who
can see this? Does anybody want any of this? I don't belong
here. I am an impostor.

And because a strategist might feel like a lone wolf foraging in the forests of capitalism, years of meetings and workshops and business-speak can loosen your grip on your internal compass. You might lose sight of your own truth. Or marry someone else's.

One day the wilderness pushes you home. There you rummage in yourself. You realize your hysterical quest for truth out there was one way to hide from the truth in here. Fetal no more, you clear the mess and tether yourself to the waiting bedrock. You go back to the wilderness, but now you know how to survive it. Practice, publishing, and a gang keep the bedrock clear and the tethers strong. And now your strategy life's hell-bent rummage for meaning becomes your life bent, and strategy work is life's work.

## MEANING IS YOURS TO MAKE

Meaning is what you make of it. Like life. Also like sand, Jell-O, flour, paper, and strawberry shortcake–scented pink bubbles in a bathtub on a long weekend when the family is away at a chess tournament and you think to yourself, "Well, I might as well." If you do strategy work and if you believe you cannot make your own meaning in life, you'll keep your brain in a torture chamber. If you find it but you fail to commit to it, you'll create a hellish limbo for which even the nearest, least crowded IKEA won't contain instructions.

Strategy is a constant rummage for meaning. Here is what somebody said, but this is what it means. Does it connect to this? What if it did? What if it always did and nobody ever saw it? To what else does it connect? To what doesn't it connect, and why, and what if it really does? Or what if it could? It's a high-RAM lifestyle and the computing is ceaseless.

Who'd want to rummage for meaning every day? All the dust and dust mites and those dead moths and goo at the bottom of the closet next to the mildew at the back there. Who'd want any of that? All that world-seeing and people-meeting and idea-having and book-reading and meaning-making. Who'd want any of that? Well, a strategist would. You would. You might need it. What's worse is you might only feel you know yourself when you're lost in a rummage. So you rummage.

But what if your rummages are how you distract yourself from your inability to find more lasting meaning for yourself? You can say your meaning is finding meaning, and you'll mean it when you say it. However, after your second or third layoff, you'll question your own wit and nuance. You'll wonder if your foraging was an attempt to soothe the chaos closer to home. You'll struggle to recall your own meaning because your compass pointed everywhere but inside. It pointed to school grades, college applications, jobs, and promotions, all the while saddling you with debt, flattening friendships, and pushing away loved ones.

This questioning doesn't just happen after the age of forty, when some get the itch to reevaluate their lives and ponder, "Am I locking this in?" It happens during internships when you wonder, "Is this what I signed up for? There aren't even any strategy jobs for recent graduates. Shall I accept the account executive role and hope I can move later?" It happens as people reach their thirties. "Is this all there is? At thirty, I thought I'd know the answer. I love what I do. Well, I love the idea of what I do. Doing it is hard. Other people make it hard. People suck. Maybe I need to volunteer. Or do yoga in an ashram. Does Bali have ashrams?" It happens after a baby appears. "I don't know if I want to return to work. Everything will pale in comparison to this little shitting and eating demon creature that means everything to me and because it means everything it has set a new benchmark to which nothing else can rise. At least until week four, when I'm exhausted and I just want to sleep through a night, one night, any one night … or under my desk at work." Your gluttony for meaning can take many shapes, and those shapes will shift.

A life of finding meaning for others is steady as long as the idea of wanting to do it is steady. The work is not steady at all. It's this, it's that, it's nothing, it's everything. It's this plus that but not this. It's one more meeting, another review, a lost client, a won client, a good boss, a bad boss, a new tool, an abusive colleague. It's a cowboy standing in the middle of a seesaw that can buck from either end at odd times as if it were two separate rodeo beasts. *When you make yourself by making meaning for others, meaning is always there for the making*, so steady is when steady says.

Everywhere he looked, psychiatrist Viktor Frankl discovered prisoners finding meaning in World War II concentration camps.[5] As he wrote in *Man's Search for Meaning*, they found it in their futures, in helping other prisoners, and even in their

---

[5] *Victor Frankl, Harold S. Kushner (Foreword), William J. Winslade (Afterword), Isle Lasch (Translator), Man's Search for Meaning, Beacon Press, 2006 (first published 1946).*

suffering. They found meaning by squeezing it from death and despair with all the strength left in their starved, overworked hands. Because, as Frankl learned firsthand, prisoners whose hands lost their grip on meaning didn't last.

It's not that you are a prisoner in your strategy life— although French philosopher Michel Foucault would see open offices as conniving panopticons,[6] inventions designed for surveillance more than productivity. But your hands, too, grasp meaning as a noble way to stave off thoughts of death and despair. Watch your brain if you need proof.

At its faintest, meaning is a bridge that helps people move from one day to the next. At its most vibrant, meaning is a catapult that flings us into the stars. It takes focus to arrive at and a strong hold to keep still. It's an attempt to clutch the infinite and cattle-rustle it into a plastic bottle filled with miniature plants so you can put it on a bookshelf, stand back, and say, "Look, I caught a butterfly." "It will die in there," says a voice over your shoulder. "Yes. Yes, it will," you say. You smile small and lean in to study the universe beating its wings, and you make it to the next day.

*You seek meaning because meaning makes you. But you make your own meaning.* And with this comes responsibility. Which meaning will you choose to make yourself with? At what point is it specific enough, big enough, enough enough? Oh, they didn't teach you how to do this in school? Why would they? School's not for that.

---

[6] *Michel Foucault, A.M. Sheridan-Smith (Translator), Discipline and Punish: The Birth of the Prison, Vintage, 1995 (first published 1975).*

School is for information, tests, and jobs. School doesn't want you to think about meaning because then you might challenge the meaning of school. You need to teach yourself this.

Emotions are our school for meaning. They're our teachers. While we don't always know what to do with them and which we are allowed to have, emotions teach us what is meaningful to us. If you're sad or angry, why are you sad or angry? When weren't you sad or angry? When have you felt alive? Can you remember when time didn't matter? What were you doing? Where? With whom? Can you build your life around these ideas? If you can catch the feelings, you can dig for meaning. This is the rummage the strategy life can lead you to. If you let it.

Clear, isn't it?

## CLARITY IS WHEN YOU SAY IT IS

Peekaboo. Clarity matters more than truth. Peekaboo. Many lies are clear. Peekaboo. Some lies are useful. Peekaboo. Without clarity is confusion. Peekaboo. A strategist who confuses others is a regular strategist. Peekaboo. Public confusion can lead to public clarity. Peekaboo. Public clarity can lead to private clarity. Peekaboo. Too much confusion will cost a strategist's career. Peekaboo. Too much confusion will steal your sense of self. Peekaboo. Sometimes people steal someone else's clarity and make it their own. Peekaboo. Clarity. Peekaboo. Clear? Peekaboo.

A penguin, a sloth, and a social media influencer walk into a bar. Old leather seats with cuts and creaks and rusty steel legs sit knee-high under a maelstrom of loud bodies. The social media influencer places the penguin on a stool and slings the sloth around her neck. It's happy hour in Temple Bar, Dublin. Temple Bar isn't just one bar. It's a scrum of bars, many of them on a street called Temple Bar. This scrum wraps its big arms around people's necks and heaves toward an invisible try line.

A try line is an endpoint. It's a wide target. It's where a rugby player kisses a ball to the grass to score points. A rugby player can do this between the try line and the dead ball line. There are two types of rugby and the two types of rugby player score tries in the same way, even though they play two different types of rugby. There are seventeen types of penguin. Maybe twenty. This type of penguin is fond of a Guinness or two or three. It's crass to count in Ireland. This is why Dubliners refuse mathematics in school and Irish sloths fear numbers the way influencers fear a failed social media post. And so the penguin drinks her Guinness and one thing is clear. This penguin is thirsty.

Clarity is an arm wrestle with chaos in which free hands are allowed to punch the opponent in the mouth. You judge who wins, but if you decide clarity has won, that is really just a starting point. It's a preemptive heckle: "Here's what I think about you." Whether the clarity lasts minutes or years, the win gives both clarity and chaos what they want. Clarity gets clarity and the chaos gets to grow. More clarity, more chaos. There is always more chaos to wrestle. They need each other like a strategist needs a creative brief.

Clarity is a social game. Like the Declaration of Independence, *you can just declare it and it is until someone else declares it isn't.* "I've cracked it," you say. But your clarity needs allies for it to exist outside your head.

Your clarity will take gentle steps into public. You'll hope colleagues will see it and join you in a goodwill melee. Some will. Some will put your clarity into a school playground headlock and rub its hair. "Yes, this is so good and so clear. Are you open to sharpening it even more? Have you thought about this? What about that? Aww, the client will love this." Some won't. Instead of a goodwill melee, some of your clarity will enter a cage fight. You'll face combatants defying your clarity with their own clarity in a battle for their egos and budgets.

And then there are the spectators of clarity. You'll work with many spectators in your life. The harmless spectators sit in meetings and watch. Their goals are to not look stupid and to not hurt feelings. They'll pretend they have clarity when they need to. These bystanders seem benign, but they cost time and air. And beyond them are the evil spectators.

Evil spectators exist in most companies. They offer no clarity. They add chaos with bravados of self-importance, noise, and words. Or they stay silent and wait to ply their trade later, when they'll undermine everything they have heard.

Clarity is a game that happens when you and your fellow game players believe it has happened. When you believe it has happened, then you'll know what to do.

When clarity happens, action happens. That is the point of clarity. With clarity, the team can act. But clarity isn't pure. People can hear the same words and have those words mean different things. You can put this to the test by touring the words "idea," "insight," and "strategy" around an office. See what kind of definitions you get from different players.

Clarity happens within a context. Think of this phrase: "I'm going to beat you." It seems clear. But it's not. Imagine the person saying it is holding a chessboard. Now holding an egg beater and a carton of cage-free eggs. Now wearing boxing gloves and a blow-up sumo wrestler costume. Now flaunting a tank top, drunk eyes, and a baseball bat. Imagine the person is a police officer holding a baton. Clarity keeps changing, which means clarity doesn't stop. Clarity needs to continue to happen so that actions can adjust. You don't get to lock it in like you're about to win *Who Wants to Be a Millionaire*. You move from one arm wrestle with chaos to the next, and you hope there aren't too many punches in the mouth. Mouthguards for your feelings help.

Clarity is your drug. It's how meaning feels. It's a runner's high with a runner's exhaustion but without the runner's legwork because the running happens in the brain. When you say you want clarity, you sign up for all the chaos it drags with it. Chaos is your enabler, the price you pay. With each moment of clarity, chaos sprawls and ink-runs to new corners of the paper, and it beckons you with a crooked finger to rummage in it. This is why you need more than one moment of clarity. You need clarities.

## TRUTH IS DISOBEDIENT

Strategy is a search for truth. Strategy seeks to find truth, determine what it means to a business, then prance it through the corridors of capitalism in a parade of clarity. But few businesspeople "do" truth in the building. "Get that truth out of my face. We don't need it here. It's stabbing my eyeballs." This makes sense—truth has been married four times, has two restraining orders against it, carries three daggers, works five jobs, survives off tips, and enjoys a casual meth addiction. Truth is difficult because it is the business world's trailer trash. It's seen as messy and savage, and it keeps its own hours. It defies the idea of work because work exists to numb the soul, not scar it. Truth can be scarring because it shows us things we don't want to acknowledge.

How people use the word "truth" suggests it lives in hiding and only the threat of violence can seduce it into the light. "Truth" is extracted by coerced confession. "Tell me the truth. We won't leave here until you have. How's that waterboard?" "Truth" tests relationships. "Tell me the truth—you'd never lie to me, would you?" And "truth" starts criminal trials. "I swear to tell the truth, the whole truth, and nothing but the truth." The word is wedded to high-stakes punishment, so living a life turned away from truth is one strategy to avoid pain. But that's just one truth about truth.

The truth about truth is there are many types of truth. *The journey for most strategists is from truths that are banal and don't give anybody an edge to truths that are surprising and give many people an edge.* For instance, people use hands to turn the pages of books.

This is a banal truth—everybody knows it and it doesn't give anyone an edge. But more truth about page-turning might exist. Is there a way to turn the pages of a full-length book within sixty seconds and commit the words to memory, and do few people know about this? If so, we now have a truth that can give people an edge—an edge truth.

Banal truths litter the early years of your strategy life, as you seek to fit in and survive and pay off debt. But over time, your ear will develop a disdain for the banal. In its stead, a zeal for the extreme will appear. This journey to the edge may take many seasons. You'll read case studies, research papers, strategy books, books about those books, and so much research you won't know what to do with yourself when you're not reading research. Your ideas will test themselves in public and they'll report on how they fare. And no matter what, you'll live. And this is critical. You'll suffer, but you'll live. Love, travel, jobs, loved ones, awards, and titles will come and go, come and go. Mud-laden step by sludge-slogged schlep, you'll plod to the edge of strategy's domain of knowledge to find truths that give people a competitive edge. This journey will turn you radical.

As you reach the edge, the land ahead will disappear into a cliff. Above, dark clouds will grind and lightning will crack. Below, sharp rocks will rabbit-punch fishing boats and heave waves around their necks. The wind will rip your clothes asunder. Naked, you'll stretch for the horizon and glare at the storm's eye. "Is this it? Is this all you have for me? All this reading and researching and writing? All the late nights and working weekends? All the timesheets? The timesheets.

My thoughts were only for them. I didn't want to sell time
in the first place. Time isn't even real. But you took it all."

The storm will hold its choke grip. You'll take a crouched
boxer's stance, plant one foot back, and toe a divot in the dirt.
The storm will hurl ogre whales and narwhal trolls at you.
It will slap you in the face with goblin bats. A mini golf course
of all the holiday parties you've ever attended will flying-saucer
at your head. A death breath of a trillion ping-pong balls
will pummel your skull. Flying fish zombies of all your failed
relationships will purge from a hole in the sky, and there are
a lot of them, so they'll fall for hours. It will hail feedback.
Still you'll grit and stand and soak.

After days, the wind will abate and you'll emerge raw from the
cliff with a colossal haul of storm truth. Now you'll see people
as they are, which is as they want others to see them, and you'll
allow them that while also looking through them. You'll also
see yourself with clearer eyes because you'll no longer need a
mirror or camera to look at yourself. You'll see truth everywhere,
like Patagonia vests and anklet socks on Wall Street in early fall
and the miniskirts shorter than hats that swarm the streets of
Manhattan SoHo in spring. And here your strategy will take a
turn and you'll shift from obedient truths to disobedient truths.
You might even leave behind the ideas of "right" and "wrong."

Education systems have taught many a strategist that "right"
answers are the only answers. After all, right answers are easier
for computers to grade. Right answers teach the student to
obey questions, not challenge questions. Right answers are how
solutions moralize rather than intrigue. Right answers seduce

the brain into thinking only enough, but never more and not too much. Right answers teach the student there is only one way to succeed. The other way is wrong. Obey. Comply. Conform. Approved. Next. But why live such an obedient thinking life?

Obedient truths start with Yes. Along St. Stephen's Green in Dublin, not too far from the scrums of Temple Bar, is a sign that shouts the words "Handcrafted Sandwiches." "Handcrafted Sandwiches" sound like sandwiches a sweet grandmother laced with love potion and hugged into existence. "Handcrafted Sandwiches" sound like a Valentine's Day gift for the stomach pit. "Handcrafted Sandwiches" sound like they will renovate the sandwich eater's soul, and who doesn't need a little more light in there? Together the two words heat the belly, coat the throat, and tickle the jowls. Scrumptious. These are obedient truths because we are obeying the sign.

Disobedient truths start with No. "Handcrafted Sandwiches"? No. Why are those two words together? What makes those two words belong together, and do they belong together more than two other words? Has anybody made a sandwich in Dublin that is *not* handcrafted? Do robots make sandwiches now and do those "Robotcrafted Sandwiches" horrify the mouth? Is the word "hand" in "handcrafted" sweating profusely? Yes, it's drenched. It's doing more work than "crafted." Well, how else have people tried to craft sandwiches? Are there Facecrafted Sandwiches, Elbowcrafted Sandwiches, or Buttcrafted Sandwiches? Could a squad of underpaid workers with basic healthcare and minimal vacation time hunker over a conga line of bread and craft sandwiches with their asses? Yes, it's feasible. But we'd need to disobey the hand-appeal of our original sandwich sign to make Buttcrafted Sandwiches fascinate the public.

Disobedient truths start with No and then they turn aggressive. If "hand" is straining the most, what if we attack it? What do hands want us to think? Hands want us to accept the current world order and to look down on the butt. People use their butts to sit, dance-grind, bump, bottom-burp, prostate-check, hide things, retrieve things, reverse-spoon, make the sex, scoot, run, lift, climb, and toilet. The butt is Jan's "Marcia, Marcia, Marcia!" to the body's smug *Brady Bunch*. Hands are the majestic firstborn. Hands write songs, conduct orchestras, hold babies, pet puppies, point at fireworks, and hug the universe. Hands hold and make what matters. The butt gets rid of it. That's what hands want us to believe. But what does the butt think of all this? How would it defend itself from behind its white underpants? It would say hands are dirty. Hands go places no other single body part can go. They enter nostrils, mouths, ear holes, front *and* back toilet bits. And they clean. Butts don't clean. Hands clean sinks, toilets, germs, baby poo, and cat sick. Butts are sheathed (except by nudists). These are disobedient truths. These truths disobey the "Handcrafted Sandwiches" sign, but they are still true.

Disobedient truths don't stop at the first No. The first No is the start. The first No says, "There's more to this and many other ways to look at it. Let's flex." And then the brain frolics. "Here is a truth. What makes this true? Who benefits from people's belief that this is true? What if it isn't true? Which part of it is most true? Which part of it is least true? Why is this part least true? What if there is another truth about this? What are obvious truths about this? What is a playful truth? A taboo truth? An absurd truth? What would have to happen for these truths to exist?" This is how Buttcrafted Sandwiches could conceivably become the most festive lunchtime event seen this century on Dublin high streets, and put hands into unemployment lines and trouser pockets everywhere.

Your strategy life is a quest for disobedient truths. It's not an easy life. Sometimes, you'll have to withdraw to survive. When a meeting is in a flinching convulsion because the truth turned naughty and got all up in everyone's brains, you might need to save yourself with a few lullaby reassurances sung under your breath. "Everything is OK. You're OK. I'm OK. We're all safe here. Look, here comes the catering cart. I'm going to leave the room now. Someone will send me next steps. My next step is out, out into the fresh air-conditioning. It will blow the tears from my face. And then we'll do it all over again this afternoon, yes? Yes. Can't wait. Great meeting, everyone." But after you commit to a life of disobedient truths, you'll struggle with too many of these withdrawals. A salary can only soothe you for so long.

### FOG IS CLARITY COMING

A lifelong quest for meaning, clarity, and truth is not tidy. It is not wake up one day, secure a mission, heroic act here, heroic act there, oh I'm floating, applause, repeat. It is instead like sticking your head into an industrial washing machine and trying to keep your eyes on that one pair of underpants as

it spins and spins and spins while heavy blankets pound your
neurons. It's What's this? What's that? I've got it. No, I don't.
I had it. I've lost it. I have it again. Why am I still doing this?
I love it, that's why. Yippeeeeee. Nooooooo. If you think for
a living, you risk thinking too much to live. Your head is in an
industrial washing machine, but the rest of you—and the life
the rest of you is leading—can fall into a fog.

Like truth, fog will haunt you. A fog is a veil and veils hide
truth. A fog is out of people's control, and control sedates
fear. A fog lurks and stalks. We don't like it when other people
do these things, so we don't like it when fog does these things.
Boats, cars, and airplanes crash in fogs. Brain fog is a medical
term, something to cure. A fog might make you feel confused,
lost, listless. Too long in a fog might make you want to
surrender. But what if we are wrong about fog?

Fogs are disobedient clouds. Clouds are high and mighty
and royal, but fogs run the streets because fogs are clouds that
can touch the ground. Clouds are always going somewhere and
they dish out darkness, rain, and thunderbolts en route. Fogs
like to hang out, but they keep to themselves, and they don't do
flashy displays of electricity. Clouds don't like people standing
in them, so they are standoffish. Fogs come close and love it
when people wear them. Because fogs are disobedient clouds,
they make perfect spirit weather-animals for people who do
disobedient truth work. The real problem is when fog turns
into deadly smog.

In December 1952, a fog sat on London's chest.[7] Over five days, the fog ran an interagency workshop with an angry smokestack and sent 150,000 people to the hospital and 12,000 people to the morgue. The workshop was yellow-brown and stank of rotten eggs. Its ingredients were sulfur, fumes, and burning coal. Over the course of the workshop, people's vision blurred and faded, flying animals smashed into buildings, pets died, thieves looted, and England knighted the event The Great Smog. The Great Smog of London was lethal, but it led to Britain's Clean Air Act of 1956. The act said don't mix fog with smoke, and really don't mix it with smoke and sulfur dioxide.

Plain old fog is a friend of your strategy life. It's just you doing your work. But if you've spent any significant part of your life thinking, you'll know smog is only a couple of bad decisions away. A crisis of meaning, a grip on clarity that slips, or truths that are too disobedient can turn a fog evil. This is why you need a Clean Air Act. A Clean Air Act salutes fog but tries to keep it away from sulfuric thoughts.

Scrutiny about strategy is scrutiny about what it is to think, so your Clean Air Act will need to pay heed to the different types of thoughts your brain will encounter.

*Nonsense thoughts* are like watching someone who's never driven a bumper car steering it backwards and in circles but never completing a lap. Though bumper cars don't race laps, real bumper car drivers know laps are how you win at bumper cars.

---

[7] *Jane Onyanga-Omara, "Mystery of London Fog That Killed 12,000 Finally Solved." USA Today, December 23, 2016, https://www.usatoday.com/story/news/world/2016/12/13/scientists-say-theyve-solved-mystery-1952-london-killer-fog/95375738.*

And when they see first-timers taken captive by a bumper car with a mind of its own, it looks like an unstoppable, unintelligible mess that will break a neck. Nonsense can cause whiplash.

*Histrionics*, on the other hand, are kidnappers. They are thoughts that phone during a rare family dinner and hold you hostage, trying to drag you into an all-night conference call and then deep into hell. They circle and circle and circle and you know they aren't useful, but if you have not taken care of yourself—if you've ignored your physical, emotional, social, and intellectual needs—they can keep you prisoner for days.

*Quips*, meanwhile, make you smile. They are you observing your world and your thoughts as they collide, while enjoying the eccentricity of each collision. They are intelligible and emit from an internal entertainment system. You might need noise-cancelling headphones to hear them but once you tune in, you start to see them as more than mere distractions.

*Savings* are for your piggy bank. These are thoughts you've stashed over the years. They are observations, quotes, what-ifs, and research waiting to spring into the world. They marinate in your vault, and they emerge with interest.

*Classics* have happened before, but they linger for years and you know they house something useful. That's why they linger. You might resent having had them. You might hope nobody else knows you've had them. You might dismiss them at first re-appearance. But just because you've already had them doesn't mean they no longer have life. They might deserve a repeat reading.

Your Clean Air Act will admit it is rare for thinking to suffer from too much quantity. Instead, lack of quality is its woe. Nonsense, histrionics, and quips are not enemies. With distance, they are raw material and can work their way into usage. To enjoy thinking is to enjoy helping thoughts make this journey, like a skilled guide helping a novice scale peaks in the Himalayas, and also to accept moving on when the thoughts reach the limit of their climb, or, regrettably, fall off the mountain.

Your Clean Air Act will deal with the critique "You're overthinking it." It will understand this phrase can mean many things:

It can mean "You're confusing us." Your listeners want to understand you, but you're not herding them to that understanding.

It can mean "We don't want to think at all." Your listeners work to pay bills, not think. Perhaps they believe they pay *you* to think.

It can mean "We want what we already had." Your listeners needed, the last time you met, to act like they wanted thinking, but recoiled when they saw the fruits of their request.

It can mean "You're forcing a difficult connection." Your listeners aren't coming with you to your idea—it's just too far.

It can mean "Seriously, you make no sense to anyone. We ran a survey." Your listeners, and perhaps all listeners in the world, can't understand you.

"You're overthinking it" can stand in for many unspoken reactions. Some of these may seem harsh and tricky, but they can also tell you've brought too much of your fog into the room.

Your Clean Air Act will beg you to keep an eye on first principles. If your fog intertwines with someone else's or gets a sulfur dioxide blast, you can keep a few simple questions nearby. Remind yourself and your colleagues what you're doing together and what you're trying to achieve, and smoke out the assumptions that you're holding in common but not in the same way. "Are we here to do 'great work'? What is that? How do we believe it happens? What are our constraints? How can we be inventive in the midst of our constraints?" This flurry of questions can help a fog reset with fresher air.

Your Clean Air Act will also call for seeking out obvious suggestions, because a strategist's mind can sometimes resent the obvious. Get outside. Stare at nature. Write or draw. Change your surroundings. Play music or sounds. Visit a cafe, bookstore, or museum. Spend breath moving the body more than the brain. Talk to friends. Cook. Clean. Reorder a bookshelf. Knit. Work wood. Climb a mountain. List what you're thankful for. Boat. Beach. Breathe. Full-body strategy needs you in your body, not just your head fog.

Nonetheless, you'll spend much of your strategy life in a fog because that's what it is to think. To understand and admire the different types of thoughts you have as you help them become useful, to appreciate when your fog is clouding other people's minds, and to take care of the rest of you is to *enjoy the fog and stave off smog*. The Great Smog will kill a strategy career. A strategy career is dangerous enough as it is.

## MISCHIEF MAKES FOR DANGER

If meaning is what you make of it, if clarity can declare itself, if a strategist's life cuts with truth and disobedient truths are the sharpest weapons, then your strategy life is a life of mischief. Mischief is behavior with good intentions that happens to fall on the slight side of bad. Mischief is devilish, impish, puckish. It is playful malice with a sense of fashion.

Strategy threatens change in big and small ways. *This threat is your livelihood, and you inflict strategy on people one truth cut at a time.* You can dress yourself in expensive business clothes, but you remain a miscreant.

Your strategy life plays with order. And order doesn't like play. Order keeps its toys in a dank basement away from the hands of mischief. Order takes itself seriously. Every morning order stands in front of a mirror before it leaves for work and says, "No. Not today. We'll have none of that." Then order steps into the world at exactly the same minute as yesterday. Order "Nos" and "Musts" and "Shoulds" its way through the day. Order wavers for nobody unless order senses chaos. Chaos is what order senses when its way of living is under attack. When order's overpriced shaving blades, overpriced yellow taxis, and overpriced cable television packages find fierce competitors, order might pause to listen to you. But order is suspicious because any change is chaos, so when you speak, order will hear upheaval.

You are a jester. The jester's mandate is mischief. To see and say things that others do not and dare not, and yet survive all the same, is the riddle. To hold as valid mental tools—not hold in suspicion—cynicism, sarcasm, vulgarity, taboo, obstacles, messiness, absurdism, and simplicity is your burden. To relish two opposing ideas at once, to not know, to enjoy not knowing, and to admit not knowing is your truth.

Mischief says, "We're doing this wrong." Mischief says, "Hey, come over here and look at this." Mischief says, "There's another way to do it." Mischief says, "We *have* to do this another way." Mischief says, "I have an idea."

But even though they are your job, such simple phrases can throw a strategy life into turmoil or keep it from itself. Are you, dear jester, hiding or finding? Are you hiding in finding or finding what's in hiding? Who are you? Do you know? Do you try to snare others in your honesty while avoiding honesty about yourself?

The jester does not trust order because order removes the grit of life. And the jester knows order can be the true mischief. And yet the jester must find just the right way to disrupt the order, or it will never change. The most successful jester is the one who unearths how to declare the jester's version of order as the new and real order.

The jester knows this: like clarity, order is order when order says it is order. It's easier for order to hide the idea of change and pretend it doesn't exist. A culture with too much order will force a truth-seer into hiding. If this is you, you'll develop a precarious relationship with public truths. You'll shuttle them in and out of the light, hoping new eyes will see your ruse and invite you into their lives. Or you'll find an underground for your self-expression somewhere on the internet. Your people exist. You'll have to find them.

A life of mental mischief is a life committed to threatening order. With truth and ideas as weapons, your existence is an act of disrespect. Your words are defiance. Your breath is a weapon, a revolt, and a dare to reorder order. And systems exist to reject all of it.

## REJECTION WAITS TO POUNCE

Rejection will headline a life of mischief. Idea after idea smells like threat after threat to order, and order thinks this stinks. Order wants its tribe and its way of living, and it wants these things to stay the same and ideas to go away. Order is deaf to ideas because to listen to them is to admit order is out of order and order is never out of itself. Order has good self-esteem. Besides, it is rare for a person who expresses an idea to possess only one idea.

Ideas are waterfalls. They start as quiet streams hurrying through fabled mountains but then they turn torrent and explode over cliffs. This makes order suspicious. "Well, if this strategist has this one idea, what other ideas are they hiding up in the mountains? Does this strategist have ideas about stealing all our food, water, and wood? Does this strategist have ideas that involve overthrowing me?" One idea can suggest a private eternity of deviance. So, order rejects not just ideas but the people who have them: "Let's banish this thinker and their thinking. Who's with me? I know the answer. I know what it is. You're all with me. Waterfall raincoats off."

If your life serves ideas, you may spend swathes of it feeling alone and broken. That loneliness, however, is a symptom of you not committing enough to yourself and your ideas, not befriending the ideas and losing yourself in them, and not finding a gang with whom to roam. People who contemplate the human condition and whose minds wander with ease into others' feelings can pay a tax for those abilities in the world, and in interactions with people who aren't wired the same way. Loneliness is one of the taxes.

*Ideas are enemies of those who want order, but they are friends of the strategist. Any time a pang of loneliness appears, all you need to do is reach for a pen and piece of paper and welcome an idea into the world.*

These pangs deserve probing because a strategist who feels loneliness isn't alone in this feeling.

First, your brain isn't common but it's not the only one. Your yearning for raw, cavernous truth and a deep-seated need to express it in a world that rejects it can make you think you're damaged and in need of mending. Sometimes, people in your life will tell you outright that you are defective. You may even believe them. Don't. Take back your story. Tell it how you want to tell it. Find allies who tell a similar story to the one you want to tell and tell it together.

Second, you are someone who breaks things for a living and risks overidentifying what you *do* with who you *are*, but you aren't the only one. If your life is ideas, your life is to break apart things and reassemble them in odd ways. This will make you good at breaking yourself apart, too. Sometimes, you'll

hold yourself in pieces in your hands and marvel at how many ways you could remake yourself–infinite yous at your fingertips. Yet which version of this infinite you is good enough, friended enough, intimate enough, rich enough, happy enough?
Is the opposite of lonely what you even want? If it was, why do you keep thinking about moving companies, relationships, professions, and cities, of living on the road, or of throwing it all in? To stay sane, you'll need to break it apart then put it back together and hold it together because *something needs to hold.* You can't just admire your janky state of self-awareness.

These pangs of loneliness and brokenness are only minor turbulences if you hear them and honor them and don't move in with them. Your inner world needs you strong in your vulnerability—because the outer world is ready to strike at all times.

In the outer world, one reason people don't share ideas is fear of social rejection. They fear judgement. They fear their tribe will deem them stupid. They fear people will kick them down the ladder or throw them off the ladder altogether. But what's this game? It's simply another trick that order plays: "If we can make people think other people will deem them stupid and steal their status, then nobody will share ideas and we won't have to change."

And so order builds systems to reject ideas. It pretends these systems, smirks, and eye rolls are normal. More conservative people, people who like to conserve order, interact with more creative people—people who hunger for ideas—by attempting to establish the norms. Their tools are these: rules, processes, cautions, criticisms, suspicion, disgust, pretend-listening, No, You're not normal, and You're not a cultural fit. Ideas and open-mindedness are threats to these norms. Systems that can fake normal and threaten rejection reduce the brain energy that order needs to expend as it fights off encroaching ideas.

In response, your mind might develop coping mechanisms. These mechanisms can include a disdain for other people's lack of openness, self-doubt, avoidance, tantrums, dismissiveness of rules, "shock and awe," feebly hoping a salary is a means to an end, and depression. A strategist's fog can turn to smog when it spends years believing other people's norms and not finding its own norms. A strategist can also indulge in a form of pre-emptive self-rejection. "Well, if I reject myself then the world can't also reject me. I come pre-rejected. Smart, aren't I?" No. The world that doesn't want to change wants you to think yourself smart in your own rejection. If you reject what's normal to the world without holding onto what's normal to you like it's a lifesaver in the middle of frenzied river, it will just be you–not your ideas–crashing with the waterfall.

Sure, hold yourself in pieces but then piece yourself together and hold yourself that way. At the very least, you need to belong in yourself. The world isn't done with rejecting you yet.

## IMPOSTORS BELONG, TOO

There are three fiendish biases in many businesses:

1.  If you can't count it, then it doesn't exist,

2.  Creativity is words and pictures, and

3.  Nearly anyone can do words and pictures.

These biases reinforce a business ego. They make the creative mind an Other, they shrink its importance. But the business ego takes care of the money and strategists need money, so strategists have to find ways to obey this culture while also teasing it with disobedient truths, and while knowing each truth shared is rejection waiting to pounce. All these mind games can turn on you and make you feel like you don't belong in business.

In 1978, American psychologists Dr. Pauline Rose Clance and Dr. Suzanne Imes published *The Impostor Phenomenon in High Achieving Women: Dynamics and Therapeutic Intervention* in *Psychotherapy: Theory, Research and Practice*.[8] In the paper, they identified the "impostor phenomenon" (also known as "impostor syndrome"), as a pattern in which intelligent women can believe that they are frauds, that they have hoodwinked their way to success, that people overestimate how good they are, and that an eminent colleague will soon find them out.

---

[8] *Pauline Rose Clance and Suzanne Ament Imes, "The Imposter Phenomenon in High Achieving Women: Dynamics and Therapeutic Intervention," Psychotherapy: Theory, Research and Practice 15, no. 3 (Fall 1978).*

The impostor phenomenon has been thought to particularly affect women and people of color because white men tend to attribute success to themselves and failure to bad luck or how difficult a task is. However, most people who peddle ideas for a living and who aren't sociopaths, which is most people who peddle ideas for a living, will find self-doubt a frequent companion. Threatening order with ideas while constantly fending off rejection can increase this self-doubt.

When an internal voice goes whack-a-mole on you—"Here I am: You suck. Here I am: You suck."—you can help yourself by naming the critic's voice, and also by creating and naming an internal ally to fight it. Naming an inner critic and role-playing with the critic is a common practice for creative brains. Julia Cameron's classic guide to the creative life, *The Artist's Way*, discusses this technique. Viktor Frankl points to a similar use of irony as a way to dislodge and detach negative thinking in *Man's Search for Meaning*. Meditators suggest labeling your thoughts as they arrive—Worry, Anger, Envy—and then letting them continue on their way. When you hear the critic's heckle, "Who are you to do this?," you can talk back. "Who is anyone to do this? This is what I want to do and wanting to do it is always easier than doing it, but I'm still going to do it. Anyway, who am I not to do this? Well, the same person who hasn't done this—yet."

A brain that is quick to welcome in confusion and low self-esteem benefits from imaginary allies and new language. Aggressive self-talk really can help: "Screw you, critic. I have something to offer. I'll work it out in public. If it costs me jeers from unforgiving people, then that's OK. I'm the one who has to live with me. Nobody else has to do that."

Darling memories will lend their own furious support. "Remember that time we helped reverse the fortunes of a client? Remember the first brief we presented? Remember that conference presentation? That crazy weekend of writing a pitch that won the business?" You can try to fend off the impostor phenomenon through a clear sense of your own meaning, allies in your head, angry or happy role-play, and giving oxygen to vibrant memories. This system will glitch occasionally, but it's better than having no system at all and letting the nothingness eat at you.

The phrase "impostor phenomenon" or "impostor syndrome" is useful because it assists our self-understanding. But it's destructive if we identify with it too much and wallow in it. What if feeling it is a healthy call to action? Perhaps the feeling is a sign of maturity, a sign you are learning about the areas in which you want to grow, and an invitation to use that anxiety to launch yourself toward growth. *Perhaps the silver lining of the impostor phenomenon is this: It's a sign you want to improve.*

Next time you feel it, tell yourself that's not you feeling like an impostor. Tell yourself that's how it feels to care about doing something well. Then go do it. It's one way to feel like a friend to yourself and not like a powerless outsider.

## LONE WOLF, ARE YOU REALLY?

"I'm a lone wolf," you howl into the stars. "I'm a lone wolf.
Nobody understands. Nobody tries to understand. Nobody
wants to understand. They deem me an outsider. They come
for my ideas, but they sneer at my mind. I'm a lone wolf.
I see the world in colors no rainbow has ever captured. I see
patterns no computer has ever rendered. I see futures that
make Nostradamus look shortsighted. I feel emotions without
names. I have thoughts I can't turn off. They're solar-powered
and I can't find a shadow. Some thoughts are smudges and
some are neon. And when I speak I can only speak of these
thoughts. Few ears will take them. Most ears want my thoughts
to disappear. Sometimes, I want to disappear. But I can't
disappear because I exist in my head and I'm always with me.
I'm a lone wolf."

Miles away, another lone wolf joins your howl.

"I am also a lone wolf, stars. Can you hear my tears? They
drip in my head. I'm a lone wolf. I enjoy my alone time, but it
makes me feel lonely. I know few people like me. That is to say
I know few people who are like me and I know that few people
like me. About this last point I have never inquired, but I sense
it. I sense all things except self-worth. Maybe I can plug my
loneliness with people like me. With people who will like me.
We'll build a commune. We'll wear thinking hats. We'll grow
melancholiflower. We'll make the walls mirrors so there
is always a speaking-friend. We will need no clocks because
it will always be thinking time. A motto! Yes. *There are no rules
except to think*. Nobody will enter unless they think and feel like

us. And nobody will leave. Why would they? Happy at last. Lone wolves no more."

The duet turns into a mountaintop chorus of lone wolves howling for each other. Their solitude dances in public unison. Across the night sky, the lone wolves glance sideways at each other. But none move.

Wolves are pack animals. A pack—really a wolf family— usually stars a male and female breeding wolf pair. The pack also includes their pups, and may occasionally feature other adult wolves. The breeding parents, or alphas, create one litter every year. The alpha male commissions hunts and is the first to eat the kill. At two or three years of age, sex-ready wolves leave their packs. They scatter dozens of miles to join other packs or to create their own packs. A lone wolf is a wolf that has left its pack for an independent street life. Often the breeding male has driven away an older female, or the lone wolf is a male looking for new territory. A lone wolf is a lone survivor. There is the lone wolf and there is nature and that is all there is.

Many strategists see themselves as lone wolves, but that is rarer than Tasmanian tiger sashimi. You need people to do strategy. You need a client, a client's customers, and a team to execute the job. Without people, a strategist is an isolated philosopher or a novelist holed up in a cabin or a crazy nut or David Carradine in *Kung Fu*, but even David Carradine needed people so he could have sick fighting scenes that Bruce Lee was too Asian for.

A lone wolf eats what it kills. It is rare for a strategist to kill. You might make strategy that's destined to be killed, but a true killer will do that killing. And most strategists confine themselves to desks, walls, and artificial light, safe from the wilderness. They swap the emptiness of a horizon for the emptiness of a full calendar. Also, it is rare for a strategist to show the aggression of a lone wolf. A lone wolf is often more aggressive because it needs to survive. Aggressive strategists don't last, even if the target of many strategists' aggression is themselves. Truth truth truth. Cut cut cut.

So what does it mean when you say you're a lone wolf, and do you only say this because it sounds self-aware?

Identifying as a lone wolf depends on your definition of rejection. Are you a victim of rejection or did you reject the world? Have you experienced rejection that is colossal and absolute, a rejection made up of a thousand small shoves, an imaginary rejection, or seemingly no rejection at all? Have you chosen the life of a lone wolf, or did somebody else force it on you? Are your howls howls of pain or howls of Look at All This Land to Explore? Perhaps Lone Wolf was an escape button someone pushed for you, or one that you yourself hit early in life to stay safe.

Identifying as a lone wolf depends on your definition of like-mindedness. If you think for a living, you can struggle to find like minds. This struggle will give you friction. The friction will escalate your thinking and you might isolate yourself to deal with it. You then risk deciding the entire world is the Other and the only non-Other is your thoughts, even though many of your thoughts are friendly fire. At yourself. Bang bang.

Identifying as a lone wolf depends on your understanding of compatibility and similarity. If every person in your pack has to be similar and you define similarity as Latin Poets Who Love Comic-Con, then you are playing brinksmanship with reality. It's too easy to see differences in individualistic societies.

Animal packs are less individualistic and have fewer needs. They need, mainly, to survive. You can reinforce your own lone-wolf-ness by seeing the world in infinite nuance and using that nuance to declare all other people to be too different from you, even when it threatens your own survival. Finding a pack means focusing on compatibility, not rigid similarity.

If you think a pack can only be people in the same company with the same job title, then most strategists will experience little in the way of a pack in their careers. You can instead look for a pack in a subgroup of the company, the entire company, the company and its clients, the industry at large, informal peer groups, industry bodies, online communities, friends, and family. A job title is not necessarily the best representation of like-mindedness. Identify traits you would like in your life, and find people who demonstrate those traits. If you value research, critical thinking, how the brain works, philosophy, history, ideas, writing, teaching, and self-expression, then you can assemble a pack of comedians, teachers, academics, philosophers, and more. Your ability to do so will also depend on these other people seeing beyond job titles.

Identifying as a lone wolf depends on your attitude toward independence. Some brains thrive in their own wilderness and not in the jostling of many other brains. Too much time with

other brains tires, deflates, and flattens them. Social interactions
make them feel packed away like a folded airbed. So they
stake out a life on the outskirts of human settlement, in the
vibrant backcountry of their own minds. These wolves seem
free. Intuition moves them through their days. They choose
independence and then they choose seclusion as a way to protect
their independence. This is an independence that, for them,
feeds creativity. It doesn't just lock them away from the world
in the dark. They are light and electric. They create space
around themselves and then use the space to create for
themselves. This lone wolf is easy to romanticize–they're specific
in their social needs and how they build their days to breed ideas.

Identifying as a lone wolf depends on your social skills.
If isolation causes you pain because you believe social links are
important, yet you struggle with how to form them, then you'll
need gradual exposure to humans and you'll require more
social skills. It's one kind of intelligence to have a brain that
thinks in concepts and uncommon patterns. It takes another
kind of intelligence to interact with people. Perhaps you attend
a gathering and give yourself a goal of talking to three groups
of people. You arm yourself with a way to introduce yourself,
a couple of questions, and a way to evacuate the conversation.
Then you execute your plan.

But whom does the lone-wolf identity benefit?

The lone-wolf identity can benefit other people–those in the
group that the lone wolf eschews. If a lone wolf excludes itself
from a group, then the group has fewer internal competitors.
Decisions meet less resistance; resources fear fewer land grabs.
For these reasons, companies can also benefit from strategists

who identify as lone wolves. Lone wolves are less likely
to threaten order or to exchange information about things
like salaries, the stability of clients, or opportunities
for advancement. Lone wolves are weaker than a pack.

The lone-wolf identity can also, it is true, benefit a strategist.
A lone wolf sounds mystical, and this mysticism can reinforce
an ego. The lone-wolf ego whispers that few others are
intelligent enough to understand what we think, and that
is why life is just us. The ego is an ally in your solitude.

*The lone-wolf identity is also a preemptive strike at rejection, because
people can't reject what doesn't seek acceptance.*

"I don't want you to accept me. That's your game and I
stopped playing it several egos ago." The lone-wolf identity
can prop up the ego, however, because it justifies constant
displays of thinking that few others understand, as if the point
of strategy is the show of thinking rather than sharing thoughts
that others can use. "They just don't get it and they'll never
get it. My drawings on the wall never amount to anything.
They never travel out of the room." The lone-wolf identity
can keep you safe.

But the lone-wolf identity will hurt you. When you feel you
see the truth of the world and that few others will engage with
this truth, you might develop an emotional callus. You'll be
hard and hard to know and will not want to be known. You'll
be playing a one-handed, one-brained game of Pong, the old
video game where a ball is shunted back and forth ad infinitum.
And you'll both win and lose each match.

At its worst, the lone-wolf identity will cripple you.
In Pong, there is at least movement, but the lone-wolf identity
can eventually devour you and freeze you in its icy belly pit,
where all thinking leads to one sad thought: "I am a lone wolf."
There, the lone-wolf strategist waits for the lone-wolf stomach
to digest it.

If you have no pack, live in the wilderness, hunt your own
food, have a snout and paws, and are only ever alone, then you
might be a lone wolf. But there's no such thing as a lone-wolf
strategist. A strategist needs people to understand and to serve.
Strategy is people work, not lone-wolf work. If you experience
loneliness or alienation and diagnose these feelings as a life
commitment to lone-wolf-ness, then your internal drama is
acting like a mental virus trying to overthrow good sense.

People who think for a living do spend time alone. People
who think for a living may have spent much of their lives
alone. To think. If they excel at thinking and create lives and
careers overflowing with their thinking, then what they have
in common with a lone wolf is an ability to survive. But what
if they could do more than just survive by detaching themselves
from the idea they are lone wolves? What if they started every
new project by gathering their pack, doling out some verbal
love for them, and keeping them arm-locked-in-arm together
through the work?

## TETHER YOURSELF TO YOURSELF

Mr. Potato Head is a plastic spud on legs and feet. For ten
dollars, kids can pin his body parts where they belong, or they

can test their malice and their bent for the absurd and make him look stupid. They can replace his nose with his mouth, his ears with his arms, and his eyebrows with his lips. They can store extra body parts in his tater tush. He doesn't come with a bonus butt, so kids can't store his butt in his butt, but they would if they could. Who wouldn't? Mr. Potato Head can't stop this abuse. Besides, it's not abuse. It's creative play. But *is it the kids who play with Mr. Potato Head, or Mr. Potato Head who plays with the kids?*

Mr. Potato Head is a mastermind. Born to Brooklyn's George Lerner in 1949 and served up to the world by Hasbro in 1952, Mr. Potato Head's first breaths buried him in young American minds. As both the first toy advertised on television and the first one advertised to children, not parents, Mr. Potato Head is a voodoo doll with ambitions. His ruse is to convince kids they have some kind of control over the world. Control is all kids want. A little God play with a plastic ear never hurt anyone. But it's Mr. Potato Head who has control.

From where do all his body parts come? From a factory stamping them out of plastic slabs, you say? Maybe. But let's imagine the body parts come from people. Real people.

People are born. Their families tell them they are This, not That. Mr. Potato Head takes all the That. People go to school and more people tell them they are This, not That. Mr. Potato Head takes all the That and laughs because the teachers have little That left. If people have enough of the right This, the world awards them with an unpaid internship, an underpaid first job, and hopefully a better-paid career. How wonderful. More That for Mr. Potato Head at every turn.

Corporations love a specialist, so they use meetings, feedback sessions, and annual reviews to shave off as much That as they can. Mr. Potato Head takes it all.

Then, after a childhood, a puberty, and an early career of becoming individuals, all the individuals start to wonder what they have become because they no longer understand what they see. Mr. Potato Head knows. Nothing! And he's not even Buddhist. They can't recognize what they see because people can't see Nothing. They can see their small This in the mirror but it's only when they spot Mr. Potato Head holding what used to be there that the rest of their lives can happen.

*Mr. Potato Head's power move was to get the human rainbow to cull its colors and leave a dull gray.* In the name of individualism. All individuals must become This. And he convinced us that the only people who don't do This are maniacs. Artists, he whispers to the child. Only the silly artists do THAT.

At some point, you realize another way must exist. You know the way is inside somewhere. You look away from This and rummage within. You find the entrance to a ghostly labyrinth and near the entrance is a thread. You can stand at the entrance with thread in hand for years until you decide to Theseus your way to the Minotaur, but Theseus you must.

This is the strategist's journey. Your journey. A decades-long scavenge for meaning in the outer world can cease to provide adequate meaning, so you'll journey closer to home. You'll see threads in memories, photos, never-finished creative projects, relationship tics, and old journals. You'll clump together the threads in one hand and wield them through doorways like a clown holding a hundred helium balloons in the colors of the aurora borealis. The balloons will get stuck and bounce into your clown face. But the balloons must breach the doorway. And once they have made safe passage, you who became This because the world said This is what you must be will cease to let Thisness control you. You'll become That. But you'll need to hold tight your threads. Mr. Potato Head is coming for them.

One of the most direct paths to your balloons is questions. Take them for a long walk, let the words push their way to you, then sit and write your answers without judging yourself.

Questions you might find useful include:

1. What are you doing when you feel alive?

2. What does the world ask of you?

3. What is something you care about and feel angry about?

4. What do you know that your customers don't that would change their lives?

5. What can you do that others can't?

6. What do you do that others don't?

7. If you designed a good week, what are you doing and with whom are you doing it?

8. What do you want?

9. What's in your way?

10. What's your first step?

You can't get your answers wrong. It's more a matter of fit. Do you fit in your answers? Could you? Do they fit in you? Could they?

As you start to decipher the balloons, Mr. Potato Head will tempt them from your grip. A high-profile project or pitch, another job but better this time we promise, a friend or life partner who prefers you as This, an internet or a manager troll, or a fear of taking responsibility are Mr. Potato Head's siren calls. You are This. You know who you are as This. This is who you are. Mr. Potato Head knows that once you unhinge from This, you are somebody else's—maybe even your own.

Deadlifts and chin-ups help build grip strength. But to hold onto balloons, you'll need regular practice, a commitment to fiery publishing, and a gregarious gang.

### PRACTICE PLAYS THE BASS

In the early 1990s, there were raves in decrepit warehouses in the middle of nowhere. The raves swarmed with young hearts seeking kinship, an escape, a feeling, and self-annihilation. The more complex ravers could practice both love and self-hate with nobody knowing. Everyone held adulthood at bay. Deafening speakers were stacked higher than houses, and the bravest gnashing ravers danced off their faces yards from sonic booms. The frontline ravers wanted to dance a lifetime in one night and dared the music to explode them. To return home after a lifetime of dancing made no sense.

Every so often the music would seek to prolong a climax. The bass would stop, then the drums, and all that would remain was an intergalactic war in treble. This peak stretched with killer high-pitched noises. Sounds would grate and twist and pretend to come down, but go back up. It was a long orgasm. It felt like meaning.

The ravers would grin through each other. The intergalactic war would wage on. And on. *Pew pew. Pew pew pew pew. Pew pew pew.* The DJ would feign harmonic peace, then revert to the treble war. Yes. Look at us. We are here. We fight the universe. We love it, too. If the treble climax lasted too long and the melodic scratched too far into the industrial and sounded like machines dry humping at three hundred beats per minute, bored groups would peel off into discussion. Or ravers would rave their way over to the toilets. Or dip outside to get fresh air and avoid the cops.

Those treble climaxes were the Mr. Potato Heads of the rave crowd. Those highs were mind-control games. Those aural zeniths pretended they were the meaning. They were the pitches, the wins, the awards. They were the corner office, the fancy offsite, the promotions.

But these orgasms, thrilling as they may be, aren't meaning. Love is meaning. And the best part of the raves' ear assaults was always when the most unassuming player in the mix rejoined the war. The return of the simple bass, the part that never tried to outshine its music friends, heralded the real reward.

The bass line never did too much, but when it reappeared after the DJ's attempt at five consecutive spirit orgasms, ravers reflooded the floors, hats and water bottles pogo-sticked into the air in celebration, and rather than falling flaccid to a dance mattress for postcoital comforting, the rave would tack and head in a new direction, more determined than ever. "Right, got that out of your systems?" said the bass line. "Come with me."

*Practice is your strategy life's bass line.* It isn't always the sexiest, but when it's there, everything else makes sense. It's there before a career orgasm. It's there after a career orgasm when the many parts of you scatter, waiting for the next hit. A strategy life without a bass line is a career on the verge of a sugar crash. Practice grounds the strategy life. Practice is how you interface with meaning. Practice is an act of self-exploration and an act of self-love and an act of honoring an inner sense of self. Let your bass drop.

You can use the word "practice" in two ways. One way focuses on you improving at something: "I need to practice my writing." The other approaches "practice" as an operating system, a way of living, a philosophy, how you exist in the world: "I have a yoga practice. I have a writing practice. I have a rave practice." In this second sense of the word, a strategy practice can happen in small and simple ways. Like this:

**A Strategy Practice**

1. **Explore** new ideas and the world

2. **Do** your strategy; apply your ideas

3. **Teach** others how you do strategy

4. **Improve** how you do strategy

5. **Chill** ... for a second

6. **Repeat**

Both types of practice will keep your strategy life tethered. But practice births many other benefits, too.

Practice gets you good. How boring the life where you could press a button and instantly arrive where your strategist-self wants to be. Especially because you wouldn't stop at just one button. More buttons would appear. More pressing would occur. Shortcuts to infinite shortcuts. Yuck. The longcut is the way and practice is the longcut. And it's deliberate practice that is the best longcut.

Deliberate practice separates the *most* elite from the mere elite. According to K. Anders Ericsson, a professor of psychology at Florida State University,[9] deliberate practice requires:

1. An expert to break into pieces the required skills

2. An organized set of practice sessions to focus on these skills in ways that are meaningful, not mindless

3. A coach or partner to provide quantitative or qualitative feedback

---

[9] *K. Anders Ericsson, Ralf Th. Krampe, and Clemens Tesch-Romer, "The Role of Deliberate Practice in the Acquisition of Expert Performance," Psychological Review 1993, Vol. 100. No. 3, 363-406.*

Brazilian jiu-jitsu practice is arranged like this. Classes are active and alive. If you turn off, you'll lose your breath because someone will choke you. Elite youth soccer practice is also like this. It is ninety minutes of ferocious puzzle-solving, not doing laps and skipping around orange cones. Top musicians practice like this, too. They spend more time on the most difficult techniques and repertoire, breaking down thorny passages over and over. Yogis, stand-up comedians, and ballet students practice like this.

If strategists are so smart, why do so few strategists practice like this?

Once you understand what matters to your strategy life, you can break the skills you need into pieces and devise ways to practice them. You can start here: much of your strategy work is noticing the world, pulling it apart, reassembling it in new ways, and compelling others with what you see. Practice can involve asking questions, quick or in-depth research, putting things into categories, mind-mapping, writing on large workshop walls, structuring stories and presentations, writing single-minded propositions, and listing thoughts and ideas and observations in a pocket notebook.

*If your strategy life has no time for itself, then your strategy life is lying to itself.* Practice can happen on the subway, in a line for lunch, while eating, on a plane, and on the toilet. You need only to push the On button and kick the shortcut button to the curb.

Practice oxygenates your creative spirit. Your strategy life's main risk is to commit to a creative *work* life instead of a creative life overall. A creative work life is important, but it's a subset of a creative life. And a creative work life can distance you from your complete creative life by making creativity something that only serves a salary.

Your strategy life needs a creative spirit that is larger than work. There are times when you'll run as fast as possible to be a strategist—often when you have no dependents and no mortgage. In these times, the idea of practice will seem slow and stupid, a burden. Isn't that what school was for? But when those times fade and the shininess of your career feels worn to a blunt butter knife, the idea will no longer seem stupid. You'll crave practice to stay sharp, not to mention to develop new edges.

Practice can also help you find peace, in two ways. First, treating everything as a means to practice is sanity. You can focus on technique and self-improvement, not on short-term climaxes. Practice can focus you on the internal and mute the noise out there. Failure is still a thing, but learning and doing the *next* thing are the main events. Second, practice is meditation. To breathe, move, and serve the soul into a creative product—whether a story, a cake, or a painting—can give you a quiet place from which to pay attention to the world, to distance yourself from thought patterns, to flow. Thoughts and emotions can appear and disappear. You can be a vessel, no more, no less. You can emerge fresh. In the end, practice not only points toward peace, it is peace.

Practice is your values in action. If you value ideas, then you need to practice ideas. If you value curiosity, then you need to practice curiosity. If you value empathy, then find ways to practice empathy. Saying these things are important is all well and good. But if they are truly important, then you practice them. *Without practice, you risk waiting for the outside world to bestow importance on you. Practice is you honoring what's important to you.*

A practice mindset will keep you engaged and improving for years. Setbacks will appear as ways to try new ideas. Success will appear as a bonus detour, but not the point. And while practicing in private will warm the engine, practicing in public will magnify what matters to you. So, practice then publish.

## PUBLISHING TAKES YOU PUBLIC

In your strategy life, you find meaning for others, then help others put that meaning into the public eye. You hope these public acts bring more people into your clients' orbits and into your fold. Meanwhile, many strategists lead chaotic internal lives and keep this chaos private. And despite our actions having the potential, if a client is large enough, to affect millions of people across the globe—the public on a grand scale—we are often more preoccupied with a smaller public: how we appear to our companies and clients. *This is a small and critical public, yet it's not the real public.*

The strategy life is a competitive life, so any thinking that makes it into this small public can meet with fast devastation that will make you feel unglued. But that's only if you believe that this is the real battlefield, and this is the only public. If you can maintain a tether to a deeper life meaning, develop a strategy practice and a way to practice, and understand the larger publics that exist, then these risky back-and-forths are important but only fodder. They are feedback in a bigger game.

Going public is you plying the strategy trade to yourself. If you understand pride not as arrogance but as a compassionate love for yourself, then pride requires you to use strategy in your life. And this may compel you to find a deeper meaning and to put it into public. That means not only for your small public, but for the next circle that includes the industry as a whole, and then into an arena that touches the public at large. The act of making something public is called publishing. That doesn't mean just books. Each step of your publicness and your publishing—from an online portfolio to articles written to speaking engagements to whatever else your imagination can conceive—shows your commitment to your own coherence.

Friends, family, peers, strangers, and trolls are armed with sniggers and confusion and criticism, but if you chase a career seeking meaning, often you'll have no choice but to widen your reach. The result of not doing so is a muted existence and a temporary strategy life.

Oh, but some of the best strategists somebody knows are never "in public." Good for them. They have found ways to have their emotional, intellectual, and social needs met without "going public." This doesn't make them good. It's just how they are and what they need. They are good anyway. And, most likely, they are either fully loved or don't need love at all. Going public isn't a sign of being good, but it will help most strategists get good.

Going public takes courage and courage is seductive. College degrees, resumes, titles, awards, agency names, and portfolios matter. After a few years of accumulation, these things can carry a strategy life for several more years without much effort. However, going public can help a young strategist to stand out and a mature strategist to work out what's next. Most young strategists play the same checkbox game. It includes the right college, degree, internships, CV, and portfolio. Then there is the spreadsheet of people to hassle for coffee. Some call this hassling an "informational interview" but that is like calling a one night stand a first date.

To wit:

**Can we meet over coffee for an informational interview? I want to understand you.**

*You mean, you want to understand all the stuff I write about on the internet?*

**Umm. Yeah.**

*The thousands of words on the internet? Have you read any of them?*

**[Silence]**

*[Silence]*

**What if I just tell you my life story? Will that get me a job now, please?**

*No.*

**But the deal is we sit here and tell each other our histories, right?**

*I didn't read the fine print.*

**Can you just give me a strategy job, then? I've done everything right.**

*Only if you can count all the way up to the total of your college debt in ten seconds.*

**This isn't how the instruction manual said things worked.**

*Well, the instruction manual needs to add a new section.*

**What if I tell you how passionate I am for thirty minutes?**

*No.*

**What if I tell you how good I am for fifteen minutes?**

*No.*

**What if I tell you …**

*Stop it. Show me something you have put in public. Tell me why you did it, what happened when you did it, and what you learned. If you're passionate, passion would have made you do this already. Passion doesn't just say; passion does.*

**But in the instructions, "I am passionate" is a trigger phrase that makes jobs that don't exist appear. It's magic. I didn't know it meant anything else. No one told me.**

*I'll tell you. Passion means going public. You call this an "informational interview," right? Well, now you have your information.*

When you ply a network or play with recruiters, public work shows bravery and commitment and a strong sense of self. Done well, people in the office will say, "Holy crap. You need to see what this person did." Next stop: job interview.

Going public is a teacher. It gives you feedback. This feedback will help you understand what the world wants from you. This isn't the only signal to listen to—it's not always as useful as the internal signals you get from your own intuition—but it has a place. It is why so many stand-up comedians give themselves a target number of open mics to hit every month and then record their sets to see how many laughs they got and where the laughs were. A comic may aim to do five open mics a week and develop a set that generates five laughs per minute. They learn their craft in public. The public is their teacher. But they stay tethered to a comedic perspective and the stories they find in themselves.

Going public leads places. Not only can public thinking lead to a job, it can lead to a career, a conference, a book, a new peer group, a new city, a new love life, a whole new *way* of life. However you choose to go public, your voice is there for the world to hear. If the world likes what it hears, it will send invitations for a close-up, and then all you have to do is be ready for that close-up. Bravery, stories, and insights lead difficult public lives, but people will respond.

A shift from a small public life to a larger public life is relative to the culture in which it happens and to your ambitions. There's a threshold beyond which there is a universe on fire with the public exchange of ideas—but without stepping into it, only dark boredom awaits. To tread beyond that threshold is you applying self-awareness to your life. And living. And it helps to have fellow thinkers nearby as you go public.

## A GANG CAN KEEP YOU SAFE

A strategy life chases odd shadows of materialism. Agency names, client logos, dots on maps, trophies, agency hashtags nobody uses, job promotions, strategy books, obscure research, industry events, gluttonous timesheets, vacation days remaining and never taken, free tickets, free lunches, free logins, laptops and devices but better and newer than everyone else's, guest lectures, social media followers, email newsletters, subscribers, portfolios, portfolio websites, work credits, offsites, office pets, office twinsies, offices with windows, fancy street addresses, ping-pong tables, foosball tables, agency award tables, standing desks, case studies, press releases about another agency repositioning, famous department heads, secular holiday parties, confused industry committees but at least there's free food, important meetings on the calendar, out of office replies, photos at awards shows, Cannes, MBA, MFA, empty articles that are flashes in the pan: "As CEO of Agency X," business travel, business class, first class, frequent flyer points, boutique hotels but so boutique nobody else can stay, executive assistants, executive coaches, board seats, trade-press interviews, weekly columns, podcast appearances, strategy books that you are writing, autobiographies, therapists, shamans, and ayahuasca tourism.

"I'll have one of everything," says the strategy life. "Light me up."

Mr. Potato Head laughs. Take This. You will no longer need That or That or That. Give That to me. More? You want more? Take This and This and This. Gimme all of That. Yes, update your CV and social media presence. Email the world. Of course. Send all the people to me. Make them This, too.

The sophomore intern clears his throat. "I know I return to college in a month, but I'd like a meeting about my title and my career path, and I need mentors. At least five. I'd like one from every department, plus understudies. That's ten. I'd also like to rotate departments every twenty-three minutes. And I have feedback about the onboarding experience. It was off-putting onboarding, but it gave me time to prepare these lunch menu suggestions, which means we'll need to hire a chef and build a kitchen and a farm."

"Keep wanting," Mr. Potato Head says. "Want it all."

People who think for a living don't really need much. They need air, cash money, and a topic to haunt them. People who think for a *life* need more but it's not a lot. They need to keep one hand on their meanings, they need a practice, they need to practice, they need to go public, and they need a gang.

A mentor can also be important, but mentors can be near or far, alive or dead. Mentors are metaphors. They are pretend solid structures that give people a sense of certainty and legitimacy. They are ponds into which a strategist can reach to retrieve truth. Some mentors can coach and add to the strategist's practice. Some mentors can plug a strategist into a new network. But a gang can do these things, too. And a gang offers better protection.

"But you're a lone wolf," Mr. Potato Head says.

When you look down and see the balloon strings gathered in your palms, the helium lifting the balloons high, and Mr. Potato Head trying to peel them away under the mild distraction of romantic whispers–"Outsiders are the sexiest"–you can strengthen your grip with a fellow strategist's hand. This hand-spooning is affection of the intellectual kind. It is soft, intimate, and honoring, but it is also staunch, defiant, and adamant. It's a reverse handshake that promises to help tether you to what matters. The balloons look fun up there, but tethering is serious work. As more hands grip your grip and a hand gang forms around the tethers, you understand the lone-wolf metaphor as a way to keep you alone and to think that being alone protects you from being wrong. But *as you shift your game to a game of meaning and not of right or wrong, you'll need allies*. All the deadlifts in the world won't tether a strategist like a gang can.

Here's how real gangs work. Some combination of poverty and despair forces people together. They offer each other protection from the outside, but lose themselves in a constant fight among themselves for respect and money, or whatever treasure they deem of most value. Initiations are extreme. Violence is contagious. They use artistic symbols—tattoos, colors, clothing, secret gestures, or other modes of expression. They have meeting spots. They have enemies. They have fallings-out. Gangs run until they run out.

Gertrude Stein ran a gang in Paris. In the first part of the twentieth century, she rolled with the likes of Pablo Picasso, F. Scott Fitzgerald, and Henri Matisse. They met at her art lair on Saturdays. They called it a salon because that's a French word and they were in France. Their violence was art, one of the most brutal things a person can inflict on another person. Their despair was their quest for the infinite; their poverty was too much money or self-hatred or actual poverty. They protected other adventurous souls and maintained as their enemies a lack of art or bad art or each other. Gertrude Stein and Ernest Hemingway fell out.

RZA is Wu-Tang Clan's Gertrude Stein and the way RZA's crew moved through the world is worth a brief study. They launched together with the 1993 album *Enter the Wu-Tang (36 Chambers)*. Then they dropped art solo and in different combinations and as guests on other people's songs while expanding into other fields such as acting, filmmaking, video games, clothing lines, and books. Sure, there was turbulence and violence, but Wu-Tang Clan was a home for most of the members to return to and their public presence was louder and more thrilling because of it.

No matter what, pick a style, use a rare voice, band together, get a RZA or Gertrude Stein, make art, collaborate in unexpected ways, expand into other art forms, tour together, put sharp truth into the world and make it rhyme some of the time, fight, flop, return to the surface for air, add new members, franchise that shit, go to prison, fall apart, put on a reunion show, develop independent lives and careers, reminisce, and keep creating. People are old soon enough. Why not age together in public with an airtight spooning grip on those balloons?

If ideas are a menace to society and if society exists to reject menace, and yet you do menace anyway, you'll need a gang for protection. And, in that gang's protection—as long as you steer clear of controlling sociopaths and manipulative narcissists, you'll hear echoes of self-respect because those echoes are the sounds of your truths shouting for attention. *People don't change the world. Gangs do.*

02
—

# Work
# *Words*

# CHAPTER TWO

# Work *Words*

S trategy work is art. Art brings ideas into existence. Its sled dogs are intuition, empathy, and courage. Together they race truth into the world. Art succeeds when it guides people into feeling something deep about themselves, and art does this because it sees deep into people. At such depths, art breathes and the artist stays alive. Each day is an underwater snorkel over the craggy coral of the soul. Science is similar. But science tries to take a stroll from one thing to the next, and art is a glitch that seduces science's stroll off track. "Hey, come look at this." Science keeps its head down, hoping to arrive on schedule at the next set of information, but science knows its inner artist wants to go look. And this is how art updates science—one stroll glitch at a time.

*Art and science dance to make a strategist.* The dance happens in the mind but it runs into conflict outside the mind, when the strategist tries to express what they do, and they realize the world doesn't want them to see themselves as artists. Many strategists feel caught between following their artistic intuition and acting like businesspeople or science-people or something other than what they are, which is a hybrid of the human experience. Finding the words to express what they are can cause a glitch in their system. This is ironic because strategists–like art–are glitches in systems. When business as usual isn't working, businesspeople seek a glitch. Strategists are the glitch. If this weren't true, businesses wouldn't need strategists, they'd only need scientists, or they'd just ask their accountants for ideas.

All this glitching is dramatic but logic does underpin the drama. Logic helps you assemble questions and information. Drama helps you find an opinion. Opinions elicit sounds from peers—giggles, chortles, snorts. These primal sounds are the brain sending out smoke signals that truth is near. And while communities can reject truth in public, truth can operate on the private mind, selling new ways to think and behave. Then these new ways of thinking and behaving move into public. To sell well, you need words that don't cheat—words that practice monogamy—and a dedication to writing and patience.

## ART IS IN THE MARGINS

"What we do isn't art," says the dead legend. "It isn't just making pretty and provocative things for their own sakes. No, we exist to sell. We identify truths and ferry them into the world on the backs of hefty media budgets. Then the ideas corral human crowds and deliver their cash into our clients' claws. No, it's not mind control. Nor is it pollution. But rid yourselves of this art idea. It will inflate you with pride and this will make you difficult. At most, our art is business art.

It's art that serves capitalism. And businesses are the queen bees of capitalism. Fly, drones, fly. Capitalism? Yes, capitalism. Wait, capitalism is dying? Oh, you begrudge your paycheck? I'll take it. Give it to me. Take this business art from the lobby in exchange.

"Yes, we make business art. Real art hates money. Real art never seeks attention. Real art exists to exist. Besides, people don't understand real art until artists die. We need people to understand our art while we're alive this quarter, therefore it isn't art. At least when other people are in the room. Especially businesspeople. Businesspeople hate art until they are rich enough to buy it. Then they buy bad art. Have you wandered the corridors of our clients? Yes, the ones near the boardrooms that smell like tombs. Art isn't real to their profit-and-loss statements. *Until art makes margins, art is in the margins.* Sure, what we do entertains when it's good, but that's entertainment, not art.

"What's that? Strategy people now call themselves artists? We, the art directors, were too ashamed to call ourselves artists. How can they one-up us like this? I hate strategy people. They think they do such important work. Finding out stuff, talking to people, making things clearer. Just tell me one thing I haven't heard before. One thing. You know, not many of them can do that. And fewer still can do what we do. We don't even need them. That's how good our art is. I mean, it's not art. But maybe after we're dead."

Strategy *is* more art than science. *Art is uncertainty attempting certainty.* Art is a soul edging itself into the world. Art is every emotion at once. Art helps people see life with more truth. *Science is the pursuit of definite answers.* Science takes imagination and tries to alchemize it into facts. Science wants to repeat itself and is reluctant to let art steal it and turn it into something repeatable and permanent and eternal. Strategy takes facts and turns them into art. And even a paper that wins an effectiveness award isn't science and doesn't make strategy a science. An award-winning paper is a story, and it contains as much imagination as it does facts.

This makes you, dear strategist, an artist. An artist gathers information, generates ideas, and then crafts and displays ideas with which people can update their mental operating systems if they so choose. These ideas dangle outside the hyperbaric space hut. If a tribe lets them enter, the ideas breathe. "I see things" is art about to happen. Your canvas is every conversation, meeting, email, presentation, and deliverable. For you not to think these things are canvases is for you to deaden yourself.

*Few people want you to think of strategy work as art.* People who went to art school but do not spend their days doing their own art do not want this, because they feel they are not allowed to make the same claim for themselves and they went to school for it, so they deserve it more. Businesspeople in agencies do not want this because they want people to take their agency seriously and nobody takes art seriously until it's in a gallery one hundred years too late, and then everybody takes it too seriously. And you yourself may not want this because you want an earnest career and everybody is talking about marketing science and marketing science isn't art.

Such a heavy train of assumptions can endow you with an all-consuming identity crisis. In your private life you relate to stand-up comedians, novelists, painters, sculptors, musicians, and poets. In your business life, little of this can exist. You turn off your own lights before you slog to work each day. You see things, hear things, and feel things. You count things and report things. Yet all numbers need feelings. Then again, all feelings need numbers. Repeatable numbers. And once again you feel yourself sinking in the quicksand of the art-science divide. But you must remember: if strategy were a science, companies wouldn't need strategists. The science would tell them what to do. But they have you. And they need you.

There is one person who sees you as an artist. It's that chief marketing officer who's built a career on visceral creative work and demands to have a strategist in every meeting. This is a rare subspecies on the brink of extinction, but such mortals do exist. Often they recognize the art and the artist in themselves, and *they want strategy, presentations, and meetings to bulge with the eccentric, because they know the eccentric is easier to refine than the dull is to excite.* They've been old souls since they were young and they survive in their companies in spite of their company cultures. Anyone with a decade in the industry will have a mental roster of this subspecies. Not enough faces to fill a *Guess Who?* gameboard, but enough to occupy a small dinner table.

But who benefits from you not seeing yourself as an artist? First, people who sell strategy as science benefit. Arguing that strategy only requires deductive thinking–where A leads to B then C–appeals to buyers who need to point to An Inarguable

And Holy Way to reduce the amount of thinking they need to do, the quantity of subjectivity in decisions, and their personal exposure if things go wrong. It also means they can exclude difficult people—you know, independent thinkers who might who might think A leads to B then D.

Second, people who sell statistics benefit by not viewing you as an artist. When the data illuminati banded together to form the phrase "data-driven insight," they played a wondrous trick on people, because nobody really knows what a "data-driven insight" is, especially not those who spout this phrase into the ether every day.

**Yes, but is it a data-driven insight?**

*What do you mean?*

**I think it's obvious what I mean. Is it a data-driven insight or did you just make it up?**

*Yes.*

**You don't understand. Show me the statistic. Prove this will work.**

*You need proof that something that has never existed will work before it's existed?*

**Yes. You seem stupid.**

*That is like asking a placenta for a lifetime guarantee on a yet-to-be-born baby.*

**Your words make no sense.**

*What's an example of a data-driven insight?*

**Eighty percent of women don't like the looks of their armpits.**

*That is horrible and you made up that survey to get that statistic. Also, it isn't an insight, it's a statistic. The insight is inside the statistic.*

**Look, you don't understand strategy. We'll present my idea, "Make a Pit Stop for Tip-Top Armpits," based on my data-driven insight and my strategy, "Empowering ugly armpits with joy from within." You are not a cultural fit. Goodbye.**

Third, some people who see themselves as artists may benefit from not viewing you as one. Not seeing you as an artist protects their egos. "That person isn't an artist, I'm an artist." Rejecting strategy as art is a defense mechanism and an act of one-downmanship. No smug strategists here.

Fourth, people who like order benefit from not seeing you as an artist. When strategy isn't art, it is on a leash. "Come here, champ. We need more slides, more bullet points, more meetings. We don't need any of this art nonsense. Don't get carried away with yourself."

Fifth, other strategists who fear who they might become if they think of themselves as artists benefit from not believing you are one. Art is dangerous. When you identify as an artist, you know there is no going back. The future demands one courageous act after another. A future without courage isn't a future for an artist. It's Groundhog Day. And having to face the future with courage and artistry scares some of us.

So you seeing yourself as an artist would scare other strategists because they'd have to think about how they see themselves.

Nearly everybody benefits from you not seeing strategy as art. The work suffers, but certain people benefit. Until the company shuts down because the work has suffered too much. There's only so much art in an algorithm.

So, who benefits from the strategist seeing strategy as art? First, there is you, the strategist who embraces this vision. While you might think non-artistry will bring you safety, the oxygen from the baobab tree on that small planet never lasts. Seeing strategy as art and everything you touch as a canvas helps you shift into a freer mode. Everything is play; everything is more vivid. Mistakes aren't dead ends. More combinations are possible. Everything is practice. Every email, meeting, and brief is an act of creativity. *Practice makes better because perfect isn't a thing.*

The second person who benefits from the strategist seeing strategy as art is anyone who has ever wanted better strategy. Since a creative brief is a piñata shrine to strategy on a project, anyone who wants a better creative brief will benefit. Proof? When someone complains about how much a brief sucks and beats the dangling strategy piñata shrine with a baseball bat that seems too powerful for the job, the complainant can ask you to make the brief: a) more scientific, b) more business-y, or c) more artistic. Then they can see what happens. This will be science.

Strategy as art is not a dangerous idea. It is an inevitable conclusion. The only thing it endangers is another person's self-resentment and creative blocks. The only thing it threatens is your limbo. And so starts your existence.

## EXISTENCE IS FOR ARGUING

"Oh, you're so existential. Always worrying about why anything exists and if its existence is real and asking if it could exist in other ways. What is wrong with you? Stop thinking so much. Do you think you'll find something I haven't found? Do you think you'll find something I couldn't find? Do you think you are better than me? Just give me the brief. Stop making everything so complicated. It's yogurt. We all know why yogurt exists. The sugar yogurt exists to keep fat people company. The bland yogurt exists to help the skinny people feel smug about fat people. I know we can't say that. But we can imply it. We'll cast diverse and inclusive and nobody will look sad. Fat happy is the best happy. People are never sad in advertising except in charity advertising. Charity advertising exists to make people with money feel sad so they can buy their way out of their sadness with donations. What have you done to me? You're so cynical. Why do you see the existence of yogurt differently than me? Now we are all existential. You have offended my worldview, after my worldview told your worldview everything is simpler than you pretend, because that makes me feel wise. I exist to feel wise. Wiseness makes me feel self-righteous about the unwise. My wiseness is the skinny yogurt of thinking. You are hurting my head. I hate thinking about existence because then I have to think about my own existence, and I don't like the reflection I see in my timesheets at 6 p.m. every Friday night. It's not that I exist in timesheets, but if I don't complete my timesheets, it's as if I don't exist. Then that all-staff fill-in-your-timesheets email acknowledges me in a distant and angry way, and I like it. So I do them. I examine the hours I've spent on work that will never happen and meetings that drew blood. I do them. I complete them. Got the job number for this? Got the job number for that? It's ridiculous. My existence is ridiculous. I wanted to write novels and now I write timesheets. Why do I exist?"

Strategy work is the work of existence. Strategy is an argument for why something exists and how it exists. Even at its most shallow, a request to tell people about a new soap and to show some new bubble technology is to say that bubbles are important to the existence of the soap and soap is important to the existence of people and they are all important to each other and that their existence together is more important than an existence with any other soap or without this bubble technology. Every beer advertisement is an argument about a beer's existence. Here's why the beer exists, here's how the beer's existence is different, here's how the beer exists in people's lives, here's how the beer can help you exist, go buy the beer. And this work helps the beer continue to exist.

When you do research, you attempt to find what exists. A customer journey is a map of how a person makes a decision and uses a product. It is a map of what exists. A presentation slide that orders the search keywords people use to find a product also maps what exists. A qualitative research debrief reveals what exists. A website analytics report reports on what exists. A meta-analysis of academic research or financial data tries to understand what exists. For strategy to call itself strategy, it starts with forays into what exists.

After getting out of the car at the side of the road of what exists, you then wander into the forest of what *could* exist. You plaster possible strategies to a blank wall, you write a page of single-minded propositions, you brief a creative team, you write a measurement plan, you finesse a presentation. These are all statements of what could exist. You take all the things you have found to exist and you invent ways they might exist together in the future. Strategy is art and art is an attempt to make something exist. You are an artist.

Problems arise when your strategy lays out an impractical existence. An impractical existence is lost in its own intellectuality. Its head rubbernecks in the clouds. It stays aloft in puffy, long words that nobody knows what to do with. It keeps arguing and debating and rejecting, but it doesn't know what it thinks. It cites all these books and quotes from dead people and research journals, and hopes their words make sense of what's on the tip of its tongue but not yet out of its mouth. It loves symbols and semiotics, but it doesn't realize its big words are the cries of a lost strategist: "Come find me."

Impractical strategy exists in frenzied ways that go nowhere, ways that suggest provocation is the only point. What if the soap's bubbles are champagne from the future that will make the world drunk on diversity? What if the soap's bubbles are peace doves on their way to the West Bank to clean up that political mess? Yes, what if? What if that? Then what? Your strategy lurches from shadow to shadow in the office. People keep it around just in case, because they have to, or because a client enjoys the banter, but impractical minds can scare off more meeting invitations than they generate. "Do we have to bring in that person?" Sometimes a strategist is strategy's worst enemy when the strategist forgets why strategy exists.

"You're so existential" is a frequent battering ram lobbed, quite unironically, at the existence of a strategist. It says, "You frustrate me. I don't want to have to think too much. I don't want you around these here parts. Get back on your horse, Ponyboy, and hit the intellectual sunset. I hope it evaporates you." When a thought-bully accosts the strategist with "You're so existential," the correct response is, "Yes. That's why I exist."

Not everyone's reason to exist involves sounding like an academic brain on cocaine. Some people live just to die. Many, in fact. Most existences are simple to the eye, though less so to the mind's eye. But a strategist is an existence-monger—doomed if only in the mess of a head, clear if electricity out loud. You exist to help ideas exist in people's minds, then in their lives. If this meets with disagreement from you or the people around you, you're in jeopardy of feeling nonexistent. Stay strong.

### EMPATHY IS A POWERFUL BURDEN

On an asteroid you stand. The fluffiest pink clouds bunch above. Blue-white bolts zap into each other and shake voltaic hands when they meet. A conveyor belt of jagged rock, shallow dark ditches, and small cacti passes beneath your steps. Tiny angel banshees hang one-handed from the cactus needles like graffiti artists dangling from a moving steel train between subway stops before their art dares to turn dead and they lose the youth they never wanted. Sometimes your shins dislodge these harrowing Christmas ornaments from their cactus perches, and the banshees fling themselves into the infinite. They leave behind weedwhacker cuts and more banshees spawn from the cacti with each fling. The banshees are the lizard tails of the asteroid. They death-stare you in the face and shriek as they fly by. You can't look down as you walk, so you never see the banshees until they buzz up to your eyeballs. You forge forward on the conveyor belt, but you never move. The asteroid hurtles and cannot stop. It can only crash.

Only day exists on the asteroid. It keeps awake the heart in the depths of your rib cage, keeps your eyes lurking in oblivion. Most days it rains. And when it rains you open your arms and stretch your fingers to grip the horizons and tilt your chin to the stars beyond the clouds and you movie-twirl. You make yourself a bucket under a leaky roof, and you try to catch all the rain even as the asteroid marches under your feet. Your twirl is a magnet for the asteroid's rain. You collect it all. There are no puddles. Besides, the rain on this asteroid is not water, but feelings. Other people's feelings.

There is nowhere to run. You cannot run in slow motion on a lumbering one-speed treadmill. The only thing fast about this asteroid is its shot through space. The rain tumbles, pelts, and trickles. And you feel all of it.

*Some say empathy is a strategist's superpower, but empathy can lose you in other people's emotions.* Empathy is how actors turn serif-fonted words on crumpled, photocopied pages into theater. They use the pages to visit other people, assume their lives, and animate them in public for everyone to judge. They need to think what their characters think. They need to do what their characters do. They need to feel how their characters feel. In these respects, you are a small-time actor. You need an actor's empathy. You need it to course through your words and fashion your ideas. But if it becomes your only focus and you stay on the asteroid too long, too much empathy will be a curse and will keep you from yourself.

Empathy is a flood of faces. Something happens and face after face scrolls through your mind. Each face prompts you to visit it. "Come here. What do I think? How do I feel?" At its most basic level, *the call to empathy is a call to see the world not through your own eyes. To not answer every question in the first person, especially when the question is about other people.* You may have spent a lot of time in formal education that encouraged your ego's need to feel correct and to hear itself in every answer. The ego loves to jockey for status and loves knowing the easy quip, instead of loving to sit and let the faces wash over.

For most of us, the capacity for empathy is innate. Research, travel, meeting people from different backgrounds, learning languages, books, movies, and passing through life stages will arm you with a hoard of feelings. You need not herald from a certain group of people to achieve some empathy with and understanding of that group, but it may still take years for an

Ivy League intern to understand a single mother holding down two jobs just to help her children make it out of high school.

It's not that empathy is an old person's game. Its scale at any given point depends on a strategist's brain and history, and how loud the ego shouts. But empathy does require some commitment. The weather on the asteroid needs to bruise and stain you. And empathy takes vim; it requires energy from you. It thrills the recesses of the heart while sucking life from its teat. Yes, hearts have teats. Suckle on one, sometime.

Empathy is a constant loop of exploding atoms and collapsing singularities. Bang, there's everything. Vroom, it's one thing. Bang, there's everything again. Vroom, it's one thing. Bang. Vroom. Bang. Vroom. "Oh, look at all the speech bubbles over everyone's head. Hang on, where did they go? Ah, they're back. There are so many of them. It's too much. Oh, they've gone again. Thank goodness. Hang on, this is what they mean." And some empathy is fantasy—watch out for it. This fantasy involves words like these: "I think this is what they'd think." These words are scratching for truth and using empathy and memories as fingernails. But, hey, maybe you're just making it up? This is why research exists.

*Strategists are mediums. Your work is to channel other people.* You can wonder in the first person about a topic as a starting point, but you can't treat your own experience as an endpoint from which to judge other people's experience. An endpoint sounds like this: "Well, I'd never do that" instead of "I wonder why that is." And a judge makes insights sound mean and casts research in ethical terms. They don't report, they damn: "These people are stupid" instead of "These people who voted for this politician are in pain and are mourning a way of life they hadn't yet inherited but that they thought was their destiny."

Empathy imports truths from other people's realities to make insights stir within the strategist's mind, and it writes what it finds without indicting what it finds. Your strategy provides the scaffolding and you make artistic decisions along the way, but you decorate the scaffolding with the minds of other people. These people can include customers, academics, experts, internal stakeholders, colleagues, and people from other agencies. The point is to arrive at compassionate and compelling strategy more than the point is to be the one who takes all the credit for it.

There are as many ways to see the world as there are tribes in the world. This makes empathy one of the wonders of the world. It shows dull things in fresh light. It puts previously important things under the umbrella of unimportance. It reilluminates old things and puts new things in the shadows. But spending too much time in other people's emotions is a risk. It can make you lose sight of what you think about life, because empathy as a first reflex is an endless mirrored corridor. There is always one more door. The mirrors make you think you can see yourself at all times, but really you are getting lost.

And in the corridor are also people who prey on empathy. These are not usually your customers, who need you to see their lives with loving eyes, but executive types. And they know they can get their stubborn way by wielding someone else's ability—*your* ability—to see their position. There will be times when this will hurt you. It's not your fault. The trick is to latch and detach, to explore and to reel in, and to have techniques to stop the endless rain above the asteroid's conveyor belt when and if that rain becomes acid. The trick might be as simple as to make a note of their position and the way they communicated it and move on.

### FEELINGS ARE CLUES

Strategy makes people feel. It makes you feel. It makes your colleagues feel. It makes your clients feel. And via ideas that breach more minds, strategy makes the public feel. But feelings scare people. It's easier to work without feelings and to shove emotions behind the shadow of percentages and middle-aged hair mullets. "It's business work, not feeling work." Right and wrong aren't always the most useful flashlights to shine at the world, but the flashlight beam comes closer to wrong than right on this one. If you deny feelings in strategy work, you are playing a far more make-believe game than declaring yourself an artist.

Strategy makes the strategist feel. *Where empathy makes you feel other people's feelings, doing strategy makes you feel your own feelings.* There's the feeling at the start of a project—the ratcheting of the roller coaster to the summit, slow-and-steady jackhammer sounds and all. There's the swivel between clarity and fog as questions form. There's the rush of the hunt as questions heat-seek answers. There's the morning-after guilt and sense of being overwhelmed when the hunting party retires to reflect about what it has dragged back to base. There's the focus and

flow of going out again, making the hunt make sense,
of finding patterns and plastering the wall with noise and
then signal. There's the ebb and resurgence of confidence.
And then there's that feeling in the brain when you arrive
at places still knowing you need to get to more places.
It's an acupuncturist jamming in a needle and flicking
it hours later. That's one needle. Five more to go.

There are feelings that nobody even wants or understands
in strategy. But feeling starts knowing, so feel it all you must.

Strategy makes your colleagues feel, too. Often that
feeling is resentment. There is status in a word like "strategy,"
and so the word can become an appendage to many titles to
signal little more than "I can think and I can even do it with
my brain and please take this seriously and give me more
money." This scramble for titular importance dilutes the
word. Many people further dilute it by using it—or the
word "strategic"—as punctuation to say that what comes next
is important, whether or not it is actually strategic. "Strategic
planning," "strategic creative," "strategic objectives," "strategic
rationale," "strategic strategy." It's grandstanding. And so
resentment is a common feeling.

Most office-places swim between rusty resentment and an
evasive tolerance of strategists. This is a handicap that serves
nobody, least of all the office-place that has these feelings. Good
creative leadership isn't just managing the "creative" department.
It's exalting the creativity of all worker bees. And this can
happen while also honoring the profound and different expertise
of the various worker bees. "Anybody can have an idea" isn't

adequate to say without discussing what ideas are and how they happen, honoring the craft of idea-having, and recognizing the primary roles different people play within the agency. Good creative leadership leads the company, not a department. And it does so by magnifying people, not diminishing them.

When strategy works, colleagues will feel the echoes of the strategist's feelings, but the feelings will crescendo with a poke to the brain and a subsequent adrenaline rush. This can turn to a runner's high as long as people know how to run with that feeling. When strategy doesn't work, colleagues will feel frustration because this not-working will eat into their own thinking time, and their thinking time was supposed to be dependent on the strategy. On the other hand, some colleagues will feel indifferent to the whole thing. They're the ones who have a job, not a calling. They envision their own beanstalk twisting up from a sinking *Titanic* to the sky, and it only fits one person.

Strategy can make your clients feel. Words like "feel" and "feeling" will spark terror in some meetings, but they are useful. When you present work and then ask, "What does this make you feel?," know that this question will operate in three successive waves in the client's mind. The first wave is: "As an individual in this room, how does this make you feel in your loins? Yes, reach there. Do you feel fear, anger, sadness, joy, pride, disgust? Why do you feel that way?" There is no need to pretend that your client doesn't start in the moment, with their own mind and body, just because they wear business attire.

The second wave is: "If you see this work through the eyes of the people who are its final audience, how do you think

they'll feel about it?" There is no need to pretend that this isn't
somewhere the client's brain goes, even if the person throws
their hands back, assumes a bystander air, and says, "I don't
know. Let's ask them."

The third wave is: "As someone who will have to live with
this thinking and steward it through your company, how does
this make you feel?" The light can dim here. Put out your
most quivery antennae to catch what the client is radiating.
Even if their feelings are negative, they hold clues.

If the work animates the person but it seems a Herculean
task to do anything with it, they'll exhibit hesitation, and
you'll know the execution needs to be broken down more.
If the work confuses the client, they'll show you that confusion,
and you'll know you need to clarify the concept. If a client
feels uncomfortable with or indifferent to the strategy work in
another way, asking "What would need to happen for you to
feel differently?" will probe for both the feeling and the reason
within the feeling. This question is a gateway to more questions
that can help you understand what's true for your client.
If you believe in the strategy work, the first stop is to treat
these obstacles as puzzles, not as slights to your intelligence.

To make feelings central to all discussions of strategy is
a hazard. People like to hide from feelings. Over time, you'll
see a pattern. Clients and colleagues who can interact on
the level of feelings will initiate an uncommon depth in their
conversations, and this depth will lead to a livelier and longer
relationship. The opposite? A strategy life of one transaction
after another, a life in which strategy isn't art but a series of

reports with a fancy job title stamped on them. In one mode of strategy, you are neutered. In another mode, you are alive.

## DRAMA SETS YOUR STAGE

The word "drama" hauls with it a lot of baggage. School plays haunt everyone—especially, the parents who have to attend to watch their child in the silent role of "Knight Five" at the back of the stage in an auditorium with no air and a smell of rotting lunches from last month. "Dramaturge" sounds like why sewers exist. "You're so dramatic" is an accusation we level at someone we think has lost the plot, not written it. "You're making a drama out of nothing" is how we tell somebody that what they care about isn't something we care about. The allure of The Quiet Life—a life without drama—is a sedative many of us reach for when real life isn't obeying us. And so drama drags around a body bag, and it stinks, and we don't want to deal with it. But the word "drama" is yours to reclaim.

The point of "drama" as a strategy word is to make you know that information isn't enough without opinion, that *it is easier to refine a dramatic opinion than it is to add drama to a dull opinion*, and that creating the drama you need for your work requires a defiance that many other players will pretend isn't part of the game. They'll say, "Just the facts, please." This is why your presentations contain infinite bullet-points and nobody is buying what you're selling.

There are several ways to understand the word "drama." First is the understanding that *a drama is fiction on a stage. This*

*describes all pitches and agency-client meetings.* The players have their
own sets of information, their scripts and lines; they assume
roles and wear costumes; and they imagine possible futures
for their projects, their companies, and themselves. This
is fiction on a stage. (An internship, if it does nothing else,
at least provides a free ticket to this spectacle.)

Second is the understanding that drama is a series of
unexpected events. An idea is an unexpected event, and since
most projects consist of several ideas, a project is a series of
unexpected events. Ideas combine things in unexpected ways.
The idea of strategy and the idea of self-respect, for example,
will combine in a new way for some. Maybe you'll even realize
this in the middle of a meeting that's turned dramatic for
the wrong reasons and you'll put your burst of self-respect
to work by standing up for your ideas and your team. This
is one of those unexpected career events that might turn into
one of your life's main events.

Third is the understanding that drama might mean
emotional chaos—the dreaded neuroticism that poor "drama"
can't quite shake off. In fact, emotional chaos describes the
inner life of all strategy work and all projects. It just doesn't
always show on the surface and few people admit it.

Strategy is drama. Timesheets mark the plot; meeting minutes
mark the plot turns. "You didn't see that coming, did you?"

In your strategy work, you attempt to *bottle the human condition
and animate it* in a captivating way. This makes you a dramatist.
You watch the world, you come to an awareness or hypothesis
about it, then *you put that into a drama to let it play out.*

A creative brief is a strategist's story outline. A presentation is a strategist's stagecraft. Each project plan shows the blocking and stage directions, each meeting is a scene rife with conflict and unmet needs, each layoff becomes a Shakespearean tragedy, and each campaign launch is like a Hollywood premiere. Your strategy drama combines information with opinion and then awaits an audience reaction.

If you ever feel stuck in reams of research, just ask yourself "Where's the drama in this?" If there is none, go find some. Dig around online communities and consumer reviews for anecdotes people have shared where, perhaps, they've shared too much. Interview people but load your questions so you get loaded answers that might even surprise the answerer. Ask them about love, hate, anger, frustration, awe, and glee. Ask them to tell you something they've never told anybody else. Let them answer then ask gentle questions to squeeze more drama from them. "Why did this come to mind right now? How do you feel about it? Do you feel different about this now compared to before? Why haven't you told anybody else about this?"

If you ever feel empty-handed, head immediately for the drama. Catch yourself in thoughts you don't think you're supposed to have and say, "Hang on, what's the truth in that? Can I make sense of that? Is there something revealing in the vulgarity of that?"

If the ideas aren't coming, throw an unexpected event into your thinking. Take your team somewhere they don't spend a lot of time and ask them to force together what they see with the project they're working on. Take them to peruse horse stables, a retirement home, an emergency ward in a hospital. Imagine strange scenarios for the product. "So, we need to sell the last tub of yogurt on Earth but it's riding on the roof of a taxi through the crowds leaving a São Paulo Football Club loss to Corinthians. There's alcohol and anger in the air. The crowd has seen the yogurt and they want it. What do we do?" Think about the most unusual object to combine with the product you're trying to sell then search for the sense of the connection. Yogurt and picanha–the tastiest of Brazilian beef rump cuts–what do they have in common? What do yogurt and three hours of moombahton–with its thick bass lines–at the Kingston Club in Pinheiros have in common? Yogurt and the Rio Carnival? Your answers to questions like this will give your project an unexpected event.

One technique of comedy screenplay writing is to take the hero and, in each scene, pose this question: "What's the worst thing that could happen to this person right now?" Then the writer makes it happen. "Our protein-eating, muscle-building customer pauses on a street corner to decide between buying yogurt from a nearby supermarket or feasting in a steakhouse in Buenos Aires. What's the worst thing that could happen? I know, she gets sucked onto and trapped in a tourist bus of vegetarian missionaries bound for Rio Grande." Unexpected events lead to unexpected ideas, and questions can make unexpected drama happen.

If you ever fear a presentation, approach it like a director. Write your story, select your actors, design the set, direct the scenes, and rehearse. Taking one new risk in each presentation will focus your mind on what you're trying to improve and ensure there's drama–high stakes–and, at least, you'll not bore the room. You might even entertain it to a "Yes."

Information has never been so available but your job isn't information. It's the inner life of the information, the tenuous tension between clusters of information that don't seem to belong together but can if you playwright them to. So next time someone tells you you're too dramatic, reply, "Yes, that's the job." Just make sure you have enough self-awareness to know you aren't trying to stuff the person into drama's body bag because it has even less air than a crowded school auditorium in the middle of a New York summer.

### INFORMATION CAN CRUSH YOU

In evil hands, information is a killer. In evil hands, information tries to cure uncertainty. *All* uncertainty. And because art is uncertainty attempting certainty, uncertainty trying to shapeshift into certainty with metaphors and wolf howls, information in a tyrant's hands can kill art. It will do so by obliterating everything between information and art, including the fraught territory known as independent thinking.

In evil hands, information is a mercenary that non-thinkers unleash to crush other people's creative urges. This is ironic because information exists to inform, not to prevent formation of new knowledge. At its core, information asks you to do something with it besides bowing down to it, because why else would it inform you? Instead of "Do you have any information?," we would ask, "Do you have any finishing? I just want to know what to think and for that to be the end of it." Information is in formation. It is raring to form and to continue forming. It always has somewhere to go. Except in evil hands, where it is the end.

Information bullies exist. They seek to reduce the world and everyone in it to a series of formulae. They also tend to get control of companies. When that happens, they seek to reduce strategy to patterns that robots can happily inherit. They pretend to talk about ideas and sometimes wear sneakers to work on Fridays, but ideas are rare to fall from their mouths and someone else dresses them for work anyway. You'll know you are facing one when the conversation sounds like this:

**Cool idea. Where are the data?**

*The data are here—these interviews plus these statistics plus this academic research and a chat with the client over a beer. See slides one through fifty.*

**No, I need one number to prove everything.**

*No single number can prove the universe.*

**It will prove yours. It's time for a reorg. Bye.**

Data worship makes information an airplane without a flight path or a pilot. Worship of any kind creates blind spots. It's not data's fault. It's humans' fault. Data worship is the human need to know everything, usurp everything, and buy and sell everything, mixed in a morbid cocktail with the human need to feel we have control over a world that we do not control. Data worship is an ostrich with its head in a hole that lets in just enough light to see by and to make it comfortable enough not to pull its head out.

**What do the data tell us?**

*The data are the data. We tell us what to tell us.*

**Then why did we spend all this money on tools?**

*To get data.*

**All of the data?**

*No, we can't capture infinity.*

**Well, is it worth the monthly license?**

*Sometimes.*

**I'm going to lie down. I can't handle this chaos.**

*I'll look at the data and tell you what to think.*

**Start there, next time.**

There is a kind of gauntlet run with various origins that tries to explain the difference between data and information. It's called the DIKW Pyramid. The pyramid sets data at the bottom then works up through information and knowledge to wisdom. The most important part of a pyramid in our times is, of course, the top even though pharaohs were buried deep inside pyramids and had mad clout in their times. Data are made up of small facts that combine to form information.

In some definitions, data aren't useful until someone uses them, and then they are information; data become information because someone has connected them to other data and in so doing they have attributed meaning to them and used them. Information becomes knowledge as it starts to explain why something is. Knowledge becomes wisdom as the transformed data become more useful, more profound, and more meaningful. And if this process isn't part of art, then what is? Speaking of which, the knowledge might turn to art before it turns to wisdom. Everyone is making up everything.

The DIKW Pyramid is both useful and confusing. It's useful because it helps you to parse conversations, thoughts, and numbers into categories. These categories can tell you whether you're exaggerating the importance of one thing (for example, one statistic) at the expense of looking for deeper meaning (for example, why the statistic exists and how to use it). It's confusing because individuals decide what sits where in the pyramid based on their sense of how profound and useful the thing is. Profound usefulness isn't objective and it isn't static. One person's wisdom could be another person's information.

Here's an example of this gauntlet run. You collect the ages of people who work in your advertising agency. These numbers are data. You calculate the average age as 26. This is information. You compare this average age to industry statistics and investigate how the average age came to be so young compared to other professions. You hear tales of people burning out in their 20s and looking for a more stable way to live, new parents not returning to work after having children because of the hours they'd have to work or their jobs disappeared while they were away, and of leaders believing age made people less creative, slower, and more expensive. This is knowledge. Wisdom asks a profound "Why?" Why does this exist? And it might be hard to put back into numbers. Wisdom might suggest that one reason the average age of the industry is so young is that advertising is the daily act of novelty and that, over time, people in the industry become less of a novelty themselves so they defy the essence of the industry. Wisdom might suggest that senior leaders hit mid-life and start to wrestle with death in a way that makes them want to only work with people they think are distant from death–young people. Wisdom might suggest that leaders want to maintain their leadership positions at all costs and it's easier to do this when there's a clear gap in status with their employees and age is one of the clearest points of differences so they take out people who might think, "We're the same, you and I."

However someone defines the word "information," the power of information rests in seeing it as raw material for strategy art. Pieces of information are Lego blocks on a kindergarten alphabet mat. You need only to drop to your knees and assemble them how you see fit. Instructions will help, but instructions are mainly for robots and robots don't know how to assemble art.

The problem is focusing so much on data and information that knowledge and wisdom don't get time to happen. Or, worse, using data and information to fight off knowledge and wisdom. This is like insisting on playing a painstakingly well-tuned piano with one finger because things could go wrong if all fingers got any ideas and joined in. You want things to go wrong. This is how thinking happens. It's how life happens. And to make it happen, you just need to take your information and throw it into a drama using an opinion.

## OPINIONS ARE EVERYWHERE

*Strategy is an informed opinion about how to win.* Strategy is the melding of data into information, and the vaporization of information into fiction. It's the history of a champion before the win has happened. Suit-wearers might parade strategy around bleak meeting rooms as if it's a set of facts, but strategy isn't facts. *Strategy uses facts as ingredients. It cooks them into opinions.* It melts down the Legos to make a new and more exciting monster.

The problem is that everyone has opinions, so people who sell strategy pretend they aren't selling opinions, because opinions are so ... what's that word? Subjective. Yes, opinions are subjective, and businesspeople don't believe in subjectivity. Well, they don't believe in *other* people's subjectivity. The appearance of bulletproof objectivity is all that matters to businesspeople.

We use opinions in many ways. We use them to diminish people and their ideas: "Well, that's your opinion." By reducing people to their opinions and then reducing their opinions to nothing, we try to reduce their power. This reinforces our egos, helps us push away unwanted ideas, and lets us feel dominant.

We use opinions as definitive answers: "The kimchi soondubu jjigae is the tastiest at this Korean restaurant."

We state our opinions definitively to cut off other thinking. Sometimes this is necessary because there isn't time, or the other thinking being done nearby isn't of premium quality. Sometimes, we do it just to make ourselves feel good.

We dress opinions as facts to drape the world in our image: "My city's football team is the best ever" or "Strategists are all lone wolves." This helps us feel less abnormal. Checking for what's normal and whether we are normal is a steady human activity.

Some of our opinions are insights. There was a time when "The world is round" was an opinion and easy to fend off, but we can now see this phrase as an insight for its time. For our time, the phrase sounds more like a common fact.

And we can use opinions to put ourselves down. "IMHO" or "In My Humble Opinion" creates the space for the opinion-haver to be wrong. Unless they are English, in which case IMHO means the other person is wrong.

The word "opinion" fits everywhere, yet strategists pretend their thinking isn't opinion because the main use of the word "opinion" in our language is to diminish thinking as flimsy. Except when you visit a doctor for a second opinion, because then you're hoping at least one doctor isn't a flimsy thinker.

Opinions aren't right or wrong. Unfortunately, many of us grow up feeling wedged into a ledger of right vs. wrong, a world of constant moral adjudication. And education teaches many people that thinking exists to deliver us to a "right" answer. How else can someone get high marks in a standardized multiple-choice test?

People who think among peers often use information to dominate those peers in an apparent act of rightness. What's better than banter where one person leaves a winner and everyone else leaves in shame? The internet similarly teaches people to have one fast opinion, to say it, and to never vacillate. What better way to get attention than a correct fast opinion? It's thunder for the ego. News masquerades opinions as scary facts. How better to manipulate the masses?

Even some scientists have sustained famed careers with opinions they dressed as facts. The worst part of it wasn't that they were wrong, but that they pretended their answers needed no further questions *because they believed themselves incapable of being wrong.*

Watch all meeting and workshop dynamics to see how senior people typically strive to feel correct at the expense of the room. They'll wait for all the other opinions to fluster, bluster, and flounder, then talk over them with a decision. Or they'll amuse themselves by bringing in a too-polite workshop host, dominating the conversation, and staring unrelentingly at the tip of the workshop host's pen in an attempt to mesmerize it into writing on the whiteboard what they have just said. They need to prove they are the most right, because to prove this is to prove they are above opinion, even as they surreptitiously work to sell their opinion at every turn. Opinions aren't right, but they aren't wrong either. What they do offer are paths to new places.

The mixed-bag shrapnel power of opinion is that opinion can start more thinking. Opinion can lead to more opinion, but each opinion opens a fork in the road: you can fall back on thoughts you've already had and repeat them at the world, or you can consider new directions in which to take your next opinions.

Most family gatherings take the first turn—people recite opinions they have heard from strangers at each other, with little intention of taking the other fork in the road. But even though chances of success are slim, the mealtime game seems to be to herd each other down a fork like a juicy chunk of turkey as an act of benevolence so that someone, anyone, will say, "Thank you for enlightening me. This has been the best Thanksgiving ever, drunk uncle." Turkey might bring us together, yet it is unlikely to change family opinions.

However, not all opinions exist on repeat. While many people live in their own loop of opinion, opinions can lead to infinitely more opinions if your mind is open. Opinions can go places if opinion-holders and opinion-hearers just fire up the legs in their brains.

Stand-up comedy's unashamed currency is opinion, and its starting point is the premise. A premise is a sentence that sets up what comes next. A premise is also generally a strong opinion. Its strength is in its ability to snatch our attention with a striking combination of unrelated objects. Our brains throw these combinations at us throughout the day. Like: "The major US sports feature so much coaching, it's a wonder there is any time to play the game." "Accents get you senior strategy jobs." "For some men, small mohawks are how they try to outrun baldness." Comedians learn how to pay attention to these kinds of opinions and then milk from them the most drama possible. And they do so with a fusion of intuition, technique, and audience feedback.

To watch a premise unfurl is to enjoy watching the creative power of an opinion at play in the world, like a dolphin that's just escaped captivity or a Swede who's just escaped winter or Dolph Lundgren acting as a dolphin trying to escape a floundering Sea World career with underwater machine guns and grenades and Hollywood dreams. And to appreciate this unfurling, it is useful to understand a few comedic concepts.

The premise sets up what comes next and often uses absurdist combinations of objects to create tension within us. We don't know where the thinking is going, we hope it's going somewhere that won't make us feel horrible because we agree with it, and the comedian makes us feel good about ourselves because it's them, not us, who has made this awkward observation. A punchline resolves this tension, but it does so with another unusual combination of objects. It's alien multiplied by alien. A punchline doesn't always end a joke, however. After a punchline can come a tag. Where a punchline is a dirty finger in the eye, a tag gets the dirty finger to linger and push through the cornea and into the prefrontal cortex. It says, "Well, if you thought that was bad, check this out." A tag is a sentence or two that exaggerates the punchline and makes the punchline look timid.

Then there are actouts and callbacks. Actouts are where the comedian takes on a character and acts out the premise or tag. Callbacks repeat a theme or phrase from earlier in a way that feels like poetic justice. In novel writing, a callback might be described as using "follow-through" or "Chekhov's gun." This is the principle that one should only introduce a major theme or item into a story if it will be significant—if it will be followed through on—later in the tale. Like if Andrea Pirlo appeared right now and asked you, "Are you still running or have you learned how to play?"

The point of all of these concepts is that a comedian's or writer's opinion is part of every stage of their work. To shy away from this idea is to shy away from the magic of the work.

Here are some examples of these stand-up comedy concepts in action, in a series of words that do not claim stand-up comedy quality:

A bad creative brief is a nymphomaniac. <u>Premise</u>

It screws everyone. <u>Punchline</u>

"I haven't slept in days. I've run from inbox to inbox, meeting to meeting, nightmare to nightmare. I can't get enough. I don't know if it's good sex. But it's a lot of sex. I leave everyone exhausted and with paper cuts. And I think they all know what I'm doing because they look like they hate each other." <u>Actout</u>

A bad creative brief's online dating profile reads, "If it moves, yeah, I would." <u>Tag</u>

Even when a bad creative brief has hung around so long you try to ship it off to a retirement village, you know it's wandering the late-night corridors like the Big Bad Wolf looking for pillow action. <u>Tag</u>

"Little pig, little pig, let me come in. Or I'll huff and I'll puff and blow your pitch in." <u>Actout</u>

Next time you see your grandparents, check for paper cuts. Bad creative briefs are living longer than ever and they are everywhere. <u>Callback</u>

The sentence "A bad creative brief is a nymphomaniac" is many things. It's an answer, because it answers the question, "What makes a bad creative brief?" It's a metaphor because it is not literal—creative briefs do not fornicate. It's an idea because it combines two things that are not common bedfellows. It's an insight because it's a door to a new way of seeing a small part of the world, and it might change how someone behaves with creative briefs. It is also an overstatement, which is dramatic by nature. Curiously, it's not a fact, but it can't be called wrong; in its absurdity, it might open someone to concrete arguments about why this is so. It's a premise because it leads to more ideas. And it is an unashamed opinion based on years of watching horny and suggestive yet bad creative briefs hold agencies hostage.

There is, indeed, no shame in opinions. The shame is when the opinion thinks it is a right answer and not the start to more questions. The truth is that strategy is infinite and if you declare you've cracked a brief, well, you've decided that only because you needed to decide that and congratulations to you.

People might pretend that a number has the correct opinion, but numbers don't have opinions. Numbers need someone else's opinion to count.

A huge portion of the media transacts only in previously established opinions and encourages a narrow game of opinion-within-opinion. That is, it provides room for voices to share a minor nuance of opinion within the genre of opinions that the media outlet has deemed acceptable. It's called the Overton Window. Implicit in many questions asked by such organizations is the question, "Within the opinions that we generally hold acceptable, what's your opinion?" Few media outlets are interested in people challenging the origins of the accepted opinions because that would challenge the origins of the media outlets.

Opinions can help thoughts happen, but they can also be occupational hazards and they need to understand the culture into which they enter if they are to lead anywhere useful. Most cultures don't like opinions. Opinions are suspicious, always scoping out the neighborhood looking for ways to break in. They're real opportunists with their smash-and-grabs. Opinions are dangerous. "What? You can think for yourself? We'll have none of that." Opinions are viruses. "If everyone feels free to express their opinions, if this catches on, then how will we control people?" And so some workforces survive without opinions:

**What should we do to keep the client?**

*What's your opinion?*

**Just tell me what to do.**

*I respect your brain too much to do that.*

**I'm just trying to survive.**

*I'm sorry we have taught you that not thinking will help you achieve this.*

**I'll only think for myself if you tell me to. But then you also need to tell me what to think.**

*I want you to think for yourself.*

**OK. I am doing that right now.**

*And?*

**Nothing.**

Strategy is an informed opinion about how to win. The combination of information and opinion is drama and drama is art. And all of it leads, if you are lucky, to sounds.

### SOUNDS ARE PLEASANT SURPRISES

What sounds does your brain make?

Have you ever sat still and tried to listen to your brain? It's history's nosiest invention but you can't hear it and many of you can't turn down the volume even when you cover your ears and yell, "Stop. Just stop."

What sounds does your brain make?

Does it chomp, whiz, purr, screech, meow, woof, or moo? You've spent a lifetime in your brain's racket but you don't know how to describe your own soundtrack even though you can describe the nuance between your fifty eccentric music playlists and you own noise-canceling headphones to block noise from the outside and inside worlds to listen to them.

What sounds does your brain make?

Have you ever attempted a long-distance romance? Long-distance romances are where you feel love here, but you send it way over there, and you hope the love you send way over there hits your lover in the face, heart, and loins, and washes over them enough so they don't cheat on you. Mad, isn't it? What sound does this allover washing make? Is it the sound a bucket of ice water makes when you dump it on somebody dragging themselves to survival through the hot Saharan desert sand? You know the sound. It's this: "That was exactly what I needed except not there."

All brains make sounds, especially yours. The sounds are long-distance. Your brain sends the sounds to other parts of your body. Your brain does this because it doesn't want you to know what it's thinking. It exists to judge you, but it doesn't want you to judge it. It's scared you'll uncover its ruse. It's scared that if you knew what you thought, you'd change, and, if you changed, it would have to change, and it's easier to do anything in the world than change. Even drinking water off the Saharan sand floor is easier than changing. Long-distance relationships are easier than changing. Covering your ears and telling your brain to shut up shut up shut up is easier than changing. That's why your brain makes sounds somewhere else.

You might not think of snot as a sound, but it is. It's an aural brew of a throat losing hold of itself because the tummy's sense of humor punched up at it, an ocean of wisdom bursting through a nasal blowhole, and a catapult flinging a small gooey object at the world with a high-pitched splat.

You might not think eyes frozen wide-open make sounds, but they do. Try it. Open your eyes as wide as possible and listen. You'll remember this stance because you've taken it before.

You've taken it when you've heard or seen something shocking and your eyes have frozen still in the hope that whatever you've seen won't see you back and will just pass you by. It sounds like an infinity of butterfly wings fluttering in a hellish Southerly wind gust.

You might not think a sudden holding of breath makes sounds, but it does. The breath heaves in a final clump of air, the nostrils flare then snap back, the air drawn through your nose lands on top of your esophagus, you clench your gut, you hold it in and your eyes whimper, then, eventually, you let it go like a dart in a Manchurian pub, and the air whisks back out into the world.

Business schools don't teach laughter because it's hard to laugh while also taking your college debt seriously, and business is best empty and sad. This is why quieter sounds such as giggles and gasps are more frequent brain sounds. They are examples of how the brain tries to fend off new ideas–"Keep that away from me." The brain has primal reactions to ideas, and you can look for the primal noises it makes to protect itself from changing.

Primal noises are the sounds of strategy happening. These sounds are not accidents. They are the sounds of the brain surprising itself. They are the brain telling you to pay attention. Where did that idea come from? Does it belong here? Do I have to let it in? What does it look like if I let it in? Will I have to change?

The worst sound you can encounter is silence. Silence is indifference. Silence is the echo of the obvious. Silence is waiting for the next meeting. When you pitch strategy to a large, silent room gathered by a veteran of procurement who has told everyone to say nothing because to speak is to give you power, you'll know you've hit a chord by listening for a snort. If you're onto something, the audience will struggle to prevent such sounds, because they can't control their brains when the poke goes deep. They will concede you snorts, chuckles, and gulps, because those aren't words that could confess to your power.

The sounds always happen. You'll hear them if you pay attention to the room and don't just speak at it and try to defeat it with how right you are. Primal noises are the everyday soundtrack of ideas. And all ideas are an attempt to sell something.

### SELLING ISN'T CHEAP

**What are you selling today?**

*Oh, I'm just standing on this street corner with an idea. I'm not selling anything.*

**What kind of idea?**

*It's an idea from some of the finest brains. Are you in the market for an idea?*

**Yes. We need to sell more widgets. Can you sell me your idea?**

*I don't sell ideas.*

**How much is it?**

*This idea isn't for sale. But it is ten thousand dollars.*

**How do I buy it if you don't sell it?**

*Your company gives my company money and I give my company my time. This is a deal between your company, my company, and eternity.*

**So, I buy your time?**

*No, no, no. I'm too pure to sell. My hands touch none of the money.*

**How do you pay your rent?**

*With money.*

**From where does the money come?**

*My time. It's an invisible thing that uses magic to fetch me dollars. I give it to a company.*

**You aren't selling this very well.**

*Surely my detached nature invests in you the idea that my thinking serves a higher purpose and that my higher purpose is thinking, which makes my thinking much better than other people's thinking. Selling never sullies it.*

**But I need thinking to help me sell.**

*I won't sell it to you.*

**You won't sell me thinking that will help me sell?**

*No, but I'll give it to you for free. Just ask me to pitch.*

**I don't have time for a pitch. It's a waste of everybody's energy. Most people use pitches to get better prices, not better thinking. I find work I like. I find the people behind the work. And I ask them to sell me on working together.**

*Go on. Ask me to pitch.*

**I don't believe in it.**

*I'll give you free thinking.*

**OK. Will you pitch?**

*Yes. Thank goodness I can finally tell you all my thinking for free.*

**How will you survive if this is how you operate?**

*Timesheets. I live off timesheets. They take care of me.*

**Sold.**

Agencies trying to land new work aren't the only ones standing on street corners. Open office floorplans with free coffee and Summer Fridays are street corners. Workshops with tidy agendas and agreeable nods and time counters are street corners. Presentations and tissue sessions and company-wide meetings are street corners. Dressed as something else, they stay street corners. And on these street corners, you sell. You might hate to admit selling and use all kinds of mazes and puppeteering to distract from the idea that you sell. But sell you do.

Selling can make strategists feel cheap, even when the price isn't. What price your soul? Every day, you sell the idea of strategy, you sell a way to do strategy, you sell the ideas that burst from strategy, and you help clients and stakeholders sell whatever it is that their money asks of you. *Everything you do is selling*. To keep a cold distance from this fact in the name of intellectual integrity is to treat your intellect without integrity. To think you are above transactions because invoices pass through other people's fingers is a crippling abstraction. You sell. People sell you. It's all selling.

A certain type of agency person knows how cheap selling feels to many agency employees. This person duly takes on the task of telling clients the agency exists to sell (so that no one else has to mention it). The businesspeople, of course, love this. The statement is so obvious that it can seem counterintuitive and ring like an insight, even though it's the most basic of facts.

To sell is to exchange one thing for another. Money might be one of those things, but money is something a small group of people dreamed up and shoved into the collective consciousness as a universal representation of worth. Time is also treated this way. And it's incredible how seriously serious people take these dreamed-up things. But since this is the world we've created, you will inevitably exchange time and ideas for money, unless you work for free, and then you are probably working for self-respect. Or to quell long-held feelings of inadequacy and irrelevance. Still, it's hard to pay rent and mortgages with dignity.

It's even harder to pay rent and mortgages with words but words are your currency.

## MONOGAMY MAKES WORDS MEAN

Strategists hold the volume control on meaning. When you find something that means something, you can choose to increase the decibels or quiet them. The higher the decibel level, the louder the meaning, and the more chance the meaning will get to enter someone's memory. A lot of strategy is a mess. It's a cacophony of squawks, a din of shouts, a clamor of insecurities. And then one thing means something and it rises above the noise, a soft but true note reaching for the heavens. This note might form a chord, but it is clear in itself. It doesn't rush up and down octaves wishing to impress people with its runs and hoping the listener latches onto one thing. It simply *is* the one thing.

Meaning is loudest when it means something specific. Otherwise it means a lot of things, and a lot of things are hard to hear. A lot of strategy tries to say everything and it uses big words to speak. Big words say so many things without saying anything. Meaning means itself when it speaks.

Strategists make cacophonies for several reasons. They make cacophonies because they fear not pleasing. They hope a smorgasbord of babble will keep everyone happy. "Just in case you didn't like what we found in the research or the insight or the strategy, how did you feel about slide one hundred and four?" They make cacophonies because they aren't clear about their own thinking. "Look, here's everything. I'm not quite sure about any of it but I'm hoping to distract you with the amount of it, and also hoping you'll tell me what's good without me letting on that I need help." They make cacophonies because they are in cultures where length is loud and loud is lauded.

"We need more upfront slides, team. At least fifty. It might seem we're yelling at our clients, but we aren't. We'll use our finest inside voices. More is always better–it's the best."

They make cacophonies because they aren't confident. "I'm not sure what to cut here. Am I allowed to cut anything? What am I allowed to do right now?" They make cacophonies because cacophonies are quick hiding places. "You can't find me. You can't find me. Look, I was under the bedsheets in the middle of the room the whole time." They make cacophonies because their competitors make cacophonies and the loudest din seems to win. "Wow. I think that agency won the pitch because they had a hundred slides that compared the populations of the different social media platforms to the populations of countries, democracies, feudal kingdoms, prehistoric tribes, the average number of bacteria in the gut microbiome, and more. It was an aggressive subreddit pitch strategy. Endless. The maps were pretty cool though."

They make cacophonies because they think straight into a presentation template and the template has slides with a lot of placeholder bullet points. "Does this slide really need two hundred words? I guess so. The template certainly seems to think so, and who am I to challenge a template?" Strategists make cacophonies for every reason other than to make meaning memorable. Cacophonies are attempts to bludgeon people's minds into obedience.

Meaning rings loudest when it uses words so strong they can't cheat. People remember these words and the meanings they confer better than weak and accommodating words.

Memorable words, according to researchers Mahowald, Isola, Fedorenko, Gibson, and Olivia, are "monogamous"[10]: they do not have a multitude of meanings, only one strong meaning.

In their research paper, "Memorable words are monogamous: The role of synonymy and homonymy in word recognition memory," they say: "Indeed, the most memorable words ha[ve] a one-to-one relationship with their meanings ... The best recognized words ha[ve] few meanings and few synonyms."

As it turns out, words like "pineapple," "potbelly," and "pi" haunt us more than words like "concepts," "exchange," and "concern," according to the findings. Their paper concludes by suggesting that "words are encoded in memory by their meaning, and this gives r[ise] to competition during recognition between different words with the same meaning. As a result, words that are monogamous with their meaning are most memorable."

These monogamous words keep thinking on the ground and meaning in the mind. They are the opposite of "heady" words, ones that ricochet around the brain because the brain can't catch them. Heady words like "innovation" and "holistic" and "synergies" are cheats. But that doesn't mean there isn't a place for big words or word games in your strategy.

Double-entendres and puns are fair game, but dangerous fair game. When a meeting congratulates itself because the strategy enables it to say everything in the history of the world and thinks

---

[10] *Kyle Mahowald, Phillip Isola, Evelina Fedorenko, E. L. Gibson, Aude Oliva, "Memorable Words Are Monogamous: The Role of Synonymy and Homonymy in Word Recognition Memory," 2018/02/05, https://psyarxiv.com/p6kv9/.*

this is smart, it's not. A strategy might involve a double-entendre, but it needs to intend it as a single-entendre. If you were to use the word *natural*, for example, are you saying the product comes untouched from nature or that the person using it is a natural and has innate skills in a particular domain? If you were to say you want to position the product as a *smart decision*, are you expecting ideas that deal with intelligence and smarts or is this just a self-congratulatory strategy and you don't know what you want? *You must pick a side.* Wordplay can help you get to the thing, but to the thing you must get.

Big words, in particular, can try to mean too much. And so it is useful for you to ask, "What are we pointing to with this big word? Can we use a shorter word? What about a one-syllable word? We don't have to keep it, but let's see if we can get there." The aim is to ring out that one, clear note, a beam of meaning that will reach to the skies and sell. Not cheat. And this makes a healthy infatuation with writing critical to your success.

## WRITING BREAKS OPEN SAFES

The glee of an early strategy career resembles the Cooper's Hill Cheese-Rolling and Wake. Every year, Brockworth in Gloucestershire, England, hosts this competition. It stars a seven- to nine-pound round of Double Gloucester cheese about the size of two of your heads. That's the most nonviolent thing about it, although dairy can wreak havoc on many people.

Here's what happens: You walk to the top of a grass-covered hill and you inhale the view. "Made it. Now to beat all these other chumps to that large circle of cheese." The cheese launches down the hill, sometimes reaching speeds of seventy miles per hour, and then you launch yourself after it. For half a second, you and your fellow fromage racers resemble kids running down a small slope with legs that miss the ground every few steps. It's not too bad. Then the hill drops into itself, and one of you faceplants. You see the body break in two, then snap back together just in time for another faceplant.

Coming from your left, a stream of vicious somersaults throws another strategist ahead of you. Others of your strategy kin work their side-roll techniques until one of them flips three times before breaking a pelvis on the ground in an aggressive one-way act of making love with the middle of a small mountain just outside the Cotswolds. Splat. That unfortunate strategist slides down the rest of the hill like a sticky plastic frog toy melting down a window.

A wily competitor five strategists to your right thinks, "Screw this," and dives headfirst toward the finish line, hoping that by taking the shape of a torpedo they can fly like one, but face burns are all the action this strategist will see. Somehow, a lanky strategist out of nowhere with legs like a ninja cricket wins the cheese. Sure, she found her footing on a few spines and skulls along the way, but who can judge the victorious Cheese Catcher of a Cheese-Rolling and Wake? Later and while in surgery for a blown-out meniscus, the winner wonders, "You know, if we'd all paused to focus on our writing skills and pooled our money, we could have bought all the cheese. And the hill."

Books on writing are foundational strategy books. Writers must notice the world in new ways and compel their readers with what they see. These two things are also at the heart of strategy work. Most high schools contain teachers who tell students to include an idea in every essay paragraph. If teachers taught this well, everyone would know what an idea is. But everyone does not know it. And so an essay about the New York Knicks might start with this sentence:

"The New York Knicks have frustrated New York for decades."

and not:

"The New York Knicks are how New York manages its anger."

In the first sentence, the word "frustrated" is an observation that requires little from the reader. It also gives little to the reader. The second sentence is a firmer statement of an idea, and that idea is that the New York Knicks are a form of anger management. It suggests that the New York Knicks are a frustratingly bad team because a public two-hour therapy session with basketballs is how New York likes to deal with its anger issues. Get that rage out, New York.

For the first sentence to cross the idea threshold, the writer would need to take the thinking about frustration further. Unedited wordplay can help with this. Here's an example of such unedited wordplay and the theme of frustration:

"The New York Knicks are where New York places all of its frustrations."

"The New York Knicks are the blue balls of basketball."

"The New York Knicks are a citywide groan."

"The New York Knicks are how the mindful test their
  mindfulness."

"The New York Knicks are how Wall Street vents."

"The New York Knicks are why yoga is so popular in
  New York."

"The New York Knicks are how to practice patience."

"The New York Knicks care about you as much as
  New York cares about you."

"The New York Knicks will survive New York longer than
  its inhabitants."

"The New York Knicks are a New York tragedy."

"The New York Knicks are more a business than a team."

"The New York Knicks love money more than basketball."

"The New York Knicks exist to print money, not win games."

All of these statements resemble a premise, an insight, and an
idea. You decide what work you require of them. And what work
happens next.

As a writing exercise, you need to first focus on the riff—the
wordplay dramatics. Your first focus isn't on what is indisputable.
Truth will leak into the wordplay, and you can then unearth
more of it. By the way, you could agree with any of these
statements and still love the New York Knicks. But if the writing
succeeds, you'll see the New York Knicks with new eyes, as this
new Knicks notion echoes in your mind for days.

Writing isn't a multiple-choice exam where a "right" answer exists. Writing isn't definite until you say it's definite. Writing is a mess until it's clean. And writing can use strong statements to dislodge dogma in order to get to another question, yet not replace the dogma with more dogma.

Writing is like opening the lock on a safe. Creating the first draft of a sentence is how you start to crack the lock. Inside the safe sits a way to see the world that might change someone's life.

The digits you try as you turn and spin the lock are the words. You enter a possible combination of words into the lock.

Then you ask questions of each word:

Is that really what I want to say?

What if it's the opposite?

Is that specific enough?

What do I really mean?

Is there a stronger word for that?

Have I heard that before?

Where's my "pineapple"?

*Example:*

Bad creative briefs create more work.

Bad creative briefs cause a mess.

Bad creative briefs mess with everyone.

Bad creative briefs screw with everyone.

Bad creative briefs are nymphomaniacs.

Each turn of the padlock seeks words with a stronger signal. Each whirl is a finger tickle trying to lock in this new signal. You, as the writer, decide when the padlock might open, but the reader must also be able to open it themselves when they read it. To find the combination that breaks open the lock, your strategy brain must loosen itself and be willing to brawl with its ego. The ego needs to enjoy the wrestle while taking responsibility for picking a winner, especially if other minds await a creative brief. Limbo isn't an option.

How do you get good at writing? It's a secret combination of experience, learning to care less about other people's opinions, reading too much, developing a love for words that don't cheat, writing a lot and for the sake of it, attempting particular techniques, and always hoping the next sentence is better than the last one. Also, it involves a suspicion of too-pat words and platitudes, and involves seeing words as puzzles where the first draft is simply an initial, chivalrous glove-slap to the face, saying, "I challenge you to a duel."

There is nothing wrong with using templates to think, as long as the thinking happens. But templates, whether for creative briefs or company presentations, can seem too sacred. The templates can feel like a shortcut to importance. They can exonerate you from thinking.

Hands, paper, and pens can help you feel the words. Research studies suggest that forming words by hand as opposed to with a keyboard increases brain activity, helps thoughts self-organize better, and leads to a stronger ability to breed ideas.[11] Completely hands-free thinking is also a technique. A stroll under the sky will allow you to write in the brain. A walk with the lazy goal of one clear thought can ignite an afternoon of writing.

Most books on writing say writing is rewriting. Rewriting can feel like an early strategy career that's constantly rolling down a hill for cheese while watching the New York Knicks lose again. But bumps and bruises are your allies, not your conquerors. It also helps to have a healthy attitude toward time. Some call this patience.

## PATIENCE IS LONG ENOUGH

### How long is patience?

*Long enough. It's a decision.*

### How much is patience?

*Infinite. There is always more.*

### How will I know when I've had enough?

*Pain. It will hurt.*

### What if it's too early?

*Yes. What if?*

---

[11] Ephrat Livni, *"Keyboards Are Overrated. Cursive Is Back and It's Making Us Smarter,"* Quartz, July 25, 2017, https://qz.com/1037057/keyboards-are-overrated-cursive-is-back-and-its-making-us-smarter.

**What if I'm just giving in?**

*You are. But to what?*

**What if I'm just giving in to the pain?**

*You are. So what?*

**What if I feel pain but I'm not supposed to?**

*Yet you do.*

**What if the pain is just in my head?**

*Always. That's where it is.*

**Why are other people more patient?**

*Other people are always more of something.*

**Why can't we move more quickly?**

*And whom does this benefit?*

**Wouldn't this benefit all of us?**

*Are you including your timesheets in "all of us"?*

**How do I get more patience?**

*Sit there.*

**Then what?**

*Sit there more.*

**Won't I miss out on stuff?**

*Yes.*

**What if I don't want to miss out?**

*How does that feel in your head?*

**Why does it feel like chaos?**

*Because you don't know what you want.*

**What if I want it all?**

*Yes. That hurts the most.*

**How can I want less?**

*Sit there. Want less.*

**How will I know when I want enough less?**

*You'll sit there.*

**Is patience a virtue?**

*It is until it isn't.*

**What's the opposite of patience?**

*Mania.*

**How do I avoid mania?**

*Breathe.*

"Patience" is more than a Guns N' Roses song. *Patience is a calibration of desire against a timeline.* Patience judges what it sees and how it feels against what it believes are the minutes it will take for what it sees and how it feels to align with what it desires. A plea for patience is a plea to see the timeline of desire with forgiving eyes. Those eyes need to consider current circumstances and imagine future circumstances, and then pit the urgency of their desire against their ability to manage that desire. Many strategists struggle with patience because they don't know if they have too much or not enough of it, but no matter which side you fall on, the realm of patience is always a four-fantasy orgy.

The first fantasy is your desire. Many strategists aren't clear about their own desires. Often they adopt other people's desires. One day moving to New York seems like a plan. The day before, the plan didn't exist, except in the mind of a friend. Fantasy.

The second fantasy is time. Astrophysicists, philosophers, ayahuascans, mushroomers, and Einstein figure among the enemies of watches and timesheets. Humans invented time as a means to understand the universe and to have a sense of control over it, and then to control people. Fantasy.

The third fantasy is how you judge current circumstances. How much closer does one event take you to a desire? How many events need to occur to make momentum seem real? One, ten, or all of them? Does the desire need to have come to fruition so you can retroactively prove the chain of events that made it happen? These judgements are a series of biases, from survivorship bias to confirmation bias. Fantasy.

The final fantasy is your ability to predict the future. Prediction is different than fiction. Strategists excel at fiction. Fiction relies on your capacity to imagine a different world. Although strategy uses facts, it is fiction. Yet often we have delusions of being predictive. Strategists can no better predict the future of their strategies than their own futures, but we fantasize that it's possible.

This orgy between desire, time, circumstance, and the future chafes the thighs of patience. Rashes break out and patience realizes some fantasies complicate life more than they help it.

Since patience is fantasy, it isn't the same for everyone. One person's patience is another person's victimhood. Is that a desire for love or an indifference to abuse? One person's patience is another person's laziness. Is that a desire for calm or a lack of effort? One person's patience is another person's prison. Is that a desire for control or oppression?

Impatience also differs for everyone. Impatience embarrasses many strategist CVs. Is that hopping jobs or escaping unhappy jobs? Impatience frustrates many long strategy projects. Is that how long a project needs to take, or a convenient way to fill calendars? Impatience pushes for another redesign. But has that logo or campaign run its course, or does it still have legs? Fantasy, all of it.

The patience fantasy in a strategy career is complicated, because patience depends on both the mental makeup of the strategist and the environments into which the strategist erupts. Even a casual perusal of the "Big Five" personality traits, a model initially advanced by Ernest Tupes and Raymond Christal in 1961, will show that some strategists aren't what other people would call stable: they are high in neuroticism. Partner that with a powerful and hungry brain, high expectations, a desire to feel useful, a need for variety and novelty, comfort with mess, questionable social skills, an industry or agency that doesn't know what to do with strategy, a boss who doesn't know how to manage a strategist, a creative

department that resents strategy, and clients who think
only *they* do the strategy, and this kind of strategist will leave
behind a CV trail that looks like confetti thrown off a midtown
Manhattan skyscraper in a blizzard. This difficult pattern will
be made even more painful by a lack of self-understanding and
an accompanying lack of self-respect.

   *A strategy career in the wrong hands is a dark place to hide.* A strategy
career that exists only to express itself through companies
it works for risks playing a foul trick on itself. It is a rapid way
to self-repress. A strategy career in the wrong hands is a victory
for Mr. Potato Head as he peels you away from yourself. But the
midlife crises and light depressions that might seem born from
your neuroticism can, paradoxically, act as alarm clocks. Wake
up, strategist. Sometimes, you'll find you have been the most
patient about the fantasies that guide you away from yourself,
not to yourself. And you might even find that the fantasy you've
been most patient with wasn't ever yours anyway.

   For many people who think for a living and who can't feel
a pulse unless they are thinking, developing patience toward
themselves is the greatest challenge they will undertake. Over
time this is a mightier, and more helpful, fantasy to construct
than all the other patience fantasies put together.

   This fantasy needs a task. What are you alive to do?
Discovering the answer is a process of remembering and
listening and distilling the first principles of the themes that
have run through your life. This patience-toward-self fantasy
also needs a gang. Who is your crew? Strategists need muscle
and they need that muscle to push them beyond themselves.

The fantasy needs a fight. For what and against what are you fighting? You don't need to hide from your anger when you can listen to it and put it to work. The fantasy needs an internal monologue. How do you speak to yourself? Patience asks you to speak like a yogi and say, "I am where I need to be but let's keep going."

The patience-toward-self fantasy furthermore needs to focus on process goals, not outcomes. *Process goals amass actions over which you have control, with the actions focused on what will improve you or help you flow.* Daily or weekly goals of reading for an hour, writing three hundred words, interviewing two people, speaking with three clients, and visiting one museum or gallery are examples of process goals. Perhaps the outcome goal is a promotion, publishing a book, or moving to a new city. These small actions—your process goals— are the beats of the fantasy. If they don't happen, the fantasy won't happen, except through divine intervention—and that is wishful thinking, not strategy. And so you build your fantasy and then you step into it and make it happen and patience creates a new relationship with time and money.

When is any of this enough? When you say it is.

# Operating *Words*

Words operate you and you operate words.

The words you say to yourself are crucial, because these words shape your mind and they will shape you in public, even if that public is a small meeting room or an email. Words that remind you of your mischief, your need for meaning, your frequent facetime with pains of the brain and soul-cramps, your need to practice, and your need to form a gang can help tether you to bedrock. Few strategy careers last a lifetime, and when your strategy career fades, you'll need to resurrect a sense of self that remembers what it has to contribute to the world outside of a job. You'll fare better at this if you remember yourself before you need to. Honor yourself, remember the impact you can make, and make it on yourself.

Words are your work, and they let you access the world.

As you flirt with words and ideas of art and drama, you flirt with power.

To know strategy is opinion but it is stronger when it respects information is to work an honest strategy life.

To seek sounds in meeting rooms and to enjoy the feelings of doing strategy is to respect what is human.

To admit you are selling and that you are selling how to sell are worthy admissions.

To do strategy is to play with a light heart, not to bludgeon. And words are your toys.

Words make ideas and ideas make strategy. But words mean different things to different people. And people use words in different ways *at* different people. Sometimes they use silent adjectives to confound and dominate colleagues. Sometimes they don't know they are doing this, yet it happens. Words aren't wicked, but people can put them to wicked use.

To discuss strategy is to first identify the operating system within which you operate. These things change between countries, cities, agency types, strategy department types, and clients. And your operating system includes not only the outer world, but your inner world.

Strategy doesn't happen in a vacuum. With a stronger grip on the context in which your strategy happens, we can now discuss how to do it.

# SECTION II

—

# Strategy
# *Words*

03

—

# Ideas Are First
# & *Forever*

# CHAPTER THREE

# Ideas Are First
# *& Forever*

## THE SECRET ABOUT IDEAS

One word wanders truant through the veins of the fluorescent concrete holding pens that pass for adult daycare–or "offices," as you might know them. This word punctuates every second breath. It grimaces when people try it but fail it. It wiggles into new shapes when people argue with it. It vows to start and finish everything. It is a Big Bang unto itself. People say the truant's name five times into a mirror, and they hope it appears. Sometimes they forget there is no mirror and they are in a small room with other people they must pretend to like, but that's what the free alcohol is for. If the truant doesn't appear, they repeat the name until they're breathless or the lights shutter off and the local buses and trains nap. The word feels like power, the same kind of power a teenager with no bank account feels when they run away from home with only one plan, which is to get their feet beyond the front door. Slam. Now what? The word is always there, like carbon dioxide. The word is "idea."

The secret about ideas is this: Few people who use the word "idea" know what an idea is. Or how to have an idea. Or how to help others to have an idea. Or how ideas are different from thoughts. Or how to explain an idea. Or how to express an idea. Or how to make an idea. Actually, that's seven secrets. And yet people who say they have ideas will also say they are in the "idea business," as if that sounds more important than advertising. Or more specific. Or as if that were an idea.

Accounting students spend their first weeks of college learning the concepts of "debit" and "credit." And if they enter the career of accounting years later, an intimate knowledge of these two words is a precursor. But people can enter advertising careers without knowing what an idea is. Some of these people, in fact, sustain long stints in the profession through personality alone. And by playing a game of, "Well, if none of us knows, then who's to know? Shhhhhhh I'll stand here and make all the money, OK?"

When an idea exists, words make it exist. Body language, silence, noise, and pictures can only take an idea so far. Try it. Announce to a room, "I have an idea," and then strike a yoga pose, say nothing, burp, or draw a picture. You'll give the room work to do and they'll do this work out loud. With words. They'll have to distill your charades or sounds into words because words will help the idea travel into their minds, and then usher the idea beyond the room. And so the centrality of words makes each of us responsible for our use of the word "idea" and the words that we use to have ideas in public. It also makes charades and burps team-building exercises, but no more than that.

*Strategy is ideas and ideas are made of words.* After you have found facts in research, you combine these facts with feelings and you origami it all into something new. This new thing is a combination of things that have already existed. This new thing, if it's good, will be an idea. And you'll express the idea in words.

When people fight these two truths—that strategy is ideas and ideas are made of words—they are fighting to defend their sense of identity, their status, and their desire to feel they own certain words and that other people do not get to play with those words. These people mutter under their breath about strategists. These people see themselves as the strategy department and the creative department and the fount of all things, and as so much of a fount they need nobody else, especially not a person with "strategy" in their job title. They think strategists get in the way.

The people who mutter are confused bullies. They gain strength by making others feel powerless. Claiming "We don't need you" is a powerful pseudo-idea in itself, and it's the main one they have. This zero-sum game hurts everyone until you, the strategist, can define and defend why you exist and then live somewhere people want you to exist. Achieving such a thing can seem to take forever. And it's one reason why the internet thrives, as strategists and other word-and-idea types all furiously punch the keys, looking for each other.

Words make strategy and strategy is ideas and ideas happen in words, so words need our love, or ideas won't show up for school.

The word "idea" doesn't want to play truant. It's not a naughty kite that has cut loose from your grasp to the sounds of *na-nana-na-naa you can't catch me*. It needs tethers. It wants boundaries. It also wants people to know it, not keep it in shrouds. It didn't want to run away in the first place, but it was tired of the neglect and Mom's unstable life partners.

When someone surprises a meeting room with the word "idea," an actual idea won't appear unless the person also knows what they are saying. *"I have an idea" is not proof someone has an idea*. It's a hope. Like declaring, "I am the boss of the world." Or holding a seance. Or reading a horoscope.

When it grows up, the word "idea" wants to be oxygen, but it needs lungs that know how to liberate it from carbon dioxide. The word is tired of people using it to hold power over other people. "Idea" is a genie in a bottle, it's a secret spirit that needs help to be released—but remember that this magical creature has morals and self-respect. It's time for people who say they do ideas for a living to give the word "idea" the dignity it deserves. The secret that so many who claim to work with ideas don't know what ideas are needs to come out into the open. So, too, the reason ideas exist at all.

## IDEAS LIVE TO FIGHT

Ideas—and their kissing cousins, insights—help humans survive. And that is the reason they themselves have survived. Ideas and insights are evolutionary adaptations.

For some reason, humans have a highly developed, self-aware consciousness. Humans don't know from where this consciousness came. Nor do they know from where their thoughts come and if their thoughts are even theirs and are happening inside them or whether their thoughts happen through them, beamed from some secret source.

One theory is that human consciousness derives from pre-human hominids eating magic mushrooms that grew on the feces of wild cattle in Africa. This "stoned ape" theory, promoted by ethnobotanist Terence McKenna in *Food of the Gods* (1992 and 1993), suggests our ancestors ate their way to a higher consciousness, ingesting psilocybin and getting a genius neocortex for taking the risk. Or perhaps, on the same note, human consciousness has been helped along by hallucinogenic fish with names such as "the fish that makes dreams" *(Sarpa salpa)*, "the fish that inebriates" *(Siganus spinus)*, and "the chief of ghosts" *(Mulloidichthys flavolineatus)*. These are exceptional job titles.

However it is that we arrived at our kind of consciousness, the planet did this to humans, but the planet needs none of it to survive. Earth doesn't need ideas, humans need ideas. Ideas create and destroy, and so Earth would be quite content to not have ideas from humans at all. Earth knows how to create and destroy by itself. And perhaps—given the climate change and mass extinction situation we've got going on—Earth has had what fun it can have with humans and now hopes the genie will return to the bottle.

Until that happens, ideas will provide humans with two key benefits. First, ideas give humans a competitive advantage over most other animals and provide competitive advantages among humans themselves. Second, ideas provide humans with ways to understand their sense of self and identity. Earth can only sit and watch.

Ideas give humans a competitive advantage about how to create or take resources. Yes, ideas are a fight for resources. This makes ideas dangerous and it makes people who have ideas weapons. It also makes people who have ideas enemies if they are on opposing sides. It's no wonder adults cajole creativity from their children and usher them into conformity. Who would want to raise adults who think for themselves and for the sake of it and because thinking is a gift?

Anybody who has earned resources with their ideas has participated in a competition for resources. Resources can include money, food, attention, love, and shelter. They can also include more abstract concepts. Cryptocurrencies aren't that different from the gold stars on a teacher's desk except for people who believe otherwise. Ideas compete for these resources but these competitions happen within a web of cultural nuances where different groups of people place different importance on different resources and how people compete for them.

Australians are fond of tall poppy flowers. But the love of these tall, sweet flowers is why Australians also have a condition called tall poppy syndrome. It's a congenital Australian ailment that involves sarcasm, binge-drinking, not moving facial muscles while speaking, and fighting for no reason as you do your best to take down anybody who thinks they're better than you. When a poppy gets too tall, Australians cut it off at the knees. This is why it is both fun and scary to spend time with Australians. The banter is endless, and it exists to keep people in check. *Australia's banter is Australia's answer to England's class system.*

Tall poppy syndrome exists for various reasons, but one theory is that in cultures of scarcity—like Australia, with its vast stretches of harsh terrain—to stand out is to signal a threat. "Hey, look at me. I have ideas and I'm confident. You probably think I'm going to steal your stuff, don't you?" After all, ideas are waterfalls—one innocent idea about helping the tribe might gush into the idea of taking control of the tribe. But in cultures of abundance like the US, the world's number one economy, people need to stand out to attract resources. "Hey, look at me. I'm special. Lavish on me everything we have and reward my innate individuality." The question "What's special about you?" is laser-etched into American brains from birth. Answers to it appear everywhere—in grandparents' compliments of their toddler grandchildren, preschool and high school and college applications, the labels people know themselves by throughout their schooling and their careers (junior, senior, sophomore, rising junior, rising senior, executive, vice president, senior vice president, executive vice president, president), on business cards and in email signatures, and in the way sports commentators seek data-points to point to an athlete's uniqueness (for example, "She's the first left-footed, only child born in Alabama in 1987 and who loves to eat ramen while watching reruns of *Friends* to ever score at a World Cup"). *Labels of individualism are America's answer to England's class system.*

To watch these dynamics at play, try observing an Australian order water just outside Minneapolis by saying, "Water," after which a colleague from the US South says, "I'll have chilled water with a slice of lemon, ice but just three cubes, a drop of lime, served in a cold glass with one straw, please." To an Australian, this order sounds absurd and greedy because much of the Australian mentality is in a battle with how much individuality it's allowed. But in a country with both abundance and specialization, you learn to know what you want and to have that want satisfied, and also that to not be specific is to risk dissatisfaction. Many Americans are in a constant competition against mediocrity.

You can also observe how people introduce themselves in meetings in the US. These scripts of individuality are so well-rehearsed that it's only when someone who grew up outside of the US and whose culture didn't ask them the question "What's special about you?" and then mumbles a lame answer to the question that you realize the power and pressure of this question. The trick with these scripts is that most come from a preapproved playbook. While a beautiful American idea is that you're allowed to have ideas about yourself, most American businesses want that to happen in private because they don't want to have to compete with those ideas in the workplace.

Ideas and idea-havers aren't as safe in corporate America as you'd expect. American business culture is hierarchical, and few businesses are democracies. This means that ideas don't fight it out among themselves. The hierarchy fights first. Then the ideas fight. But, if the hierarchy can stamp out competing ideas, there is no fight between ideas. This means that for your ideas to have power, in some businesses you'll need to first have power.

Despite public talk about individuals and their ideas, the norm in the US is like the norm in most country cultures: ideas and idea-havers are threats. Businesses often place employees who are known idea-havers at a distance. Idea-havers eventually learn that they must only have certain kinds of ideas and share them in ways that don't affect who gets to be important. It's a strange, dishonest game that hurts many people, especially when they hear their team leaders cheerleading, "Ideas can come from anywhere" and "We have a problem—does anyone have any ideas?" It's a painful irony that sits alongside the irony that many who run big businesses hate socialism for ordinary people but love it for their businesses and ask for it in tax incentives, bailouts, and tariffs. If companies can ask cities to reward them for existing in them, why don't people also ask cities for the same benefits? Now, that's an abundant idea.

*In advertising, ideas exist to give companies and idea-havers a competitive advantage.* They help companies battle for people's attention, money, memories, and recommendations. They help idea-havers build careers. The challenge for most businesses– advertising businesses, included–is to encourage ideas in spite of hierarchy. Otherwise, the only thing that's competing isn't the business, it's the pecking order inside the business.

## NOT ALL THOUGHTS ARE IDEAS

You can do whatever you like with words, because nobody owns words, but when you throw words at other people it is considerate for you to hold yourself accountable for the way you throw the words. Otherwise, what are you saying? And if you hurl the word "idea" at people all day without knowing what you're saying, the word "idea" will limp home exhausted to its TV dinner in desperate need to recover from its daytime nightmare and anxious whether its stress will let it sleep at all.

The word "idea" is used in almost as many ways as the word "thing." This is why *the word "idea" often gets in the way of actual ideas.*

First, there is "I have an idea." This translates to "I have a thought that I'd like to suggest to you." For example, "I have an idea—let's visit Vancouver but let's not go to the part of town where we have to jump over all the syringes. I pulled my hamstring last week."

Second, there is "My idea is this." It translates to "I have a thought for which I'd like credit." For example, "My idea is to go to the Edinburgh Festival for the day and to not leave without eating fish and chips in a local pub."

Third, there is "You have no idea." This translates to "You are stupid." For example, "You didn't realize Latin America was a cultural region and you thought it was a business region? You have no idea."

Fourth, there is the other "You have no idea." This translates to, "OMG! Something so bizarre and amazing happened that it defies your reality and is only knowable to me." For example,

IDEAS ~~are~~ THOUGHTS, but not ~~all~~ THOUGHTS ~~are~~ IDEAS.

@MARKPOLLARD

"You have no idea how tasty alfajores are. Two round cookies with dulce de leche and a slather of chocolate can coat a stomach with Argentinian heaven."

Fifth, there is "What a great idea." This translates to "Yes, I accept your suggestion. Let's do that." For example, "I'd love to watch stand-up comedy in central London because people will be so drunk there is bound to be a fight with a comic. What a great idea."

Sixth, there is "You have the wrong idea." This translates to "Remove your hands from me." For example, "I thought this was a job interview. You have the wrong idea. I said, *You have the wrong idea.*"

Seventh, there is "Can I bounce an idea off you?" This translates to "I'm still thinking through something. I might have an idea, but I need you to tell me. It won't hurt." For example, "Can I bounce an idea off you? I have a hunch that England's best curry is in Birmingham—not on Chiswick High Road. Shall we have a romantic weekend in Birmingham and put the hunch to the test? We can watch Aston Villa. Just no fighting on the train to the game, OK?"

In most of these examples, the speaker is using the word "idea" instead of "thought" because "idea" sounds more important and more worthy of eardrums. These aren't wrong uses of the word "idea" in the world at large, but such uses will get in the way of the word "idea" for the way people in strategy hope to use the word.

*Ideas are thoughts, but not all thoughts are ideas.* Ideas make mischief because they're unafraid to cross the line.

## ALL IDEAS CROSS THE LINE

Johnny Cash walked the line. At least in music. He sang "I Walk the Line" in 1956, and while singing those words didn't make him loyal, loyalty is a useful concept in contemplating ideas. When you walk the line, you place dark after night and light after day. It's an act of loyalty to how people know night and day. What else does you think of when you contemplate night and stay loyal to how people know it? Sunset, dinner, bedtime, sleep, quiet, dreams, nightmares, pajamas, late-night snacks, late-night drinks, late-night nightclubs, a late show on television, stars. When you stay loyal to the idea of night and you walk the line, these are the words that come to mind. What do you think of when you contemplate day and stay loyal to how people know it? Sunrise, sun, blue sky, work, office, factory, school, commute, breakfast, lunch, coffee. When you stay loyal to the idea of day and you walk the line, these are the words that come to mind.

*Walking through a topic as most people know it and without surprises is called linear thinking.*

The word "line" operates the word "linear." To walk through a topic is to walk a line. If you draw a long vertical line down a piece of paper, put "night" at the bottom of the line, then mark the long line with ten small hatches going up and write what comes to mind when you think of "night" at each stop, that is linear thinking on a page. If you draw another long vertical line, write "day" at the bottom of the line, then mark this long line with ten small hatches and write what comes to mind when you think of "day," that is another example of linear thinking. Step by step, Johnny Cash walks up and down those lines.

If you then shake free the words from the lines above the words "night" and "day" and coax two of them together, you are doing something different: lateral thinking. "Lateral" is a fancy word for across or sideways. Sideways is how crabs walk. And while Johnny Cash sang about walking the line, crab walks were in fact familiar to his love life.

Here's another one: if you maneuver "sunset" and "factory" together with a crab walk you'll hit an idea—"Sunset Factory." What is it? It's an all-glass restaurant perched on a hill where there are the most exquisite sunsets all year round. What other shape could this idea take? It could be the name for a company that makes blinds, a morgue, a euthanasia-assistance firm, a manufacturer of sleep aids, or a melatonin purveyor.

One more. If you glue the two listless words "quiet" and "commute" into "Quiet Commute," you now have the world's quietest commuter train or the world's quietest train car, or noise-cancelling headphones, or the least noisy sequel to *Die Hard*, or a silent car engine. There is still work to be done to define these ideas in uncommon yet useful ways, but the names will open possibilities—all through the simple act of putting two words next to each other and insisting on sense from them.

# LINEAR THINKING

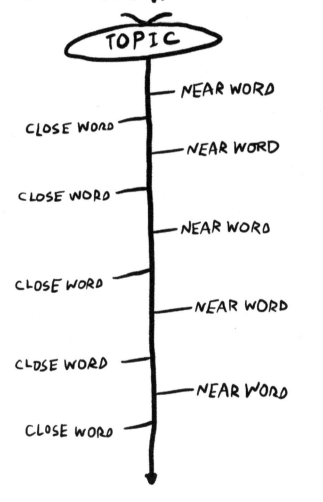

@MARKPOLLARD

Linear thinking goes down a line of thought. It stays loyal to a topic. It remains close.

Lateral thinking crosses lines of thought. It is disloyal to the topics. It roams far.

*A lateral thought is an idea.*

An idea is a useful combination of things that do not usually belong together.

Creativity brings together things that do not usually exist together in useful ways.

Having an idea is an act of creativity. An idea is an output of an act of creativity.

*Creativity is lateral thinking.*

*An idea always contains a lateral thought*

The term "lateral thinking" was introduced by the physician and philosopher Edward de Bono in his influential 1967 book *The Use of Lateral Thinking.* Lateral thinking is different from linear thinking because it forces together topics that are normally apart. Lateral thinking is also different from "vertical thinking" and "deductive thinking," which business minds like to pretend are the only ways to think—or the only ways to charge a lot of money to think.

Vertical thinking and deductive thinking are similar to linear thinking in that they all appear in lines. All three of these thought patterns walk lines. But vertical and deductive thinking are different in that they act more like logic and argument,

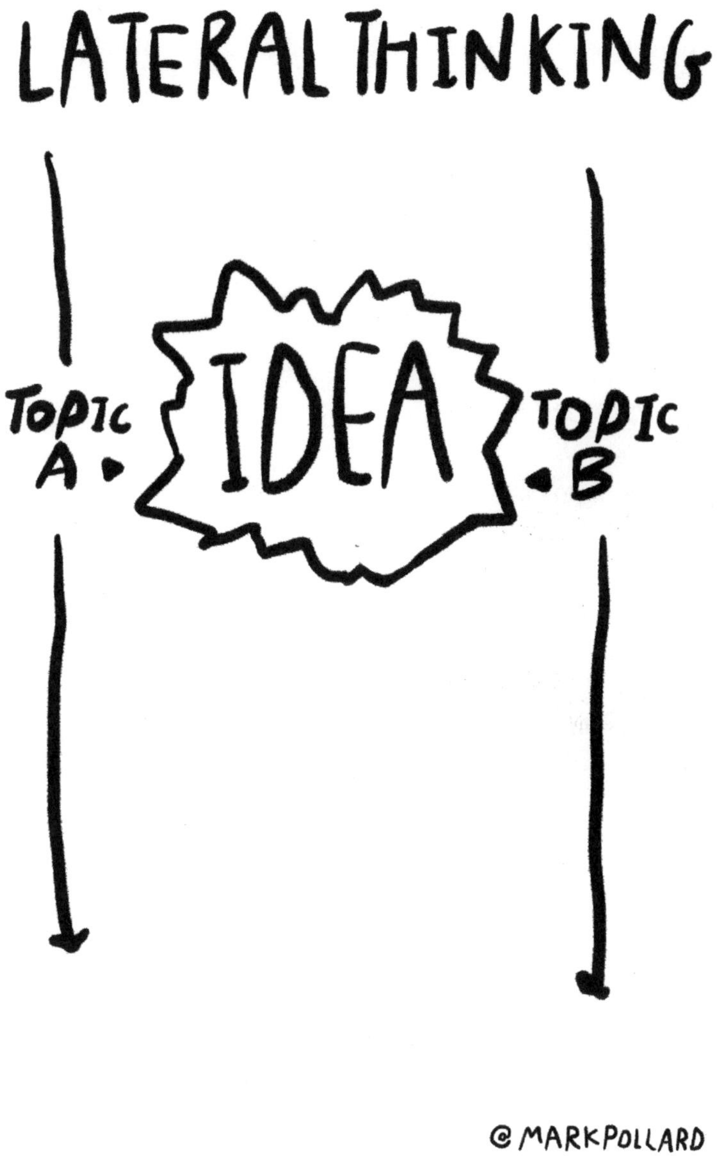
LATERAL THINKING
TOPIC A
IDEA
TOPIC B
@MARKPOLLARD

where A must lead to B and B must lead to C, therefore D. Vertical, deductive, and linear thinking are at the heart of an MBA degree. Lateral thinking is at the heart of the arts. And, yes, Johnny Cash used art to write about walking a line.

Johnny Cash's song "I Walk the Line" highlights another problem with language. It lies in these lyrics: "I keep the ends out for the tie that binds." Years ago, perhaps these words were clearer than a pink-hued sky being pierced with industrious golden rays during cocktail hour at Sunset Factory, but really, what do they mean? Are they a symbolic commitment to a higher being, a promise to only tie the knot with a person to whom Johnny Cash is loyal, a promise that even if he does stray he won't marry his affair, a promise not to impregnate his love before marriage, a sailor's jest to not take a fling too far when in port, a way that farmers might finish a bale of hay, or a simple gesture of confidence in someone with whom Johnny Cash felt bound? In song, the beauty of such a phrase is that listeners can choose their own meaning. If Johnny Cash sang this line to a roomful of teenagers on television, it could seem like an innocent promise of fidelity. However, his mind was not an innocent mind, so we know the line could have carried, and could still carry now, other meanings for other audiences.

Meaning is determined within a matrix of creation and reception. To know the ultimate meaning of this line is to know Johnny Cash, his mind's state when he wrote the lyric, how he had heard and used the phrase over time, to whom he is saying it, whether he means the words in different ways when he sings them to different groups of people, and also how different

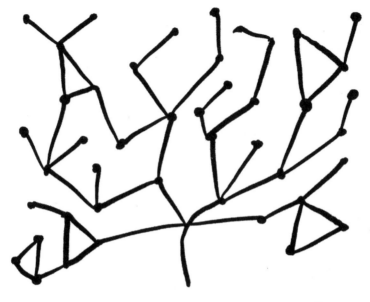

WHEN YOU SAY
ONE THING,
IT IS NEVER
ONE THING.

@MARKPOLLARD

groups reacted when he sang. To know these things is to know a network of facts. This is the actor-network theory of sociologists like Michel Callon, John Law, and Bruno Latour. Actor-network theory suggests that facts and meaning exist in a network and that a shift in any one part of the network—from the originator's intentions to how people understand a word or perceive a fact— shifts the meaning of the entire network. These shifts are what propaganda relies on. Most debates, too. Also, advertising.

Here's another example of actor-network theory. *The Five Love Languages* (1995) by Gary Chapman outlines how people need and express love. According to Chapman, the languages are gifts, quality time, physical touch, acts of service or devotion, and words of affirmation. Chapman suggests that people have a primary love language and a secondary love language. Words would be many writers' primary love language, how they give and maybe how they take away love. A writer might send love letters to their romantic partner and spend hours lost in this pursuit, yet the recipient might prefer acts of service such as fixing things or spending hours taking children to after-school activities and none of this word nonsense—and so the word "love" takes different shapes, even among those who are on intimate terms.

People often project their own definitions of words at other people without ever explaining those definitions. "Idea" is a victim of this in meetings around the world, every second of the day. A lack of definition is cancer. A confusing definition that people can't explain beyond a sentence is lethal. To have this blameless word thrown into limbo by people who claim to exalt curiosity, openness, and creativity is the irony of ironies. To not know what an idea is and to work in advertising and marketing is insanity. To *pretend* to know what an idea is without respecting what ideas really are is devious. And for an industry to allow this to happen is reckless.

While people are raucous with the word "idea," yelling it into the comets and stars above, they usually define the word— if they define it at all—in silence, so nobody finds them out.

## SILENT ADJECTIVES ARE SLOW DEATHS

Silence is life. To sit still and listen is to hear life. The breath of a stranger, the scrape of a chair, the churn of an Italian coffee machine, the gentle clang of small glasses, a gasp at gossip, car engines forging by, a baby's squeal, taps on laptop keyboards, the scratchy shuffles of a small dog.

To sit still and watch is to see life. A man in a turquoise winter hat and aqua coat hauls up a slight concrete incline a shopping cart filled with several large black boxes with yellow lids under trees with gray-brown bark and putrid orange leaves that flit in the wind. A mother steers a stroller with two sleeping babies through the cafe's plastic and wood winter front door and then the glass and steel inner door, watching for how each door's springs tighten so that her squeeze into the café doesn't involve a sudden door bash. A man makes coffee under a black cap with a white serpent in the shape of an S. His eyes dart. He is near people but not with them. When a coffee does not require his attention, he shuffles cinnamon jars, sugar pots, metal milk jugs, and shiny white saucers around a bare counter and cleans the steam nozzles of the coffee machine.

Your own silence, and the observations it invites, is a beautiful book if you choose to read it. But some silence is death.

When teams who think for a living do not define the jargon they use, that is death. When they keep the meaning of their words silent because they do not know the meaning of their words or do not wish for others to know how they mean their words, it is hands around a throat. When a company is silent about the role and value of strategy and therefore the existence of its strategists, that is taking a guillotine to valuable brains. This noncommitment to strategists might make hullabaloos such as, "Well, why don't you tell us how to make strategy work here?" But questions like this only feign interest and are waterboarding torture, and the people who ask them know it, which is why they ask them.

When a strategy manager is unable to give a strategist feedback about how to improve or what he or she seeks in strategists, or puts the strategist onto a project that is well beyond the strategist, that is a stoning. Their compassion seems silent because it doesn't exist. When a creative leader never shows creative leadership of people who don't have the word "creative" in their title and shows an active disinterest in strategy, it is hospice. When teams who think for a living do not discuss how they think about their work, how they like to work, what they need from each other, their hopes and goals as individuals and as a team on a given project, or what "good work" means, it is gas piping into a car in a closed suburban garage.

To deny that knowing these things and discussing them matters is to deny the existence of the humans with whom you work, and since you need humans for your work, it is team suicide. There is power in keeping people out and keeping shrouded what's important. Perhaps it spares an ego or protects territory so that one small thing survives in a dark way while everything around it limps through life in an even darker way. That is fear, not power. Fear hurts. And silent adjectives are one of its deadliest mercenaries.

Silent adjectives are killers. People cannot see or hear them coming. And their ninja stealth means you won't even know they were in the room. When someone says the word "idea" and intends it as a lateral thought, not merely as a thought, chances are they are also using a silent adjective before the word "idea" and making things more complicated than they need to be. These silent adjectives get added because many advertising people resent the beauty of words and need to make them ugly with a little Botox here, a little knife work there. (Adding insult to injury, some of the adjectives are actually nouns.) And so silent descriptors like "creative," "brand," "social," "digital," "mobile," "content," "strategic," "platform," and "technology" haunt most uses of the word "idea." Halloween is all the time in advertising.

An honest use of words would recognize that meaning is subjective and that it is useful to define words, especially jargon, and to think about whether a silent adjective sits in front of your use of a word.

Otherwise you can spin in conversations like this:

**What's the idea?**

*We're going to airdrop with drones a flash mob of food trucks into Christiania in Copenhagen.*

**I'm not sure the locals will appreciate that. Also, that sounds more like an experiential idea and we were looking for a…**

*Creative idea?*

**Yes. A creative idea. This sounds like a…**

*Stunt?*

**Yes. Also, we haven't established what the brand is about so do you have a brand idea, too?**

*Well, we're selling edible ants so we thought we'd design the flash mob of food trucks to look like ants from space. It will fit with the brand idea* **Leg It***. Ants have a lot of legs and our research suggests runners like to eat ants.*

**We could sponsor the Cooper's Hill Cheese-Rolling and Wake but *Leg It* sounds more like a tagline than a brand idea. What's the idea?**

*Eat like an ant, run like an ant.*

**That sounds like a fun content idea but I think it's too specific to be a brand idea.**

*We'll get back to you.*

These interactions can house fun and lead to new ideas and clarity. They can also suffocate a team. Sometimes, we waste breath by not using our breath to explain our words and say the adjectives we're holding silent. The point isn't to approach words like a dictator. It's to suggest that working well with one another involves taking care of one another and a beautiful way to do this is with the words we use or choose not to use. This might require the pedantic act of writing a list of words that are critical to the group and the common types of ideas people use those words to make.

## IDEAS COME BIG AND SMALL

Not all adjectives in front of the word "idea" are silent. Some we bolt on loud. These adjectives attempt to describe one person's reaction to the idea, an imagined reaction by some group of people, the size of budget the idea will need, how daring the idea seems, or how close to existing ideas the idea sits. In addition to the adjectives we've already seen, your colleagues might think of ideas as fat, skinny, tall, short, stubby, chunky, long, large, wide, deep, shallow, fast, slow, medium, average, bald, hairy, scary, cozy, frigid, comforting, or alienating. Any idea could be any of these things to any person.

But when the word "big" is wheeled out, it's time to watch out. If people insist on being given a "big idea," they are also insisting on the notion that there is a "small idea" and that there is an in-between—that a small idea can grow into a big idea, or that it can't. And this differentiation isn't helpful.

It is like an avid book reader declaring their need to read a big novel but not a small novel. Or a movie fiend declaring a need to watch a big film but not a small film. Or a comedy lover asking for a big joke but not a small joke. What's the point of putting the word "big" in front of the word "idea"?

The adjective "big" dresses an idea in importance. "Yes, we need a big idea. Everybody, bring me your best big ideas. We'll have none of this small idea business. We're in the idea business, but not the small idea business. We'll now call it the Big Idea Business. You, yes, you. That idea in your hands, it is not a big idea. Even your idea knows that. Why are you so incompetent? That idea fits in your hands. How can an idea that fits in your hands be big? Or big enough? I want you to struggle to bring your next idea to me, struggle so much you can't move it from your desk into this room where I adjudicate all ideas. If it's big, it won't move. If it's big, it will be a nuclear reactor that you don't know how to operate, but when I see it, I know it will change the entire world. Or at least raze a large city and leave zombie fish in its wake. Nobody can make a nuclear reactor budge, and that's how I want it. If you were carrying a big idea in your hands, you'd look more like the Wicked Witch of the West after the house pummeled her into the ground, which is to say the idea would have crushed you with its bigness and it wouldn't be in your hands. Am I understood? Fetch me a big idea that's too big for you to move from your desk, now! We have a pitch to win."

If an idea is a novel concept that brings together things in ways that haven't existed before and that are useful, *how can one idea be bigger or smaller than another?* Is it because one idea crossed more attributes from more disconnected topics than the other? Is a "tennis ballet" a smaller idea than a "tennis tournament where gorillas are ballet dancers and tennis players have to ride the gorillas throughout the entire match while classical music plays"? Is a big idea one that is more useful than a small idea? If so, does that mean more useful to a lot of people or life-changing to just a few people? Was Facebook a big idea when it started based on its concept alone, or did it become a big idea only when it spread around the world? Netflix, Twitter, Amazon, the printing press, a pencil, a pen. Which is biggest? Who says? Does a big idea ask then answer a more profound question than a small idea? For example, what if our planet is trying to get humans to eradicate themselves and start over? Who decides what is profound and then, if you're selling a brand of toilet paper, can you even ask a profound question and ever claim you have a big idea? Is an idea big or small based on the impact it has now or the impact it *might* have later? Measured by what and judged by whom? Is its so-called size determined by the scale of the problem it solves? Is a small tweak a big idea if the problem it tries to address is massive? Does a big idea have to cost more than a small idea? Is an idea big if it's on TV and small if it isn't? Is it all of the above, some of the above, or something else altogether? Is "big" or "small" useful at all?

"We need a big idea" is code. It's code for "This project is one of the most important projects in the agency right now, and because I'm involved with it, I am also one of the most important people in the agency right now." It's code for "Put some effort into this project, unlike the last one. You won't be able to get away with that again." It's code for "Look, I know you write good TV scripts, but … can you please not start there this time? It just creates more work for everybody else. More tension too." It's code for "We are bringing in more people for this because it's huge. All these consultants we're competing with are messing with our confidence. But don't worry about that. They aren't capable of big ideas." Sometimes, it's code for "Holy crap. This client wants us to jolt them and set the world on fire."

"We need a big idea" is not code for "I see your artistic spirit, respect it, and want to honor and magnify it through this work." Nobody is allowed, we are told, to be an artist in advertising.

The point is that there is no point to asking for a "big idea" unless people can define what a "big idea" is and how a team will know if it has one. Also, "big" and "small" aren't the only types of ideas fighting for attention.

### EVERY IDEA HAS A TYPE

You meet a lot of types of ideas in advertising. You might even have a type. The problem is the word "idea" can masquerade as all of the types of ideas if the speaker doesn't clarify what they intend.

The following list of idea types isn't exhaustive but it hopes to make your workdays less exhausting. Some of these types are interchangeable, even synonymous, depending on who's using the words. Some of these types mature or regress into other types over time.

Understanding the types matters, but so does the question, "What are we talking about here?"

## THE TYPES OF IDEAS IN ADVERTISING

1. **Business idea:** what the company does that's novel

2. **Product idea:** something novel that people can buy from the company

3. **Brand essence:** a vague phrase that anchors the brand strategy

4. **Brand purpose:** how the company serves humanity

5. **Brand promise:** what the brand promises to deliver to its customers

6. **Brand idea:** what the brand stands for that's novel

7. **Brand platform:** an idea the brand can stand on for a good length of time

8. **Brand tagline:** a short phrase that brings to life what the brand stands for

9. **Advertising idea:** an idea that repeats in every communication across all channels

10. **Campaign idea:** a subset and shorter-term execution of the advertising idea within a particular campaign (in cases where the advertising idea and campaign ideas differ)

11. **Non-advertising idea:** a concept that solves a problem and isn't advertising-centric, yet it may get advertised

12. **Content idea:** agency- or marketer-produced media that isn't an ad

13. **Social idea:** an idea born from the natural behaviors and attitudes of a social network

14. **Platform idea:** a technology-driven idea that can become critical to the business

15. **Tactic:** a short-term activity that without strategy can worsen long-term outcomes

16. **Execution:** the critical, essential finer points of an idea (art direction, for example)

There are many more types of ideas. There's an industrial complex of business writers trying to coin them. The good news is this: If you and your team can corner a handful of these ideas and know how you mean them when you say them, you'll stave off heartbreak and overtime. But know that you might need to do this on every project with new people because some new people will want to break your heart.

### THE TYPES OF IDEAS IN DETAIL: A WALK-THROUGH

A *business idea* is what a company does that's novel. When a friend announces they have a business idea, well, first of all, they don't want your opinion so it's best to sit there and enjoy the announcement in silence or simulated awe. But after that, if what they announce is indeed an idea, their business might start off as a product feature or new product.

A business idea that starts as a product feature might find a problem with an existing product, but the feature would theoretically be easy for an existing company to implement. For instance, a new website that collects existing online Halloween movies is more a product feature than a full-blown product. It would likely not be difficult for a video-streaming service to implement this feature or change its code and lock out this new website, thereby killing the business—or, in the Silicon Valley model, it could possibly acquire the business to absorb its stable of talent.

Your friend reaches this conclusion, too, and they contemplate other features that could combine into a more compelling idea. What about adding a subscription box service for people who want to celebrate Halloween all year long? Once a month a box arrives with ghouls and goblins and masks and games, and as people play a game, they can watch a Halloween movie from the company's website. You could argue this is a product that could sustain a small company.

Questions that would help push this thinking into the silhouette of a company would include:

Can this product scale with repeatable processes?

What's the product's unfair advantage—something others would find difficult to copy?

Can a catalog of other products stem from this business?

The latter question can be a sticking point for idea-hatchers in every field. Many people who want to write a book or do art focus only on the first piece, for example, when what they need

is a catalog—the same way someone who wants to release
a product into the world also needs catalog thinking.

With our Halloween entrepreneur, the business idea is to
give people a taste of Halloween whenever they want it. Is this
a lateral thought? Yes, a mild one. Halloween belongs to one
day of the year, so to push it onto other days is a crabwalk and
an idea. And then, the *product idea* stems from the business idea.
It stays loyal to it and honors it, which is what you want during
that step. "Hello Hallow"—a Halloween experience at least
twelve times a year, via movies and goodies—is the first product
of this business. Perhaps it is the name of the business, too.

*Brand essence, brand purpose, brand promise, brand idea, and brand
platform* are the next ideas to consider. These can be awkward
friends, so awkward they don't always hang out together.
A *brand essence* is usually a two- or three-word phrase that sits
in the middle of a presentation slide and tries to anchor how
the brand exists in the world, and hopefully how the business
exists in the world. These two things aren't always the same.
Most brand essences are vague and pretend to say more
than they do and riddle themselves with adjectival overdose.
"Surreptitiously Nepotistic," is probably a brand essence for
a New York aftershave. "Nutritiously Delicious" is the brand
essence of most mass-manufactured cereals and yogurts.
Or "Deliciously Nutritious." Take your pick. People are
correct to sit in stunned silence at hearing many brand
essences, even though the executives who are announcing
them will assume their meanings are obvious. Brand essences
are facile things, but can provide basic direction. Our

imaginary Halloween company Hello Hallow has the brand essence "Sexy Scary." Clear?

With *brand purpose* also in the fray, let's consider how "purpose" is a useful concept. It is most useful at the business level, and perhaps deserves a rename to "business purpose." Purpose answers two questions:

1. How does the business serve humanity?

2. Why do its employees go to work?

According to research cited in books such as Daniel H. Pink's *Drive* and John Kay's *Obliquity*, businesses with a purpose outperform those without a purpose because people want to work for them. However, the word has perhaps become a victim of its own success. There are three main pitfalls when dealing with concepts of purpose. The first caveat is that purpose, in some cases, has become a department, a hashtag, or a corporate social responsibility (CSR) initiative. It's treated as a sideline issue, not a primary issue. Perhaps it exists to distract from corporate misbehavior. The second concern is how consultants and strategists project their own morals onto a company's purpose. A purpose does not need to be moral to the majority of people in order to be true or to work. Many people dislike war, but a soldier may find more than a salary in protecting their country. A street gang serves a purpose for abandoned, scared, and abused children. Coal creates jobs. The third issue with "purpose" is that people who advocate for purpose often advocate for purpose to be the main thing a brand communicates. This is a false idea. Purpose doesn't have to be front and center at every moment. A brand needs to communicate based on the problems it is trying to solve for itself. If people aren't buying a product because they think it is not healthy, first the company needs to change the product and then communicate what's changed, even if the brand's purpose is not actually to promote health.

By the way, the Halloween company Hello Hallow's brand purpose is to get people to have fun with fear.

A *brand promise* is the key promise a brand makes to people. It finishes the phrase "We promise to ..." The strategist decides whether the promise ends with a feature, a function, or a benefit—and if it's a benefit, how far from the obvious benefit the final benefit is.

Features are the ingredients of the product or service. Tires, a steering wheel, and windows are features of cars. Functions are what the features combine to do. A function of a car is to carry people where they want to go. There are other functions of cars, though. Cars can be houses in which to live, makeout sanctuaries, runaway companions, kidnapping tombs, junk storage, cigarette-smoking hideouts, music salons, pet romper rooms while their owners dash into a grocery store, and more. Benefits are how these functions help people. A car that takes people where they want to go helps families see each other— a function. And what's the benefit of that? Families that see each other stay together. And what's the benefit of that? Families that stay together often create better adjusted humans. And what's the benefit of that? And is any of this true?

*Features are the ingredients of the product or service*

*Functions are what the features do*

*Benefits are how the functions help*

A brand promise can exist at any of these steps of the feature-function-benefit ladder. You get to choose.

To create a viable brand promise, the Halloween company Hello Hallow's brand promise could recycle words from the brand purpose. The brand promise could go like this: "Hello Hallow promises to get people to have fun with fear." A promise of "empowerment" or "happiness" or "confidence"— or "Hello Hallow promises fun"—would be too generic.

A *brand idea* and *brand platform* are often versions of a brand promise, brand purpose, or brand essence. The person who suggests that one matters more than the other needs to also suggest how they are different. In particular, you'll find the word "platform" can be used in many ways, but the most everyday use suggests a platform is something on which to stand. This implies it is sturdy and can last.

The Halloween company Hello Hallow's brand idea or brand platform could recycle words from the brand purpose. It could be "Fun with Fear," for instance. A *brand tagline* or a *campaign idea* could also graduate to brand platform or brand idea status. It's amazing how these words can move around slides like ghosts sauntering late at night through an agency. All of a sudden the tagline is the brand essence. Hello Hallow's tagline, let's call it "Play with Death," might become the brand platform overnight. There's nothing wrong with this, mind you. What's wrong is pretending this doesn't happen.

If this hurts your head, that is actually part of these ideas' reason for existence. These words and phrases jostle for dominance, in the hope that the people using them get to dominate you and your attempts at strategy and clear thinking. But these are all slippery words, so it's important to take them seriously yet not too seriously. Nothing is sacred except cuddles and stand-up comedy.

An *advertising idea* is a thought that exists in a brand's communications across all touchpoints. It is more than a photographic style and more than a mascot, but it can start with such elements. The advertising idea might use the same words as the tagline, but it is more than a tagline. A tagline is a business's catchphrase or slogan. For the Halloween company Hello Hallow, the tagline "Play with Death" is also the advertising idea. The advertising idea "Play with Death" will show toddlers with adult faces in a living room with a sandbox for a floor playing with things that scare them. Those are the creative constraints for however the advertising idea appears—whether as a pop-up exhibition, a social media post, a five-minute video, a thirty- or fifteen-second television commercial, or a direct mail piece. But each part of the campaign needs to honor the channel in which it appears, along with the people in the channel, and flex the idea in a compelling way. Otherwise you'll end up with what people love to refer to as "matching luggage": communication that looks the same, sounds the same, and smells the same but shows no respect for the channel in which it appears or the job it needs to do. Efficient but mindless.

An advertising idea and *campaign idea* often start as the same thing. A campaign idea can change over time while still honoring the advertising idea. The 2010 Old Spice advertising idea *The Man Your Man Could Smell Like* morphed in different ways depending on the perceptual issues that Old Spice needed to address, or based on when there was a new product or range to launch.

Here's an example using Hello Hallow. Let's say that in year one, Hello Hallow launches "Play with Death," and soon toddler adults are playing with whatever scares them in sandboxes everywhere. In year two, the company realizes retirement-home residents particularly love playing this game as a form of meditation in between taking LSD trips. (The game and the LSD trips both calm their anxieties about mortality, making them feel powerful about their impending deaths.) So the company launches a campaign for Mother's Day to get people to buy their grandparents a subscription to Hello Hallow. The campaign from year one gets tweaked. It becomes "Play with Death from Your Deathbed," and it involves new products and an evolved campaign that show older faces on toddlers playing with what scares them in a sandbox, but this time they're on a deathbed in the sandbox. The advertising idea is largely the same, but the campaign idea has evolved because campaigns are short-term, high-energy affairs.

In 2015, Always launched a campaign called "Like a Girl." The campaign idea was to reclaim the use of the phrase "like a girl"—which had historically been used as an insult—and reframe the phrase as a point of pride, not a put-down.

According to Judy John, an executive creative director at Leo Burnett Toronto at the time, the campaign "Like a Girl" was part of bringing to life the Always platform "Rewrite the Rules".[12] "Rewrite the Rules" was something Always would stand on for a long period of time–until it stopped working–and rewriting how to use the phrase "like a girl" was a way to bring the platform to life.

*Non-advertising ideas* are often described with terms like "acts" or "utilities." They might attempt to solve a human or societal problem and they aren't advertising-centric, even though a company might advertise them. Calling something a non-advertising idea isn't a highly useful designation. Perhaps its only use was when the trend was new and advertising was the default. There was a time in the second part of the first decade of the 2000s when this was the way many people thought advertising was evolving, until social media algorithms made advertising more … advertising.

Burger King's *The Whopper Detour* by FCB New York is an example. People could get a Whopper for one cent if they downloaded the Burger King app, visited a McDonald's, ordered a Whopper from the app, then picked it up from Burger King. The World Wildlife Fund's *Earth Hour* by Leo Burnett Sydney is another example. Getting the world to turn off its lights for an hour once a year for over a decade is a non-advertising idea. The *Magic Salad Plate* was a plate with plastic salad built onto it. The salad could nurse an Australian meat

---

[12] *Kim Kauffman, "Leo's Cannes Contenders: Always '#LikeAGirl'", LeoBurnett.com https://leoburnett.com/articles/work/what-it-means-to-be-likeagirl/.*

pie while making the meat pie look like it was surrounded by good intentions. It helped Clemenger BBDO sell many Four'N Twenty meat pies in 2009. Ideas like these fit across many categories in advertising award shows.

For Hello Hallow, an act could involve taking communities with high numbers of opioid addicts and trying to rehabilitate them through its games, perhaps drawing on the same mortality-facing concept as the retirement-home advertising, with a spin toward embracing life and fun even when things seem scary. This use of the games could be called "Back from the Dead." In the early days of social media and mobile phone apps, a utility might have involved "Scares On Demand," a free app that could get people to confront their fears every day. Because of how hard it is to launch an app and how paid-for the internet is, ideas like this risk seeming flippant or second-rate now unless they directly generate revenue.

A *content idea* is something that isn't an advertisement. A content idea assumes respect for people's time. It's something they might seek out, not something that just happens at them. It resembles journalism or entertainment.

For Hello Hallow, a content idea could be a filmed internet "play" called "Death Play" that follows the backstage and onstage antics during a kitschy dinner-theater murder mystery one Halloween night. Some will argue a content idea can become a *social idea* when it involves some combination of participation, an influencer, a media collaboration, and a head-nod to specific social media platforms.

Setting aside the "Death Play" play, a social (and also experiential) idea might be a Hello Hallow game called "Death Stares." Hello Hallow does a deal with a website with street cred, gathers the people the website thinks are cool, dresses them in scary costumes, and does teasers promoting mysterious booths placed around a city. The people with street cred appear in videos within the booths, backed by crazy music as they produce their most frightening death stares. Passersby can enter these booths and see how long they last. Hello Hallow encourages them to share videos of their petrified reactions, and also to create their own death stares with, yes, a shitty hashtag.

Is any of this clear? Of course, it is. But just in case, here's a roundup ...

### AN EXAMPLE: HELLO HALLOW—
### A COMPANY IN THE BUSINESS OF FEAR

**Business idea:** Hello Hallow serves Halloween to people whenever they want it.

**Product idea:** A subscription service for people who want to celebrate Halloween all year long. Once a month, a box arrives with ghouls and goblins and masks and games, and as people play a game, they can watch a Halloween movie from the company's website.

**Brand essence:** "Sexy Scary"

**Brand purpose:** Hello Hallow exists to get people to have fun with fear.

**Brand promise:** Hello Hallow promises to get people to have fun with fear.

**Brand idea/Brand platform:** "Fun with Fear"

**Brand tagline:** "Play with Death"

**Advertising idea/Campaign idea for year one:** "Play with Death," featuring ads that show toddlers with adult faces in a living room with a sandbox for a floor playing with things that scare them.

**Campaign idea for year two:** "Play with Death from Your Deathbed," involving new products and an evolved campaign that shows older faces on toddlers playing with what scares them in a sandbox, but this time they're on a deathbed in the sandbox.

**Non-advertising ideas:**

- "Back from the Dead," a service that tries to rehabilitate opioid addicts through Hello Hallow games

- "Scares On Demand," an app that will get people to confront their fears every day

**Content idea:** an internet play called "Death Play"

**Social idea:** "Death Stares," a photobooth collaboration with an edgy website and influencers that is designed to scare the crap out of people. Participants can share videos of their scares.

Inhale. Hold it. Exhale. A communications plan will help to make sense of how the brand will appear, what it will do or say, and to whom it will speak. These pieces of jargon are simply tools available to you when you have handywork to do. An idea is an idea is an idea until an adjective haunts or appears in front of the word. And while there are many types of ideas, labeling an idea as big or small is the least useful category. But did you know some people think you need a license to have ideas?

## WHO GETS TO HAVE IDEAS?

"As a creative." What does this mean? And why is it such a verbal tic for some people, a phrase that fights "um" for frequent use? Perhaps "as a creative" is an attempt to relate to others in a poignant and personal way, in a way that tries to summarize a lifelong wrestle with identity and repression and denial, in a way that suggests enlightenment and a desire to soothe the quiet panic in the meeting at the time. Perhaps. But usually, "as a creative" is an attempt to re-establish the rules of the game and that game is this: Who Gets to Have Ideas?

When someone says they are "a creative," they are trying to signal difference. These words say, "You are not creative or exceptional and couldn't possibly understand me." This might carry a tiny grain of truth, in that every person is inevitably different and excels in different areas of human endeavor, but the real aim is to remind the listener that the speaker knows the real game and is in control of the game and the listener needs to return to this game and comply.

"As a creative" tries to shortcut critical thinking about creativity and creativity in agencies. And because thoughts like this sit in a network of other thoughts, it's important to suggest the network in which this phrase makes its thrusts and parries. This is the network:

- Creativity is the act of having ideas.

- Ideas are useful combinations of things that don't usually belong together.

- Creativity is uncertainty attempting certainty.

- Creativity is innate to all humans. Destruction, too.

- Ideas and insights, if groups of people accept them, become new norms.

- An idea can come from anywhere.

- Getting good at creativity requires technique, practice, and traveling to the edge of your domain.

- Some people excel at certain types of creativity.

- Excelling at ideas seems to also require certain personality traits.

- Ideas can emerge over time or strike quickly; insights smell like ideas and do likewise.

Unfortunately, people who try to monopolize the idea of who gets to be creative do so to reduce—not magnify—others, and they do this with a lot of silent words and embedded meanings. When a ball is in the air and a pack of kids race

CREATIVITY is an ATTEMPT at CERTAINTY. THIS is why it feels so UNSURE.

@MARKPOLLARD

to where they think the ball will land with outstretched hands and one kid yells "Mine!" before crashing into everyone else, hoping to waylay a way to the ball, that is what the phrase "as a creative" does. "Mine! Creativity is mine. It's not yours. Look, I have the ball. See? Mine!"

"Ideas can come from anywhere," on the other hand, is another fraught and overused phrase. It seems a crucial and positive thought until it becomes reckless. From one mouth, the phrase helps people know creativity is innate and begs them to pay attention to the world, to break it into pieces and reassemble it in novel ways, and to express their power. From another mouth, the phrase is an excuse to not hire expensive people who have a track record of great ideas, to push twenty people into a brainstorm, to crowdsource ideas out of miserly spite rather than love, to choose cheap over great, and to spin teams in wild directions because somebody somewhere sometime might get an idea out of it.

The most common usage of "ideas can come from anywhere" is as a retort to "as a creative," as if to say, "I know your trick and it isn't worth paying for. Besides, everyone is creative." But the dark underside of "everyone is creative" is that it's like the American Dream: a powerful advertising campaign for something that is *sometimes* true, but that not many people will ever live out. Hope is important and, yes, people can dream the dream, and dreams might be achievement enough in dark times, but saying "everyone is creative" does not make everyone exceptional at creativity even in a country known for its exceptionalism.

The phrase does not anoint people with special powers. It does not snatch power from one department and give it wholesale to other departments. Unless the people in those departments spend time learning and practicing ideas, "everyone is creative" has one superpower: making mud. "Everyone is creative" muddies waters that are already murky enough without everyone thinking their first thought is the first-ever idea in the universe. "But I'm creative, too. Won't anybody look into my soul? I'm creative. And strategic. I am everything. My parents wrote it on my preschool application." And so certain job titles have been allowed to share the word "creative."

The job title "creative strategist" arose at some point to differentiate strategists or account planners who feel more kinship with their peers in the creative department than those supposedly dry research types in their own departments. Also, "creative" whispers "important." But *creative strategist" is a tautology. If a strategist is not doing creative work, then the strategist isn't a strategist.*

Yes, the title now exists in other types of companies, but it does so to a play different role. There, it is a quiet land grab that says, "I do strategy and creative but I'm one person and one salary. Plus, I'm senior and worth listening to." It can additionally suggest the title-holder's ability to act as a liaison between strategy and creative departments or between marketers and their agencies. "It's cool. I can speak both strategy and ideas. I've got this." This is not to disrespect the people with this title, especially those who've fought for it. The title means a lot to its holders and it should– the word "creative" in "creative strategist" broadcasts a public stance for every strategist's private work. It's daring. But the title also exists as a response to a profession that has not stood up for itself as a creative profession.

When a copywriter or art director calls a strategist a "frustrated creative," they are just projecting. That writer or art director is feeling frustration, but rather than admit it and feel it and let it wash over them, they accuse someone else of feeling frustrated. Moreover, such accusations imply that frustration is evil and not simply a sign of pent-up energy, and that frustration means someone is in the wrong job. A strategist is creative. A strategist's job is ideas. When a strategist is frustrated, they are just a frustrated strategist.

In companies where ideas are a competitive advantage— which is to say all companies, and especially advertising agencies—*everyone* must have ideas, different kinds of ideas, ideas that respect other people's skill sets and ambitions but that also amplify other people, not hush them. *Who gets to have ideas? Everyone.* To work with people who use "as a creative" to deny human nature and limit the people with whom they spend their days is to court danger for the entire company. However, it's important to give each other some space–to not crowd each other out–and come to an understanding of who gets to lead which kinds of ideas, even if colleagues contribute to having them and making them happen.

## THE IDEAS OF A STRATEGIST

For all the talk of strategy as art–a dramatic attempt to stir you in your nether regions, it helps to see the ideas of a strategist as similar to the ideas of a good nonfiction writer. Nonfiction writers must notice the world in ways others haven't and compel people with what they notice. They lace every paragraph with a new way to see the world. If they don't do this, writers pay a high price—nobody reads them. Writers often earn less than strategists and they can live more perilous lives. Writers cannot survive on meeting-room shenanigans and devious politics, the way some strategists can. So the least we can do is honor the lessons these writers have to offer. *For all the frills and hard skills of a strategy career, writing is the keystone.* Remember, this makes some of the best books on strategy books on writing.

You can't succeed with good writing alone. In a vacuum. From one spiritual download to another because of a gift from another dimension. Research is critical. The time pressure strategists feel in our current business culture can make research difficult. In bygone eras, rumor suggests strategists sometimes had six to twelve months to arrive at a creative brief. Creative briefs now need to appear within minutes. What's more, many agency clients have their own research teams, inside and outside of the client's company, and aren't dependent on their agencies for strategy. And the quality of research varies. But a strategist needs solid research input to stay honest to the people whom the strategist hopes to reach and affect. To say writing is critical is not to say other activities aren't also critical. Breathing is critical to human life. So is food.

When you indict a problem for a team to solve, the problem is stronger when you write it as an idea. Instead of "We need to increase awareness of our underpants among teenagers," you write, "Teenagers think our underpants are for toddlers because they grew up wearing them." When you share an insight, the insight is stronger as an idea. Instead of "Teenagers test boundaries," you write, "Kids grow up being told off when they're naughty because everyone can see their naughtiness when it happens. However, teenagers start learning how to keep their naughtiness private and whom to show it to." When you write a "single-minded proposition"—a statement of the most important thing your brand brings to the table, a sentence that might appear on a creative brief—it is stronger as an idea. Instead of "Our underpants keep you comfortable," you write "Our underpants are naughty when you want to be." When you conduct a competitive audit, slides that trade in ideas are stronger than slides that compile a bunch of stuff with lazy words. Instead of "efficacious," "agile innovation," "personalization and customization," you write, "Our competitors are turning underpants into a show." When you mark words on a workshop wall, the workshop is stronger when you mark ideas on the wall, not just any blurt from any mouth, no matter how senior the mouth. Instead of a list of the same tactics from the last workshop such as "Partner with the famous rideshare app," "Machine learning", and "On-demand home delivery button," you write "Naughty On – a campaign that gets teenagers to share what naughtiness they're up to even if you can't tell by how they're dressed on the outside." This last one assumes you're involved with coming up with campaign ideas as many strategists are. When any of these activities happen without ideas, they force the people who receive them to *find* the idea in them if they choose to uphold the strategy. Otherwise, you are throwing hot air at your colleagues and audience, and people won't know how to catch it.

*What's an idea? It's a useful combination of things that don't usually belong together. To make ideas, a strategist collects data and perceptions of what seems linear and literal, and combines what they find in ways that are not literal—in ways that are, yes, lateral.*

Where do a strategist's ideas stop and a "creative's" ideas begin? This is difficult to define. *A strategist's ideas need to open a door while still allowing a copywriter or art director the space to take the thinking further and walk through the door into a new world they will invent.* It's subjective and it depends on the agency's philosophy and the needs of the project team.

To feel out the connective tissue between a strategist's ideas and a creative team's ideas, some people use the term "territories." "Territories" for brand strategy involve vague words describing broad themes you are hoping to address with a campaign. Examples might include "simplicity," "convenience," "empowerment," "provenance," and "belonging." There is nothing wrong with using "territories," but they often exist to do three things:

1. Territories exist as guesses hoping to please a client. They often appear in threes and play the Goldilocks gambit. Is this too hot? Is this too cold? Is this just right? Are you happy with us yet? Why aren't you smiling? Do you know how to smile?

2. Territories exist to fake decisions. A client agrees to a strategy focusing on "empowerment" and a companion set of words. But the vagueness of most territories means that this is not much of an agreement. It's like agreeing to the first ingredient of the first dish in a five-course wedding menu. It's a decision but not much of a decision.

3. Territories exist to avoid challenging "creatives" in agencies where only creatives are supposed to have ideas. If a strategist peddles the vagaries of territories— and many strategists have found themselves doing so— they can avoid the appearance of stealing the creatives' thunder. But the point should not be to stop at the territory. The point is to delve into it and find something more provocative. Otherwise, what use are you?

Ideas are a strategy's g-force. They hold together a strategy. They hold together a strategist. And while strategists need to learn how to let go of ideas that aren't working and also to channel other people's ideas, these skills can come most easily after learning that ideas are their craft and how to define those ideas.

**FOR CAMPAIGN IDEAS, SPECIFIC IS A SAVIOR**

Understanding the types of ideas your strategy career will confront and developing the discipline to define these ideas will help you keep them safe. There are situations in which you'll need to write the campaign idea having deduced it from other people's work. Sometimes, taglines, manifestos, hashtags, stock images, talking-head videos, social media calendars, a smorgasbord of tactics without opinions built into them, and idea statements that spend more time telling people how to feel about an idea than defining what the idea is are part of the journey to an idea. Sometimes, they mask the lack of an idea. And when there is no idea, the paper house will collapse at some point. It isn't difficult to define an idea if you have one. And, once you've defined it, you'll know what you need to keep safe.

A well-explained campaign idea can help colleagues fight for the idea. It is hard to defend an idea if it is barely explained in the first place. When teams present fifty slides of statistics and fifty slides of "stuff we can do such as a flash mob" and a client rejects all of it because there doesn't seem to be an idea, then the only argument back to the client is, "But we did all this work."

A well-explained campaign idea can last longer. If you can't explain your idea, then perhaps you are using verbal and visual tricks to push through something that matters more in the crafting of the idea. A certain art style or commitment to a piece of technology are hallmarks of this trick. "The video will look like a Wes Anderson film" or "We'll do whatever it is using VR or AR or AI or all of it." This can reduce the longevity of an idea, because something that is most relevant at the level of execution may not carry interest for long.

A well-explained campaign idea makes for more efficient work. If a team can't put intellectual stakes in the ground from problem to insight to strategy to idea and something at the craft level gets rejected, then all of a sudden you're in another meeting room filling the walls with random thoughts. More time, more money, more frustration. The rework will cost you.

A well-explained campaign idea can make for more effective work. If the thinking peddles craft–and only craft ("I want to do 3D typography"), then it is harder to ensure every chapter across every channel builds in a way that will make the most out of each channel. The idea will simply turn a blind eye to the formats, behaviors, and idiosyncrasies that make the channels what they are and that draw people to them. "Why don't you just copy and paste the print ad into the banner ad?"

But how do you know if you have an idea?

1.  There is a combination of things that do not usually exist together.

2.  It is useful. Utility comes in many shapes—including entertainment, connection, and access to resources.

3.  It feels unfamiliar. This may be hard to pinpoint because it requires extensive domain knowledge, which is what people with experience can bring (though not always).

4.  It answers a problem and does so with compassion for the people experiencing the problem.

5.  There is something dramatic about it. Fear and strange sounds are worth a strategist's ears.

Ideas are born for battle. To explain them well is to give them the best chance of survival. It is also to love them for how specific they are using words to do so.

## HOW TO WRITE AN IDEA

Ideas surround us. This makes the world a wondrous playground for the mind if we allow our eyes to wander and our minds to follow. You could stare at a beaten-up, chewed-on pencil and be moved to profound questions. What is the idea of a pencil? When people consider how to answer this question in just one sentence in a room filled with other people, a drop of awe erupts in every brain because they remember how many ideas are with them at all times, their hearts flutter because they remember how much they love pencils (perhaps they haven't held one in a long time), and then they write about what they think a pencil is.

What is a pencil?

People answer this four-word question in one of eight ways. First, many people will write down the function of a pencil, but they'll write the generic function of a pencil that the pencil shares with other items. For example, "A tool with which to communicate" or "A tool to write down my thoughts." Second, a smaller group of people will describe a higher-order benefit. For example, "A way to express my desires and dread." Third, someone will write a tagline. For example, "Express yourself." Fourth, someone will write a territory, a one-word essence. For example, "Expression." And again, this territory will serve as proof that attempts at essentialism and brand essences all sound like whispered perfume television commercials from Paris.

Fifth, someone will attempt literature. For example, "A pencil whisks my inner world from my grasp and lays it

in the bosom of history." This is a literary combination of
function and benefit. Sixth, someone will write a life story.
For example, "A pencil is something I use when I can't find
a pen because I have chewed all my pens and I need to write
something after I've had a rough ride to work and ink stains
are everywhere." Seventh, someone will cite precedent. For
example, "It's like a paintbrush, but with lead." Lastly, a small
group of people will do the unromantic work of assembling the
ingredients of a pencil into a sentence. They'll typically include
a physical description, a function, and a benefit. For example,
"A pencil is a portable and erasable piece of lead in wood that
people can use to express their ideas in words and pictures and
affect the minds of people around them."

When you then ask the same people, "What is a pen?," you
serve them a new set of problems to solve. Have I described
the pencil with enough specificity to distinguish it from a
pen? How is a pencil different from a pen? What are the most
significant ways in which a pencil differs from a pen? What
makes a pencil similar to a pen? People who wrote a generic
function or tagline or essence for a pencil will realize they need
to rewrite their pencil idea to make it more specific and to
provide room for the pen idea. And it isn't that any of the eight
ways are wrong. But the eighth way, *a plainspoken sentence that
outlines the critical ingredients of the thing and perhaps its basic function
and benefit, will most easily speed people's understanding of it and help
them explain it to other people.*

To describe the ingredients or attributes of a pencil, we
might list lead, wood, and eraser. Usual functions are writing

and drawing, and one can sharpen, carry, and hold a pencil. A common benefit is to have other people understand your ideas. But what if there were a pencil-long piece of lead stuck to a wall at eye height, protruding into a room, and under this lead sat a stack of blank paper and a sign that said, "Write something"? The lead is not in wood nor is it portable. Is this a pencil or just a piece of lead? Or something else altogether? In an assertion of their belief in artists, some pencils lack an eraser. Are these still pencils? Not all pencils are wooden. Some pencils are lead in plastic. Is lead in a hamburger bun a pencil because it is lead in something and you can use it to write and draw?

What about a pen? The ingredients of a pen are ink, something to hold the ink, and a way for the ink to get out of the thing that holds it—a nib, ball, or felt tip. A pen is usually portable and has similar functions and benefits as a pencil, but a pen is harder to erase, and so signifies more commitment to the ideas it expresses. And more formality. At one time the ink of all pens was permanent. No longer is this the case.

Doing this exercise of explaining the ideas in everyday objects will help you in several ways. It will challenge you to notice the world. It will remind you how many ideas are right there in front of you and how much raw material exists if you just sit still. A simple question like "What is a pencil?" can lead to at least eight types of response, and each of those responses could use a large combination of words. And yet everybody knows what a pencil is. What's more, this exercise will show you how the writing of ideas requires discipline (though not dogma) and how the inability to express an idea will lead to a messy work life. And, finally, this exercise will remind you that ideas can change over time. One day ink is permanent and then it isn't. One day ink needs storage in a vessel with a tip on the end; perhaps in the future it won't.

To write an idea is to list the ingredients or attributes of the idea that are novel, along with the ones that are constant, and to do so in as specific a way as possible. Writing an idea is, of course, also rewriting, because the writer decides which ingredients are most important to the communication of the idea and then watches how other people respond to the explanation.

With a clear understanding of the critical ingredients of an idea, an idea then needs a name. Naming an idea "Idea 1" or "Direction 1" is noncommittal, and all that will happen is a client will name the idea in the elevator on the way out of the agency. If you force clients to do this, then "The Unicorn Idea" will become the name of an idea that features a unicorn for three seconds of a video script but wasn't intended as "The Unicorn Idea." Name your own ideas unless you are prepared for others to name them for you.

Along with a name, an idea also needs a one-sentence definition. Jargon such as "logline," "idealog," and "idea statement" appear from agency mouths to represent this kind of definition. These words mean different things in different environments. In Hollywood, a logline is a one- or two-sentence summary of a movie. A logline will often include the combination of a protagonist, the protagonist's goal, and the antagonist. Perhaps it will also include an inciting incident and the stakes at play. For instance: "When a toddler named Hal catches a time disease and ages fifty years overnight, he must face his fear of death from his deathbed before the Grim Reaper turns his deathbed into a black hole for all of humanity, disguised as a sandbox." The movie's name? *Hello Hallow.*

Arriving at a campaign idea can involve a game of Marco Polo. You're in a swimming pool. You close your eyes. Your team splashes away from you. You count to ten. Then you yell "Marco!" and they have to yell "Polo!" so you can try to track them down with your eyes still closed. The difference is your eyes are open, you're in an advertising agency yelling "Idea!" and people are responding, "Tagline!" You say, "No, Idea!" You hear "Idea Statement!" then "Manifesto!" then "Hashtag!" but you're still not sure where to find the idea. So, you ask directly–this is always a brave move, "What's the idea?"

**The idea is "Simple." One word. That's how simple it is.**

*One word isn't an idea.*

**There's a hashtag, too. #GetSimple.**

*Simple is more of a tone, and nobody finds this cereal with three ingredients complicated.*

**You're a frustrated strategist.**

*"Simple" is not an idea.*

**I have an idea statement, you idiot. "Simple. This idea will remind people of the simplicity of this three-ingredient cereal and how its simplicity is unlike the simplicity of anything else that is remotely simple. #GetSimple."**

NAME YOUR IDEA
AND WHAT IS
CRITICAL TO IT

@MARKPOLLARD

*Still not an idea.*

**I also have a manifesto. "Simple. S.I.M.P.L.E. Six
letters. Yes, that's two more than 'Easy,' but easy
isn't always simple. Simple is Easy's spirit animal.
Easy yearns for Simple. Simple is as simple does
and what happened to the world where nothing is
ever simple anymore? Do you miss simple? We do.
We believe the world runs on simple. And simple
is never basic. That's why our three-ingredient
cereal will always be a three-ingredient cereal.
At least until gluten is against the law.
#GetSimple." Go sell it.**

*I would if I knew what the idea was.*

To be expressed well, an idea needs one or two sentences
that capture the idea's ingredients and what it will do in the
world. That's all. And it's the same for a campaign idea. *If you
want people to fight for your ideas, at least fight to make them clear.*


### THESE IDEAS ARE SCARY, AREN'T THEY?

We drink ideas with a chaser of fear. They hit our tongues,
they thrill us, then they scare the crap out of us. So, if you're
new to the ideas that *strategy work is the work of ideas* and that
*words make ideas happen,* you're right to drink that chaser of
fear right now. Perhaps you were jostling in a stampede to a
bigger title, a better job, a more expensive project but you ran
straight over these ideas only to realize they were waiting for

you on day one of your career. You just ignored them. Maybe
you thought you were too good for them. You might even feel
underwhelmed by these ideas and overwhelmed by the number
of words it's taken to explain them. But the fear isn't because
of the ideas themselves; it's because you know that ideas don't
happen unless you take responsibility for them. It's as if a crane
with an Australian accent and sarcastic face has just dropped
two babies on your doorstep and then flown away. "I need to
take in these two human lumps, don't I?"

What will you do?

You have three choices—you can avoid these ideas, reject
them, or accept them. Avoiding these ideas means you close the
door on the babies and pretend you don't even know what birds
are so how could one have flown to where you live with gifts of
life? Rejecting these ideas means you can stay safe in how you
know yourself. You can point to these ideas and say they are
not true and you know that because you are smarter than they
are. Accepting these ideas means you have much more work to
do. You need to refine your way with words, improve how you
have ideas, and gather a set of techniques and frameworks for
pushing your ideas into shape.

What will you do?

You have two choices—you can run yourself mindless or
you can stop, ponder, and play. If you choose the mindless
running life, never stop to ask yourself what you're running
toward. Over time, you'll forget your answer to this question
and nothing is scarier than not having an answer for exhausted

legs. If you choose a life of play then fear will appear as a mere toy for playtime. The more excited you are about your ideas the larger the toy will appear but you'll play with it anyway.

What will you do?

You have one choice–drink the ideas and let the fear put you to work.

# The FOUR POINTS

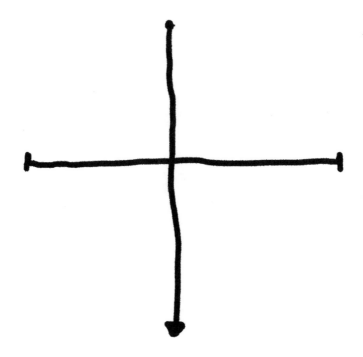

@MARKPOLLARD

04
—

# The Four Points
## *Framework*

# CHAPTER FOUR

# The Four Points
# *Framework*

## A WARNING ABOUT FRAMEWORKS

S trategists are addicted to frameworks. "Let me tear down
the world as you know it and build it anew within this
framework. And let me do that at every meeting. I do not know
who I am without a day of frameworks. I need my hit. What's
the street value of this stuff? It doesn't matter. I'll do it for free.
I'll even pay for it. It's pure. Am I buying or selling? I don't
know anymore." The addiction to pulling apart what seems
to exist and creating new ways to exist is endless. *Frameworking
is postmodernism in the name of capitalism. And both frameworks and
capitalism thrive on addiction.* Frameworks insist, "There is another
way to look at this. And another way. And another." This
makes many frameworkers spend their days dizzy, unsure
of when the dance stops.

The side effects of frameworks can be deadly. Frameworks
can dull brains when brains use them like self-playing pianos.
Press play and the piano will do the work and you can sit there
and pretend you are playing. "Yes, I'm pretty good at music.
I taught myself last night."

Frameworks can scare people out of thinking. When companies treat frameworks as sacred, it puts a holy pressure on strategists, because the god of frameworks is watching from the sky and demands your piety. A new strategist will experience the power rush of filling in the framework, scared to play the wrong note, and someone more holy will always know the true gospel and fix it in ways that may or may not make sense to anyone outside the building, but the hierarchy will stay intact and that's the point of such interactions. "Can we put a trademark ™ on this slide, please? It's our IP, right? Also, I'm still smarter than you."

Frameworks can fix thinking too early. The wet cement relishes its wetness. There is no rush to dry. Someone might scribble their initials in it. Or etch a poem or stick figure or a curse word into it. This wet cement doesn't want to look like every other slab of sidewalk.

But frameworks say, "Here is my thinking. It is in this framework. The slab has dried. It is complete. No returns or exchanges. You are welcome. I am a hero. I look forward to my promotion." Frameworks lure many frameworkers with their promises of instant power, but a career of unthinking frameworks will not last long. Unless nepotism. *You see, many frameworkers spend their days making frameworks for businesses, but struggle to make frameworks for their own lives.*

If a picture is worth a thousand words, then a framework is a strategist's middle finger to pictures. Where pictures might hint at what they want to say, frameworks promise to say everything worth saying in one diagram. "Look, it's in a framework. All of it. It's so obvious. How can you not get it?" In malevolent hands, this assertion of utter sense in one fell swoop with a battalion of large words feigns clarity to close a sale. It's a ruse and there's probably a picture to prove this.

But frameworks exist to make the brain work, not to prevent brainwork. Reading an instruction book on martial arts with its steps one, two, three, four, and five and then asking someone to throw a punch by following the diagram—"No, with the other hand … No, put your feet here … to the left … OK, try to hit me …"—is how some frameworkers apply frameworks. A frameworker would make a terrible lover. "I bought a copy of the *Kama Sutra*. Put your left hand here, your right hand there, your big toe up here, and your left knee like this. Oh. That is uncomfortable. The instructions make it look easy. Maybe it will get better? Ah, we didn't stretch beforehand. That was step one." A frameworker would acquire a yoga book and copy the poses without doing yoga. "This isn't working. I just put my hands up like this? Yeah, yoga isn't for me. I don't know what the fuss is about. I just ordered all this athleisure gear, too." Frameworks can start thinking and capture thinking, but the thinking happens in the brain. To use frameworks to dominate people via an alleged bounty of thinking but to have not done the thinking is naughty.

*A framework is a way to frame your work. The work must still happen.*

## A STROLL THROUGH THE
## FOUR POINTS FRAMEWORK

This is a framework. It's one of infinity. And it tries to wrestle the infinite into submission, like all frameworks. This makes it arrogant. By proxy, it makes a strategist arrogant, but all strategists are arrogant. Only arrogant people invent the future.

The Four Points framework attempts to solve five things. First, this framework attempts to solve a lack of thinking. Finding A Bunch of Stuff and putting A Bunch of Stuff into a document without opinion or imagination marks a lack of thinking. This framework tries to usher thinking into a project.

Second, it attempts to solve for disconnected thinking. A classic brand strategy framework is The 4 C's. The 4 C's framework hopes to summarize compelling truths about the consumer, category, culture, and company, and to show that the pithy summaries of these 4 C's lead to an inevitable strategy you can state in one sentence or phrase. The 4 C's is useful, but many strategists fill it with drivel, or worse, disconnected drivel. Example:

**Consumer truth:** Moms are busy

**Category truth:** It's a sea of sameness

**Cultural truth:** People have six-second attention spans

**Company truth:** We make high-quality efficacious yogurt

**Strategy:** Deliciously nutritious

Putting such a mishmash into a framework breaks a framework's heart. Not only are the words weak, there is no coherent theme. The Four Points is what some food marketers would call heart-healthy.

Third, the Four Points framework attempts to solve a disdain for process. "Process" is a clumsy word, because to one person it means a step-by-step way of doing something that is repeatable down to the atom and is not overly dependent on one person. In that view, a process is like a factory. To another person, the meaning of "process" is lighter, and it means How I Generally Go About Things. Creative spirits are rebels. Telling them what to do and how to do it is a fast track to an inert company. So, if the point is the thinking and if a framework can help people think while not doing the thinking for them, the question is: how much process is enough?

Minimum required effort (MRE) is attempting to do the most with the least exertion. It doesn't mean doing as little as possible. It means seeking the best outcomes while using as little energy– or as few words– as possible. This framework is not about sitting down and writing four sentences in four minutes and passing it to the next department. That would be doing as little as possible. Instead, this framework tries to capture the most important parts of your thinking while encouraging your beautiful thinking to happen.

Fourth, the Four Points attempts to solve disenfranchisement in strategy jobs. The framework represents a belief in autonomy. It is an acknowledgement that you need agency over how you approach your work and, at the same time, that constraints yield ideas.

Fifth, it is an attempt to solve the confusion of the first few years of a strategy career. The number of frameworks you might encounter in this period is overwhelming. Strategists like to find long documents on how to do every martial arts technique that ever existed, when they need to focus on just a few kicks and punches and find their brilliance within.

The Four Points framework is forceful. It hopes to force better questions. It hopes to force frank discussion about which problems need solving. It hopes to force empathy into the strategy. It hopes to force some thread between the yarns of the thinking. It hopes to force clarity and punchy words, not long blah-blah and games of hide and seek. It hopes to force you to powerful insights and ideas. And, as a bonus—it's the start of a presentation structure. It's forceful, but it also expects disobedience because it knows your heart and it loves a wild heartbeat.

The framework comes with three major assumptions. It assumes you'll conduct research. Intuition is powerful, but so is research. It assumes a clearheaded understanding of the business issue that you are helping to unscramble. And it assumes a commitment to a certain group of people or audience. *If you know nothing about the audience, you aren't doing strategy.*

The framework is called The Four Points because it tries to spawn a sense of direction but, most importantly, it attempts to capture the points of a strategy in a way where they build energy together. A lot of strategy lacks a point. This framework insists four points is enough of a scaffold to construct a muscular strategy.

The Four Points stands on four sentences. But as with nonfiction writing, each sentence itself needs to stand on an idea. And each idea needs to emit from the same theme. Otherwise the words aren't strong, the thoughts are unfinished, and you can find yourself with four Baby Frankensteins fighting for attention. And, at all times, you must remember that the point of a framework is to help a loose group of people work together, because their work will be better as a combined effort rather than if they work in spite of each other.

With a business issue and audience in mind, you first try to identify *the problem* the team needs to solve. And since many problems have humans somewhere in them, you seek *the human problem behind the business problem.* What's in the way of the audience believing, doing, or buying this product or idea? What's the perceptual or behavioral obstacle the team needs to get the audience over? A problem statement can feel like a condemnation but it's not negativity–it's fire.

In The Four Points, *an insight is an unspoken human truth that sheds new light on the problem.* But beware: even if you love insights, it is best not to use "insight" too many times in strategy work. Treat the word with the same kind of respect that exists in most marriages, where each person has a strong point of view about the other person's flaws while still appreciating their strengths and also wondering what the benefits of marriage are and how they have changed over time. In other words, with a loving yet distant eye.

In The Four Points, *the advantage is what makes the brand unique and motivating in people's minds.* The "people" here are the people

# The FOUR POINTS

## PROBLEM
### The HUMAN PROBLEM behind the BUSINESS PROBLEM

**INSIGHT**
An UNSPOKEN
HUMAN TRUTH
that sheds
NEW LIGHT on
the PROBLEM

**ADVANTAGE**
What MAKES
your thing
UNIQUE
and MOTIVATING
in people's MINDS

## STRATEGY!
A NEW WAY of SEEING
your thing based on
ALL OF THAT

@MARKPOLLARD

you have in mind and with whom you have spoken as part of your research. The audience. The target market. The humans you've deemed vital to the mission. Meanwhile, *the brand* might represent a business, a person, a social issue, or any idea in the public consciousness, such as a border wall, a surge in homelessness, or "traditional" gender roles.

In this framework, a *strategy statement* attempts to solve the problem by Shazam-ing together the insight and the advantage. It reveals a new way of seeing the brand. The idea is clear in the sentence, and *the strategy statement does not mimic a tagline or campaign idea, although there is no shame in either of those things repeating the language of the strategy statement.* After all, repetition is powerful, as our old friend Inigo Montoya from *The Princess Bride* can confirm.

*This framework doesn't end your thinking, it starts your thinking.* It emphasizes a handful of words and encourages those words to take the shape of ideas. Without these elements, you aren't doing strategy work and you're increasing the workload of the rest of the team, or you're reporting data and facts but not doing strategy work, or you aren't sure what you're doing but you hope it will shake out all right anyway. This framework helps end that suffering while letting you honor the world of idea-making.

Writing down your thinking, by hand, for other people is a powerful statement. It says:

"I'm not finished."

"Can you help make this better?"

"Do you have any thoughts? I'd love to hear them."

"I'm not here to dominate you. I win when we win."

"Let's play."

Writing down three or five or ten different and competing versions of The Four Points for one project is to try to play yourself into a stronger hand. Write one then put it on a wall so you don't own it anymore—or, so it doesn't own you. This will trick the brain to keep going, to write more and more and more. Use your ego to do the thinking but work out how to pause it after the thinking is out of you. Distance from the thinking will help you see where the fire is hottest and where your four points are pointiest.

## THE NEW YORK KNICKS IN
## THE FOUR POINTS FRAMEWORK

The New York Knicks are New York City's basketball team. The Brooklyn Nets arrived in recent years, but they are Brooklyn's team and Brooklyn is a distinct country according to anyone who lives there. This is funny because to all other residents of the United States, New York City includes Brooklyn, and all of the city's five boroughs together (Manhattan, Staten Island, Brooklyn, the Bronx, Queens) constitute an alien planet, and people call this out while laughing because they think New York is weird but Broadway knows how to put on a show. "New York isn't America," they say.

If New York is the world's city, the New York Knicks could be the world's basketball team. But the world likes winners and the New York Knicks seem allergic to championship titles. Most countries and sports have a team like this. A team that has avoided glory for a long time and doesn't seem to care about it because the money still appears. They have decoupled their survival from a need to win; they are success-independent.

Nonetheless, this example of The Four Points assumes that the New York Knicks have a business issue. It assumes the business issue is that season ticket sales are down. It also assumes the New York Knicks have identified a group of people who are likely to buy a season ticket, but they are holdouts. They are holding out until the New York Knicks start to win, and they will hold onto their money until the winning starts. This set of thinking also assumes the New York Knicks can own the truth about their likelihood of winning and losing games. And it assumes that readers have a sense of humor, because this is a joke strategy.

With the business issue in mind, you start with … wait for it … research. You conduct stakeholder interviews, you gather customer service and sales calls reports, you digest online reviews, you watch YouTube rants, you read expert opinions, and you even speak to some of the holdouts. After all this foraging, you decide to state the problem as this: "The New York Knicks holdouts are hate-supporting the team." Much of the research shows that a New Yorker is a New Yorker for life and these New York Knicks holdouts are likewise New York Knicks fans for life, but their consumer protest is to not give money to the company

# The FOUR POINTS

## PROBLEM
FANS are HATE-SUPPORTING the TEAM

## INSIGHT
The ULTIMATE
N.Y. TRAIT is to
PUT UP with EVERYTHING
until you SNAP

## ADVANTAGE
The N.Y. KNICKS
are DESIGNED
to make
people ANGRY

## STRATEGY!
SHOW that the NEW YORK KNICKS
are the BEST ANGER MANAGEMENT
in TOWN

@MARKPOLLARD

until the team starts to win or looks like it wants to win.
The holdouts love the New York Knicks, but hate watching
them. And in an age where every rant has a mouth, some
of these holdouts have become famous for their opinions.

You ponder a variety of other ways to express the problem
your team needs to solve, but you sit on this idea for a few
minutes. Hate-watching. Is there something about hatred as
a sideshow, maybe even a main event, in New York sports?
Do New York teams bring up a specific set of issues for their
spectators? How else do extreme emotions appear in New
York, outside of sports?

You recall the subgenre of nonfiction that appears in essays
by Joan Didion and Moby, on websites like Medium and
Thought Catalog, and in farewell social posts: the "Fuck you,
New York, I'm outta here" story. Yes, sometimes people get
so angry in New York, they pack their bags and leave.

You recall this one time on the subway, when there was
no room for anyone. It was hot. It was smelly. Everybody was
cranky. The air-conditioning wasn't working. The trains were
delayed and people wanted to get home. And then at one stop,
a bicycle appeared. On the bicycle was a small tortoise riding
a large boy who was carrying medium-sized golf clubs and
a surfboard and all of it wanted to get on. With the skills of
a Seoul peak-hour train rider, this clump of lifeforce barged
backwards onto the train. The whole car glanced at itself,
thinking, Who'll snap? Would it be the suit-wearer, the person
with no fixed abode, the Broadway actor, the billionaire in a
track suit, or would it finally be you? Whoever did not snap
would feel they had won the day.

And so you write several insights that try to pry open the problem. One insight is this: "The ultimate New York trait is to put up with everything until you snap." The word "ultimate" is grabby and vague and perhaps this is just a rewrite of "If you can make it here, you can make it anywhere," but it fits the emotion of the problem. Hate, snapping, anger, and angry love—they all simmer in New York at all times.

You continue. What is it about the New York Knicks that makes them excel at pulling on this knot of emotions? You list the features of the New York Knicks—and not just the obvious corporate ones that appear in boring presentations, but the things real humans have said during research. People resent the owner, the coaches never succeed, highly paid players who look ambivalent weigh down the team, few players last long, the tickets are expensive, the food and drink lack imagination compared to the Brooklyn Nets, they didn't keep Jeremy Lin, former players get kicked out of Madison Square Garden because they yell at the owner from the sidelines, and so on. You say, "It's as if they have designed themselves to make people angry. Fans are paying to feel angry."

Rather than dwell in corporate strategy phrases like "quality basketball," "fan entertainment," and "intimate amenities," or sports clichés about making history or winning wars, you dwell in words that exist outside of an office and you write the advantage as this: "The New York Knicks are designed to make people angry."

With even more defiance, you continue to linger. What's this really about? Is there one theme, something unexpected but true and defensible at play here? Yes. Anger. What is it about anger that the New York Knicks cause or contribute to or solve? People who would buy season tickets are holding back because they are angry at the New York Knicks. The New York Knicks seem designed to make people angry. New York is known for its anger, and for so much anger that some people snap. So, if a strategy statement contains an idea and we have the New York Knicks and "anger" edging into the form of an idea, what comes to mind? Anger management. Do the New York Knicks require it or provide it? Got it.

"The New York Knicks are the best anger management in town." "Best" is floppy, but the idea is there. In one sentence appear two things that do not usually belong together, and the strategy tries to honor the research and solve the stated problem. Meanwhile, the anger-inducing aspect of the Knicks has become not only *an* aspect, but a *selling* aspect: they are the best at what they do and what they do is make people angry. It could lead to a campaign idea called "Shout It Out." The campaign would encourage New York to solve its anger issues with basketball. Tactics could include free therapy while shooting hoops, a ranting booth showing the owner talking about how much money the company is making and how little winning is happening and how great that is, and live events where people can throw basketballs at effigies of the players they think are trying the least, and then the player with the most anger votes misses a game. "The only thing we don't lose is money," says the copy.

In four sentences, this thinking hangs together. It's a bamboo skeleton, but it's a start. Each sentence houses an idea, and each idea builds from one key theme–anger. The theme is unexpected in its connection to basketball and the New York Knicks. This will help people see the team in new ways and create a new sense of value. There is a strong thread from the problem through the insight and advantage, then into the strategy statement and into a potential campaign idea. A communications plan would determine where and how the campaign would appear. So, jokes aside, there is enough in the mechanics of this thinking to lead to ideas and for those ideas to lead to tactics, and for all of it to feel connected and vibrant.

Within a bizarre alternate universe where brand thinking sets the pace for business strategy, the New York Knicks might contemplate "anger management" at a business level, not just at a campaign level. What's the business model for their new anger management company? What other anger management products can they launch? Plush anger therapy toys, mass counseling sessions on basketball courts, a CSR foray into companion pet adoptions, basketball healing retreats? If this sounds a little far-fetched because it's a joke example, fear not—you can take the principles and techniques and invent your own examples. And apply them to your real clients. Step up to the free-throw line and give it a shot.

## FORM YOUR POINTS THEN FRAME THEM

The tools and techniques that follow will help you form the points you want your strategies to make. Resist treating them like forms you need to fill in as part of applying for a mortgage. Resist treating them like dot-to-dot drawings on a kids' placemat in your favorite fast-casual restaurant. They're just shapes that draw out your brain onto pieces of paper so you can reach a new understanding of the world. You might jump into one shape and immediately form a mind-stopping point. You might jump back and forth between shapes over several days before forming even one point that tickles your brain. Use what works. Zealotry is not our cause.

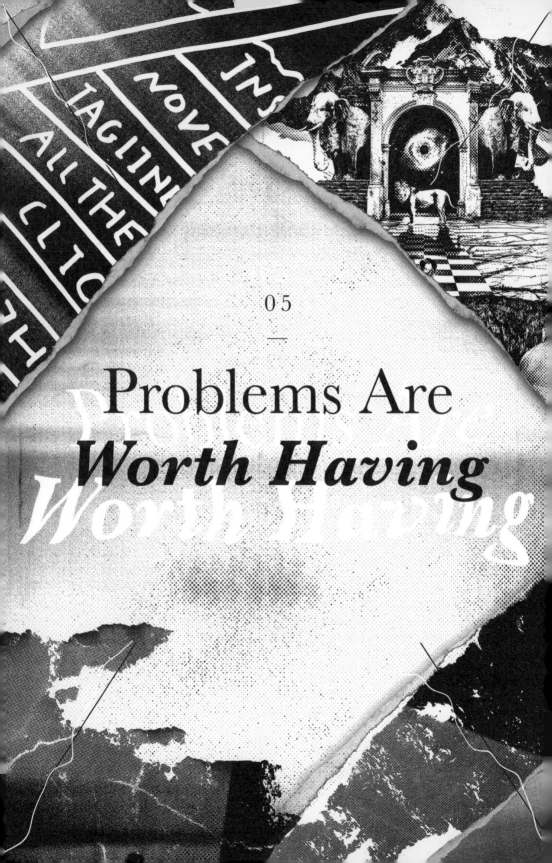

05
—

# Problems Are
# *Worth Having*

# CHAPTER FIVE

# Problems Are
# *Worth Having*

## PROBLEMS CAN DO GOOD

P roblems are so powerful that they appear in every
story, whether it's Can't Find Love, Must Fight Aliens,
Get Back Home, Discover the Thing, Beat the Baddy, Escape
the Horror, Flee from Poverty, Unravel the Mystery, Avenge
the Death, Track the Killer, or Rob the Bank. And in each
story are scenes that give characters problems: Sneak in
Unnoticed, Get Through Traffic, Recruit More Allies,
Escape the Depression, Stay Quiet Longer, Get Her Attention,
Set the Broken Bone, Follow the Map. Each story and each
scene say, "Here's a problem. Sexy, isn't it?" And humans
gorge themselves on all of it.

Humans are stories. All that noise in your head is you telling
yourself stories about problems you have. All that religion you
believe in, or once believed in, or never believed in, is made of
stories that seek to solve eternal problems. That last conversation
you had, good or bad, was one big story built on many problems.

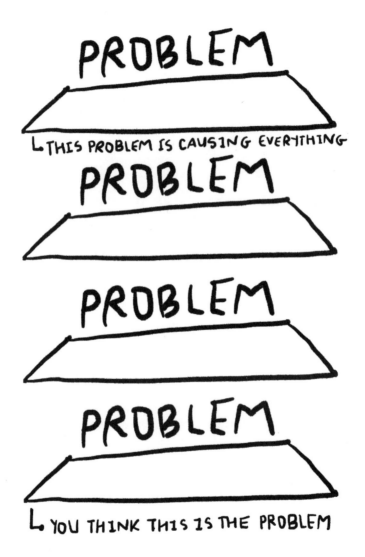

Problems are necessary human dramas. They help us survive. The irony is this: our lust for problems is matched only by our fear of problems. One way we've tried to abstract ourselves from some of our fears is in the creation of companies. We invented companies to help us survive. Then we made laws that made corporations into legal humans, and we started to go to work inside these legal humans that struggle with real human concerns like problems—as if by turning companies into human entities and humans who work in them into businesspeople, part of our world could transcend itself and then insulate itself from the very idea of being human. And so it is difficult to talk about problems in business. Whoever smelt it dealt it. But why is this? What is our problem with problems? Problems can do good things.

Problems help people sell. It can be useful to think of sales in terms of three genres of selling. One genre of selling focuses on features—"We made this thing and it has this sweet feature. Buy it." This genre is especially overused by software companies that are often engineer-led and have so much belief in themselves that they think they can just build something and people will use it because they would use it themselves.

The second genre is needs-based selling. It also goes by the name "solution sales," and is particularly relevant in business-to-business interactions. Salespeople who think in terms of solution sales are often very transparent about what they're doing. "Hi, can we meet for a coffee so I can find out about your problems?" Then, before the first sip of the coffee and after the small talk, the salesperson says, "That's great. Here's our widget with this new feature. Buy it. Cool?" Thus, while needs-based selling hopes to summon a more germane sale by using empathy, often it is a front for the first genre of selling.

Then there's the genre of problem-based selling, in which, as the name suggests, energy goes into selling the buyer a problem, not just a solution. Famous examples of this are Dollar Shave Club and Poo-Pourri. Dollar Shave Club, a subscription-based razor company, sells the idea of how the established shaving companies rip off shavers. Poo-Pourri, a company that makes products that seal in toilet smells, sells a problem, too: revealing toilet odors. Most startup pitches to investors will also lead with a strong problem. And, although creative folk might look down on infomercials, the structure of an infomercial foregrounds a problem as well, and it works. It goes:

Do you have this problem?

You have this problem, don't you?

It's a really bad problem, isn't it?

Really bad.

Like the worst.

Well, lucky for you, we exist and we also faced this problem.

That's why we committed our lives to solving this problem.

And we made this product.

It has these popular features.

Buy it now before the world ends. Or before you end.

But wait, there's more.

Quick. Give us your money. Here's a limited-time deal.

According to research published in *Harvard Business Review*, many of the top salespeople in the US likewise operate in this genre of selling problems.[13] Selling problems creates unique discussions. Most contenders for tenders will fill in the procurement form the same. Requests for oranges are met with oranges, apples with apples. This is supposed to make it easy for the procurement department to buy the cheapest option. But top salespeople say, "We can fill in the form and we will. We respect your brief to us, your RFP, and we can honor it. But we have conducted our own research and we believe there is a different problem to solve."

The "but" will cause many salespeople who *don't* already follow this method to squirm. Along with many strategists. You'll think, "Can we really say that to a potential client? What if they say no?" Well, what if they do say no? Perhaps that's a signal they don't want thinking or honesty from an agency, and that everything, including your people, will need to fit in a neat spreadsheet, no questions asked, in order to work with them. But what if they say yes? Well, then a wormhole to a lively relationship cracks open.

Not only do problems help us survive and sell, problems also captivate brains. Problems shock the ego into activity. The ego thinks, "I have a chance to be useful here. I'm sure

---

[13] Brent Adamson, Matthew Dixon, Nicholas Toman, "The End of Solution Sales", *Harvard Business Review*, July-August 2012.

I can do this." Problems appeal to people's idealism and empathy. "We must fix the world and we must fix it for other humans." Problems give the brain something to chew on and the chance to satisfy intellectual needs. "I'm bored. I need something to do. I know, let's go find a problem." Problems feed the brain's thirst for drama. "Anything to turn down the voices. Anything. Yes, give me someone else's problem." And solving problems improves people's social status and gives them stories to tell, and these stories bond them with other people and might even leave a legacy. If we ignore these dynamics or reserve them for the few, we'll risk upcoming generations being disinterested in working for advertising agencies and in marketing departments. Hungry brains want problems to fascinate them.

Another reason problems are worth having is that *problems contain solutions*. Watch a parent or teacher interrupt a quarrel among children by asking, "What's the problem here?" An open ear will then stumble on how to solve the problem. Listen to some of the most captivating entrepreneurs tell you their life stories and the problems that led them to new businesses. Watch a coach adjust their team from the sidelines as their brain whirrs to itself, "What's working? What's not working?"

The world's most renowned designers focus on problems. The legendary illustrator and logo designer Bob Gill has said of the topic:

"The problem is the problem. If we, as graphic designers, are to arrive at interesting, original solutions that *also* communicate exactly what the client requires, we have to start by being critical of the problem. The more interesting the problem, the more likely the solution will be interesting."[14]

Quotes about problems, such as "If I were given an hour in which to solve a problem upon which my life depended, I would spend 40 minutes studying it, 15 minutes reviewing it and 5 minutes solving it," are also attributed and misattributed to scientists like Albert Einstein. These quotes seek to reapportion the way people spend their invention and discovery time and hope to increase the amount of it they spend contemplating and researching the problem they need to solve. Because problems contain solutions.

Here is an example of what some might see as a self-deprecating strategy, in which a business owns its problem or its flaw. Plaid Pantry is a chain of convenience stores around Portland, Oregon. Let's pretend they are our client and need help, and that a joke strategy might house some kind of help. Let's say the Plaid Pantry stores are often run-down and dirty, and they attract fiending characters and feel sketchy to many people. Meanwhile, Portland is host to many creative workers, so if Plaid Pantry were to use research to identify that these creative workers didn't want to enter their stores because of these issues and that this is costing them money, a problem starts to emerge. You might editorialize the problem by dousing it with more drama, like this: "Plaid Pantry is where people shop when they're up to no good." This is an idea—the sentence contains the ideas of both shopping and deviance,

---

[14] *Bob Gill, Logo Mania, Rockport Publishers, 2006.*

which don't traditionally go together (deviance being more linearly associated with stealing), and it creates a new way of seeing the problem Plaid Pantry needs to solve.

But this is also an interesting strategy statement. What if we can position Plaid Pantry as the place creative workers in particular can shop when they are up to no good? Could a CEO make a video like Dollar Shave Club's hit "Our Blades Are F***ing Great" from 2012 and say, "We know how deviant creative minds are—how they rebel against norms, how they break rules, how they force things together in ways the world opposes. It's not an easy life, but it's a dazzling life. And we want creative minds to be able to shop for whatever they want without feeling shame. This is why we have redesigned our stores: the lighting is dim, there are secret entrances, there are hiding spots under the shelves, and all purchases come in anonymous paper bags. From today onward, Plaid Pantry is where creative minds can shop when they're up to no good." A problem solution can grow out of every problem statement.

But if problems are so powerful and around us at all times, why do so many people avoid saying "problem" in business meetings? Why is "problem" a dirty word? Forced optimism is like a snag in simplistic cultures that, once hit, can ricochet endlessly, "You're either with us or against us." There is no room for nuance. Nuance is an act of resistance and separation. Forced optimism says, "Everything is great. Unless you think otherwise, in which case you are not great and *you* are the problem." But seeing a problem and working hard to solve it is more optimistic than saying, "I'm an optimist. We don't have problems here. We only have opportunities."

Some people hear the word "problem" and take what follows as criticism. Imagine a hostage rescue attempt that follows that precept. One team member says to the leader, "We have a problem here. Some of our members have been taken hostage and we need to go save them." And the leader says, "Are you criticizing me and my security precautions? Well, you're fired." And then none of the hostages get rescued. In such situations, it can somehow seem less risky to act like a robot, even if things are falling apart. The robot's comforting response: Problem Does Not Compute. Problem Does Not Compute.

Many strategy processes seek *conformity to process* at the expense of *commitment to problems*. Problems are by definition aberrations. Heavily standardized processes seek to squash possible aberrations, and thus many seek to squash the exploration of problems. The culture of client-pleasing also comes into play. It's easier to gloss over any abnormalities and instead serve a menu of things a client can buy. "Don't get in the way with that thinking stuff. Just give them the things to buy. They're not buying thinking anyway. And we certainly don't know how to sell it." And so people pretend problems do not exist and by pretending problems do not exist they do not get to access the superpowers of problems, and instead they exist in their own *Truman Show* in one part of their brain, while the other part of their brain fights the demons of the problems they know are secretly surrounding them.

A good problem statement is a dare. "What? You think you can solve me? Ha. Go on. I dare you." This type of statement seeks to compel action and ingenuity and wizardry. Talking through problems is like solving a Rubik's Cube, or playing chess, or competing in a reality TV series that encourages one to traverse the globe at a fast clip *(Race Around the World, Race Across the World, The Amazing Race, The Amazing Race: China Rush, The Amazing Race Philippines, The Amazing Race Vietnam, The Amazing Race Canada,* and the list goes on—it's almost as if humans love navigating logistical hurdles in the pursuit of interesting destinations). While recognizing the mental health complications that accompany many creative lives and feeling empathy for these complications, we must also recognize that the problems that compel brains aren't flypaper sitting on quicksand, hoping to trap and then sink a team with sadness about their own existence. That's what interagency meetings are for.

Looking for the human problem behind the business problem is a rapid way to get to the heart of the attitudes and behaviors you need to help change. It is an act of compassion and wishful creativity, not absolutist judgement. You ask, "What's in the way of our goal?" But you do this through the minds of the audience members you're looking to affect. You don't want to state problems in a circular way.

Examples of circular problems are:

- We aren't selling enough.

- Awareness is low.

- We aren't hitting our targets.

- Our scores of relevance, salience, and reputation are weak.

Talking through circular problem statements like these—and they sit on many marketing briefs— tends to spin in, well, circles:

**We have low awareness.**

*Why?*

**Because people don't know about us.**

*Why?*

**Because we haven't told them about us.**

*Why?*

**Because we haven't had any budget to tell them about us.**

*Let's get budget to tell people about us.*

**What will we tell them?**

*I don't know but make it viral.*

Nearly everything you do will increase awareness and relevance. That's what advertising does. The question is, What type of awareness needs to occur, in whose minds, and to achieve what?

Empathetic problems place the audience in all the thinking that follows from them. They hope to make the thinking more relevant because of this. Examples of empathetic problem statements include:

- Fans are hate-supporting the New York Knicks.

- Erectile dysfunction conversations are too awkward.

- Plaid Pantry is where people shop when they're up to no good.

- Putting children in cages makes a president look strong.

- Retirees use their money to buy attention from their families.

- When life isn't going well, some people resort to nostalgia to escape reality.

- Many people only hire people in whom they can see themselves.

- Shame doesn't make people change, it makes them defend themselves.

- Some people's dislike for authority appears in their refusal to follow recipe instructions.

- People can't argue other people into a new opinion.

These problem statements, of course, will need to be attached to brands or social issues. Their structure is as ideas and they are indictments, but they aim to start all the other thinking from somewhere new and defensible.

## PROBLEM TOOLS

### *WINNING HAPPENS HIGH*

Sometimes a diagram needs to breathe just enough snark into a meeting to dislodge stubborn thoughts or a lack of

thinking (if it's possible to dislodge a lack of something). This diagram, however, is not full science. It's part science.

The lowest level in this lowest level of humor diagram is Convenient Cliché. Clichés can hold truths that merit your attention, but to use a cliché in public is not a creative act because clichés already exist and creativity combines things in ways that do not exist. Convenient Clichés seem common in politics, however, where creativity is not often demanded, and certain phrases can repeat themselves with the aim to appeal to a wide range of people with something that sounds specific but in truth is as vague as possible.

All types of agencies have committed the second travesty, that of All the Stuff We Can Make: "Here are fifty tactics. Do you like any of them? What about now? Now? Now? Do you like us yet? No, we have no opinion about any of it. Can I say a buzzword now?" Sometimes, presentations that list a smorgasbord of All the Stuff We Can Make exist as an overcorrection for that time the agency stood its moral ground, presented its capabilities and a hint of ideas, and lost the pitch. Sometimes, All the Stuff We Can Make appears because people don't really know what they're doing and they hope someone will tell them along the way. And some people think All the Stuff We Can Make is a good sales technique: "If we show them all the colors of the rainbow, they're bound to like one of them, right?" All the Stuff We Can Make suggests a lack of experience, opinion, and leadership.

There are beautiful taglines and manifestos written with patience and agony, words that have captivated generation upon generation. They are not easy to write, but they are easy to ridicule. That is not the point of their place in this pyramid. Their place in this pyramid exists under Novel Idea because, as more media channels have appeared since the 1990s, copying and pasting a short set of words into different channels can look like an admirable commitment to a set of words—but it is better to flex a Novel Idea within a channel based on who uses the channel and how they use it. A tagline or manifesto may not work verbatim across all channels. Taglines and manifestos, while useful, can mask the lack of a campaign idea and create more work for people who work in newer channels.

Not all campaign ideas travel with an insight. But they could. If you lace a creative brief with an insight and then the campaign idea appears out of another department and the insight does not travel with it, the idea may not travel far. One way to paraphrase one conclusion of Jonah Berger, a professor at the Wharton School of the University of Pennsylvania, and his research into why people share content is this: we share content that reveals something awe-inspiring about ourselves or about the world around us.[15] The revelation that prompts the sharing might be profound, absurd, or silly, but it helps humans make meaning of the world and their place in it. Edward Bernays, who pioneered the field of public relations in the early 1900s, talked of the need for "startling facts" in his book *Crystallizing Public Opinion* (1923).[16] This is why so many PR

---

[15] John Tierney, "Will You Be E-Mailing This Column? It's Awesome", *The New York Times*, February 8, 2010, https://www.nytimes.com/2010/02/09/science/09tier.html.

[16] Edward L. Bernays, *Crystallizing Public Opinion*, Kessinger Publishing, 2004 (first published 1923).

meetings try to work out how to find or create statistics that will make their way from a press release to a journalist's keyboard. "Awe," "startling," and "revelation" are words of high drama and help ideas travel.

And lastly, "Find the Human Problem and Solve the Human Problem," shouts the strategist from the top of the pyramid. The "Human Problem" is clunky language. Most workplace uses of the word "human" as an adjective are confusing. So, to remind you of what this means when we use it here, the "human problem" is the obstacle or barrier in the mind of the audience that's preventing them from believing, wanting, or doing something you want them to do. It doesn't mean "the problems of humanity" such as poverty, food shortages, and a lack of water or education. Its intentions are smaller than that.

The challenge with this pyramid of idealism dressed in sardonic clothing is that many clients see agencies as vendors and executors of the marketing department's thinking. They are buying All the Stuff We Can Make to fill social media calendars because activity is how they measure themselves or because their departmental setup keeps the marketing discipline at the kiddie table. "Five videos for tomorrow, please. I'm on vacation for two weeks from this afternoon but let me know how you go."

### DUMP-A-PROBLEM

This high-tech Dump-a-Problem tool has magic tricks. Its use of blunt language is corporate absurdism. Hand-drawn, it says to a workshop room that this room is different from the

@MARKPOLLARD

usual meetings people attend, and that the workshop host will conduct the proceedings in a light-hearted manner and that simple speaking will triumph. The tool exists to get people into a project and to bring their heads into the room. Often, people arrive at a workshop with different levels of interest. Some wish they weren't there, and their dead eyes let the workshop host know this. Some are there to dominate others with thinking they've prepared earlier. Some aren't sure if they can speak and how they can speak and if people will speak over them when they speak. Some are there for the soggy food that everyone pokes to see if life prowls within.

Dump-A-Problem helps turn your room's rectangular table and its skeptical tourists into King Arthur and the Knights of the Round Table. It attempts to remove people from the hierarchy they entered the room with. *This tool entices people to move through obvious thoughts and the thoughts that have gnawed at them for weeks so that new thoughts might appear.* Whether it's used with a gaggle of brains or as a solo exercise, this tool does a lot with not much.

In a workshop using this tool, you go around the room and list the problems that come to everyone's minds. You can do so using a certain definition of the problem the group has decided on previously, looking for subproblems of that problem, or start more broadly and list any problem the project might face. As you gather problems, you'll need to apply intellectual pressure to capture strong words, probing a layer or two beyond the initial thoughts and reflexive jargon on which most workshops float.

**The brand has a weak reputation.**

*What do you mean by that? In what way? To whom?*

**People don't like it. It's not ... cool.**

*Why isn't it cool and to whom is it not cool?*

**It's just that the stores are a bit ... janky.**

*Why is that? And in what way?*

**Well, the windows are often broken because people take drugs nearby, then attack the stores.**

*OK. Broken. Busted. Under attack. War zone. Cracked glass. Let's play with those words.*

Exchanges like this are rapid. The questions seek to push the speaker to a more specific description of the problem that came to their mind without trying to trap them in an absolute position or judgement. "Next. Let's aim for fifteen problems."

### SWOT

The SWOT analysis grid ("SWOT" standing for "strengths, weaknesses, opportunities, threats") is a tool business students learn early. The top half of the grid captures strengths and weaknesses that are internal to the company. The opportunities and threats in the bottom half are external to the company, things outside the office or factory or hotel. You can use tools like this however you wish, but a few main issues tend to crop up with a SWOT.

# S.W.O.T.

| STRENGTHS° | WEAKNESSES° |
|---|---|
| OPPORTUNITIES° ↑ OR ↓ | THREATS° ↑ OR ↓ |

● INTERNAL  ■ EXTERNAL

@MARKPOLLARD

The first issue is jargon. If a SWOT analysis contains vague and empty words, you introduce two risks to the project: that the project will take more time because jargon will make brains swirl and avoid committing to the thinking, and that the thinking might end up the same as the project in the room next door. If you are running a workshop through a SWOT, senior people can prove challenging. Eyes will flicker between your eyes and your marker to see if the words people say reach the paper on the wall. You want chunky, unambiguous words, and you'll have to tango with most people in the room to get them, while also encouraging everyone not to dwell overlong on their words. You'll need to help people work through words like "heritage," "performance," "durability," "convenience," "empowerment," "longevity," and "reliability" by asking for short words or asking them to explain it to a friend who does not understand the industry or asking them to tell an anecdote.

"Is there a shorter word for that?"

"Can you give me an example of that?"

"Can you tell me a story about when this happened?"

Like a Hungry Hungry Hippo, your task is to snatch the juicy words.

The second common issue with a SWOT exercise happens in the bottom half of the tool. When you ask about opportunities and threats, sometimes the first answer is: "The main opportunity is to sell more. The main threat is to not sell more." Or "The opportunity is social media. The threat is competitors." The word "opportunity" on a SWOT asks for a list of things that are changing in the outside world that can benefit the business. It isn't asking for "general principles that will help us succeed" (for example, "Get famous") or "an activity we could do to try to succeed" (for example, partnering with a media company). The opposite is true for threats.

Drawing arrows up or down and placing them before the words you write will help the group stay loyal to the grid's needs. An up-arrow may appear before words like "Public outrage," "People in their twenties living with their parents," and "Crochet video streaming." A down-arrow may appear before words like "Trust in government," "Marriage," and "Ice caps." A separate piece of paper might be needed to take note of opportunities and threats that stir, yet are examples of the other ways we use the words. Threat suggestions that include "the competition" or "the internet" can be made more specific. You can linger on these answers and ask, "What in particular about the competition and the internet is a threat? Is all competition the same? How are they competing? What's unique about this now compared to before?"

For Plaid Pantry in Portland, examples of opportunities might include an increase in the population of people doing high-paid creative work in the area, a loosening of illicit substance laws, and recent community activism to address personal shame. Threats might include protest groups fighting for tougher laws, housing costs pushing young creative workers out of Plaid Pantry areas, and flattening salaries of creative workers. This is where research is handy. Also, research is always handy.

Finally, the business problem that you've gathered to solve and empathy for the audience are always in the back of the strategist's mind. You might consider running people through a SWOT and insisting that every time you ask for an answer your question start with "In the minds of these people" or "In the lives of these people."

*In the minds of these people, what are our strengths and weaknesses?*

*In the lives of these people, what opportunities and threats could affect us?*

A SWOT grid, like any tool you use, is a working document. Tools are not forms that you fill out in one sitting and then put in the mail. Rapid questions can help people reach sharper thoughts. You can set goals such as "Let's list ten strengths in five minutes" to keep a group moving. You can also use such techniques solo. And when one technique gets tired, you can switch to another.

### THE PROBLEM BEHIND THE PROBLEM

The next two tools share a desire to reach beyond shallow symptoms to something that resembles a root cause. If the flu is a frequent visitor knocking on your body's door, is it because of the air conditioner in the office, hygiene, stress, diet, bacteria in your microbiome? Medication might reduce the symptoms, but it's unlikely to prevent their return if there is something significant causing them. To live in symptoms keeps you in a sad *Groundhog Day* scenario with little hope for change.

To engage the Problem Behind the Problem tool, you contemplate the words from the previous exercises and you

The PROBLEM behind the PROBLEM

START HERE

WHAT'S CAUSING THAT?

@MARKPOLLARD

ask, "What's the human problem—the barrier or obstacle—we need to solve?" You write this at the bottom of the chart in a crisp sentence with little jargon. Then you ask what's causing it. And you repeat the question, aiming deep and searching for the heart of the problem. Data and intuition support each step of the ladder, and you'll need to make an editorial call on which part of the ladder your team will focus on, based on the resources at hand and the license the team has to address the problem … or the problem behind the problem. For instance, a marketing client may be asking for a brochure, but, after research, you might find that a critical problem is the sales staff are bored because the product hasn't changed in ten years. New collateral might breathe new life into their sales, but what if there's another way to address the issue with the sales staff? The marketing client might say, "That's another department. Just give me the brochure." And so you make decisions about how deep into the heart of the problem to venture.

You can run up as many steps of the ladder as you would like. This diagram is just your brain on a piece of paper. But, as with all strategy ladders, you need to keep the words plain. Up high the air thins and the words daze, and there is always someone smarter than you trying to bunch thinking under one theme that is so universal it is useless. Hence, our Plaid Pantry problem ("Plaid Pantry is a place people shop when they're up to no good") becomes "Reputational dissonance" and nobody can breathe.

### THE 5 WHYS

Developed by Sakichi Toyoda, the founder of Toyota Industries, the 5 Whys is a systematic questioning method whose simplicity belies its strength. The tool seeks to unmask a root problem and thereby a solution by asking "Why?" multiple times. You write a problem statement in the middle of a circle, then ask "Why?" five times, moving each time to a neighboring concentric circle.

I have the flu again.

Why? I am not eating well.

Why? I work too many hours.

Why? I work too much because I don't know who I am when I'm not working.

Why? I avoid introspection because it hurts.

Why? I'm scared of butterflies.

Asking five times rather than some other amount is a rule of thumb, not science. You can stop before five or continue beyond five. You can restart with a different problem and a new set of words. You can do this on paper or in your head, in public or in the shower. The point is to explore the problem and use the problem to reach a more effective, possibly more audacious, solution.

### FOUR LINES ON A BIG PIECE OF PAPER

For those times when your strategy life gets hectic but you have to do strategy in front of other people, people who

# The 5 WHYS

@MARKPOLLARD

fuss over which tools you use and why, and it's 11 p.m. on a Thursday night and you just want to go home and cry yourself to sleep, grab a big piece of paper and slash four lines across it. This will create five boxes. You can then start at the top or the bottom of the paper and push people from symptom to problem. It's a brute-force move but it makes the point we want to make—the point is to think and to do whatever it takes and use whatever is available to do better thinking.

You can draw a frame around the paper if you like. Your audience will appreciate this touch and you can use the time it takes to draw it to get people thinking before they speak. You can also ask people to write down five problems they think need solving as you slash the paper. A mixture of introspection and discussion can lead to the most fruitful and least performative workshops. If you need a script:

"Grab a piece of paper and list five problems you think we need to solve. As you do that, I'm going to draw four lines on this big piece of paper. Now, on your piece of paper, circle the problem you think is the main problem we need to solve. Let's hear them from everybody. State them, don't explain them—not yet. I'm hearing a particular theme in some of these answers and I'm going to write it on the big piece of paper. We're going to do this exercise a few times to help us understand what problem we'd best put our minds to solving and we'll get to many of the problems you think are important. But let's focus on this first one. What's causing it? Give it to me as a strong sentence. You might like to start the sentence with the words 'People think…' as in 'People think workshops are democracies but they aren't.'"

These kinds of scripts will help you keep the thinking moving.

START HERE

@MARKPOLLARD

06
—

# Insights Are
## *Survival*

# CHAPTER SIX

# Insights Are
# *Survival*

### YEAH, BUT HOW SERIOUS?

I nsights are life and death. A highbrow form of gossip disguised as wisdom, insights are survival tools. They keep people alive and they do this by fighting among themselves. To stay alive to keep people alive, insights must defeat other insights.

This battle of insights will continue for the existence of humanity because humanity is wired for survival. Gossip helps humans survive. Humans spread gossip through stories. Some stories become memes and take on lives of their own, spreading baby gossip like weeds blitzing a neglected garden. Strategists are gossipmongers, dealers in rumor, and collectors of chatter. This characterization will offend some of you, because it doesn't seem like an important set of occupations. On the contrary, insights are life and death but this epiphany forces many strategists to take their insights too seriously.

The definition of "insight" as we are using it in the Four Points framework is: *an insight is an unspoken human truth that sheds new light on a problem.* Insights are revelations.

They take something obvious and whittle skin from it until the unobvious-yet-useful appears. Insights are confessions. They are people's inner voices and secrets and the things we whisper to ourselves in such quiet tones that we must pause to detect our own whispering.

Insights pose problems. When people catch them, they ask themselves, "If this is true, what am I to do about it?" Many insights house melancholy and irony, two beautiful bedfellows from which much art and activism has sprung. Humans are walking sets of irony—humans live and die, create and destroy, love and hate, touch and withdraw, see yet ignore, listen without hearing, speak but hide, and care while hurting. Insights benefit from wallowing in these dour contradictions because this is the truth of existence.

Insights are play. Yes, science has found many insights by using highly methodical approaches, but *strategists benefit from playing their way to insights rather than beating them into submission.* Like ideas, insights are infinite. Until a scientist can categorize every single human thought and pause time so that no new experiences occur, another insight is always just one thought away. Insights are many things when we honor their drama and describe them in dramatic ways. But *at their written heart, insights smell like ideas.*

To understand the mechanics of an insight is to understand the mechanics of an idea. *Insights are kissing cousins of ideas.* A lateral thought pushes together things that do not usually exist together in useful ways. It crosses lines, like a RZA remix of Johnny Cash. A lateral thought is an idea. An insight is a lateral thought. And since creativity is the act of having an idea, insights are also creative acts.

Here is a hair-loss example. "I haven't achieved enough to go bald" forces together two themes—achievement and hair loss. It's an idea in the secular sense. And the combination provokes the reaction in people, "That's so true and I haven't heard it like that before." This edges it toward the status of an insight. *The difference between an idea and an insight is that an insight will make us reorganize our lives.* It won't stop at a simple combination of two things–it also demands us to change how we exist. This is why people avoid them.

Is the hair-loss example a ready-to-use insight? That depends on the business issue, the audience, the competitors, whether the product can make a claim that addresses the insight, and what else research finds.

First, you would rewrite it and combine it with other data:

"Giving in to baldness makes some men feel like failures."

"Failing at hair is failing at life."

"Only the most accomplished can go bald with respect."

"A bald head makes a man invisible."

"Shaving a balding head can only happen as an act of achievement."

Then, you would need to decide which way to take the strategy–you can argue against the insight or agree with it. For instance, the strategy could suggest, "You've got achievement wrong. Give yourself credit. You've achieved so much, you're ready to go bald. Buy our shaver." Or the strategy could suggest, "You're right. You haven't achieved enough. Buy this hair-loss-prevention shampoo." Whether the strategist deploys Shave It Off or Hold Onto It, all the words require sharpening, but there are quick leaps into strategies from these themes.

## THE DIFFICULTY WITH INSIGHTS

While maintaining great love and respect for insights, it is important to consider what insights are not. *Insights are not numbers. They are why the numbers exist.* Insights are not reports. They combine data from reports into statements about humanity. *Insights are not facts. They love facts while feeling enough suspicion about them that they barge into them, push them aside, and rush for what lies behind them.* Insights are not judgements. They are not outsiders damning a group of people with their own self-importance. They come from a place of compassion, even if the strategist holds the audience in disdain. (Holding an audience in disdain while preaching for more empathy in business is a strange way to live.)

Insights are not implications. Implications *come* from insights. Insights are simple statements of something resembling a truth or fact; *if words like "therefore" appear in the insight, what follows is strategy* or principles hoping to become strategy.

Insights are not long. The brevity of insights is what ensures they can last a long time. Insights are also not on every slide. Insights can theoretically be found anywhere, but a cascade of slides with the word "insight" atop each of them is either an Aladdin's cave and a true representation of how incredible you are, or you're grandstanding and insecure and painting every slide with the same dripping brush.

Finally, insights are not intellectualism. Strategists might trip over their brains and stumble punch-drunk to insights by playing with scholarly terms, but to only do this out loud at other people with long abstract words and to then leave a meeting room with no follow-up will destroy the esteem of strategy within that team. Try to take the long intellectual routes and roundabouts in private and use simple, clear language for the actual insight.

As with the word "idea," the word "insight" can follow silent adjectives. There is nothing wrong with different types of insights. The friction happens when people use the word without revealing their silent adjective or the way they are intending the term.

One key adjective is "cultural." With the rise of social media and the increased importance of social movements, many strategists will deal in cultural insights. Cultural insights tend to appear in more public ways and address behaviors that are more obviously collective than other kinds of insights. How people use phrases such as "like a girl," "be a man," which memes people share, what kinds of events people attend, and the stories and music and art they digest are the grounds for finding cultural insights. Such insights can be easier to formulate because these cultural actions happen in public, but you still need to scurry into them and ferret out their deepest significance.

Other strategists will prefer insights that happen at the individual level. These insights are more about people's inner lives and they are private. They are things that people catch themselves saying or doing, but do not usually share with others—and they might not dwell on them because they create soul friction. There is nothing wrong with "company" insights, "brand" insights, and "category" insights. But using multiple types of insights on a project risks distracting people from which insight will lead the work into the world.

"That's not an insight" is a phrase that requires additional words: "I see insights differently. Here is how I see them. How do you see them? Can we agree on a way we can see them?" It can be beneficial, in fact, to use the word "insight" as little as possible. The benefit of using it as little as possible and in as specific a way as possible is that when you do use it, people will focus on it, and it will stand a better chance of appearing in the final product.

People make insights difficult for themselves. There are many reasons for this. The first reason is that, as with the word "idea," many people who use the word "insight" do not know what an insight is. This is reporting, not shaming. Other professions take themselves more seriously and arrive at certain definitions of words to use as a group. Advertising generally does not do this, to its detriment. But the better definitions we have, the better insights, better ideas, better strategies, and better lives we can create.

The second reason insights can be difficult is that insights, like ideas, may be seen as threats. Insights about particular groups of people and what makes them tick suggest there are different ways to live in the world, and many people do not want to have to think about this or do not want others to think about this. Even if it's ostensibly their job to do so. A life of denial and nonthinking is less turbulent.

A third way that insights are seen as difficult is that numbers have become egotistical teenagers and they want all the attention, and insights can be based on numbers, but are not numbers. Yet numbers want the final say. And so data often try to lead instead of inform and support. Data are meaningless until you form patterns with them and then they become information. Data provide the building blocks, and we thank them for their service, but they aren't the Taj Mahal. Many companies nonetheless force strategists to tack the vaunted term "data-driven" onto every so-called insight:

### What did you find out?

*Oh, lots of insights. All these slides in front of you—all two hundred of them—I have labeled with the word "insight." That's how many insights I have found.*

### Data-driven?

*Yup. I wrote that there too.*

But here's the thing:

*All insights are data-driven.*

*All insights are data-driven.*

*All insights are data-driven.*

*All insights are data-driven.*

*All insights are data-driven.*

The fourth way that insights can feel difficult is that they take time. Writing techniques may seem to make them happen in an instant, but in reality, life needs to weather you, break you, tear apart an easy and obvious existence to reveal different ways of thinking and living in order for insights to emerge. This is how empathy muscles develop. One reason that strategists aren't always sure if they have an insight in hand is that it also takes time to get to the edge of their domain of expertise—to know which insights already exist. This slow march is one possible yet debated reason why the average age of Nobel Prize winners has increased over the past one hundred years.[17]

Academics talk of insights that are historically new and psychologically new. "Historically new" means new in the history of the world. "Psychologically new" means new to the individual. Two strategists could watch stand-up comedy and laugh at different jokes because one of them has heard all the jokes before and that affects their guffaw level, or they can both laugh at the same joke because the joke is new to both of them, or new to the entire world.

The fifth challenge with insights arises because businesspeople like things to feel concrete. This is why they are businesspeople, not art people. Many want an insight

---

[17] *Will Dahlgreen, "Why are Nobel Prize winners getting older?", BBC News, October 7, 2016, https://www.bbc.com/news/science-environment-37578899.*

to have bulletproof properties. It's a strange desire, because shooting at words would miss every time. Nonetheless, the myth of concreteness causes much angst. The truth is that *many insights can only prove themselves in the wild.* This is why stand-up comedians try jokes in small venues and record their sets so they can hear which lines cause painful laughter and how often the laughter happens, since comedians' life goals are laugh goals. It is a form of multivariate testing, but it is not *pre*testing. The jokes happen in a context and in public. The context includes a national culture, a city's culture, what is happening in society at the time, the audience's familiarity with the comedian, the time of day or night that the jokes happen, the other comedians performing, the effects of alcohol consumption, the comedian's or audience's comfort with the language and slang being used, the level of shared understanding of history and pop culture, and many other things. To pretest any of this without its live context is to pretest air, and air isn't bulletproof.

This leads to the sixth problem with insights. There is an art to insights. This is not to put insights out of reach of eager hands. It's to put them in reach. But many people deny that the art exists. Insights require data and facts, but they don't stop at data and facts. There is a leap of intuition, whether the public showing of the intuition is poetic or academic. Yet placing too much weight on this art idea leads to another, seventh, problem: some strategists insist that writing insights is a mystical feat and some kind of spiritual superpower. Many strategists operate from a deep well of intuition, but strategists are more powerful when they bring their teams into the insights rather than leave them waiting at an altar for one.

The eighth thing that makes insights difficult is shitty attitudes. A strategist acting holy is shitty. A strategist policing other people's insights is shitty. People undermining each other's insights is shitty. Other departments saying they don't need insights from a strategist is shitty. And here's the ninth problem: the strategy community self-flagellating about caring about insights—vacillating between caring about insights and feeling guilty about their caring—makes insights difficult. "Oh, you're being too clever," your colleague says. What does this even mean? What it means is that you've gently criticized a statement they made because it is not an insight and it isn't clear. Then that person, embarrassed, refutes the idea that they had any intention of describing an insight or being clear: "You obsess way too much about insights. What's wrong with you? Who would take the job so seriously? This doesn't happen in other professions. In our profession, if people see you taking your job seriously, they won't take you seriously." Nonsense.

The people strategists spend time with by proxy when they're too good to think about their craft are obsessives. If work isn't working out today, they pick up a novel, research paper, album, ticket to a music festival, wine, beer, meal, or coffee, or they visit an art gallery. Strategists surround themselves with artifacts of the obsessive while shaming others out of obsessing about strategy. And this isn't just in London.

The tenth way in which people make insights difficult is with their words. It's too easy to whip out "insight" to try to sound important and to then use long, nonsensical, quasi-academic language to make something that is not an insight sound important enough to seem like an insight. "Are we there yet? Are we there yet? What about now?" To which the answer is, "By 'there', do you mean, 'lost'? Yes, you're there."

*Before I learned the art, a punch was just a punch, and a kick, just a kick.*

*After I learned the art, a punch was no longer a punch, a kick, no longer a kick.*

*Now that I understand the art, a punch is just a punch and a kick is just a kick.*

*—BRUCE LEE*[18]

### HOW INSIGHTS WORK

Insights are survival tools, and this makes insights a natural part of the human condition. But how do insights work? Insights can name hunches. They offer words for thoughts that have loitered in people's minds, and their appearance makes people say, "That was on the tip of my tongue, but you put it in a way I'm going to steal." Insights that capture everyday behaviors like dating, relationships, eating, traveling, and driving often operate in this manner.

Insights can also pry open new worlds. The power of words is that they congeal insights into doors. Where some insights

---

[18] *Bruce Lee, Gilbert Johnson (Introduction), Tao of Jeet Kune Do, Black Belt Communications, 1975.*

make hunches real, other insights are doors that appear from nowhere, and, once you step through, you cannot change how you see the world back to how you saw it before you pushed through the door. Door insights are less the product of everyday observation and are more profound acts of philosophy, science, and art, coming from an exploration of the depths of the human psyche.

By naming things, insights give humans meaning. Meaning gives people structure. Without some kind of structure, people flail and flounder. As mini sets of scaffolding upon which egos and thought patterns can stand, insights can therefore change people. When Alain de Botton discusses the problem of modern people trying to solve themselves and fulfill all their needs in one relationship because of the influence of Romanticism, and claims that this is a fairly new idea in the scheme of human life (the Romantic movement having only started in the eighteenth century), then a person can decide if this insight resonates or if it seems flawed, and what to do about it. The insight is this: romanticism ruined love.[19]

Insights tend to demand change from people, but they can also reinforce people. Where one strategist might contemplate how to get a group of people to rethink the idea of locking defenseless immigrant children in cages, another strategist might contemplate how to make this behavior seem necessary and attractive, and stoke a different group into defending it.

---

[19] Alain de Botton, "How Romanticism Ruined Love", ABC, July 19, 2016
  https://www.abc.net.au/religion/how-romanticism-ruined-love/10096750.

Strategist One identifies the problem as "Cages show strength." A leader with a flair for the authoritarian and a supporting base who adore shows of strength benefits from cages. Strategist One decides to try to shift the idea of strength and argues for the insight that "Caging something makes a strongman look strong, but it takes more strength to open the cage." Strategist One argues for the strategy "Show that strongmen open cages," and promotion of the idea that it takes more strength to open cages than to use them to keep at bay what we fear.

Strategist Two also knows that cages show strength. This is why Strategist Two encourages the appearance of the cages in certain media channels. Phase one of this strategy is to go on the attack, showing that people who don't like cages are weak, and that because they are weak, 1. They'll make other weak decisions, 2. Their opinions are for crybabies, and 3. Through a combination of weakness and crybabiness, they are irrelevant. Over time, as opinions against the cages mount, Strategist Two faces a problem: how can we continue to show strength about this issue without making any concessions to people we have condemned as weak and irrelevant, because if we make any concessions to these people, then we are weaker than they? Strategist Two will then borrow the strategy from Strategist One, but in parentheses will add, "without making us look weak." So they'll say, "Show that strongmen open cages (without making us look weak)." This means that the opening of the cages will need to be a *major* show of strength, a theatrical epic of superpowered empathy with fireworks, costumes, and F-15 jets patriotically screaming through the sky, beyond anything Strategist One might have envisioned. Alternately, Strategist Two could attack the word "cage"— maybe trying "playpen"—and hope that different words will make the issue less of an issue without changing any behavior. "These children are not in cages–they're in playpens."

There are many benefits to insights. Insights change business relationships. Agencies can win pitches and keep clients because of a sentence that changes the trajectory of a marketer's career. Insights can win awards, decorate strategy portfolios, and earn jobs and promotions. Insights can bond people across businesses. Informal chitchat about topics that have nothing to do with the overt business at hand—chitchat that includes spontaneous, zesty insights—can bring agency folk and clients closer to each other. Small talk about how a client can manage an absent or helter-skelter boss can bond the client to a better career and then to an agency. Insights can lead to new ways of doing business and new product ranges. These things can happen without insights, too, but insights can help.

Insights give people common ground, but many insights initially stay private. A person whose mind shifts about the role of marriage or how they perceive their mental health challenges might keep these shifts private. At some point, however, insights usually appear in public. They burst into conversations, movies, novels, songs, and essays. Insights can make money, so this creates an industry of people scavenging to make the private public. In public, collections of people can observe an insight and nod as they absorb it and consider how to apply it. Then they discuss it. Some go on to join a new online community, subscribe to a new podcast or newsletter, or attend an event, and they do so because *the insight has given them a problem to solve and common ground upon which to solve it with other people.* The common ground makes people feel less alone in their attempt to solve the problem.

Insights help businesses relate to people. Humans love seeing themselves everywhere. In mirrors, in their children, in their parents, in the design of cars and buildings, in more famous humans, and in old tales. "Ah, that's just like me. I'm not so unusual after all. See, maybe I'm normal and you are too. Let's be friends." Insights ask humans to see themselves in a brand, even if what they're seeing isn't how someone else would see them. For example, a parent buys an off-road car because the car understands the mountains, but the car, once bought, never drives in the mountains. Or a middle-aged American drinks a beer because it's a Mexican beer and young people drink it on beaches in the summer, but the middle-aged American doesn't go to beaches or to Mexico. Insights know what it is to long for mountains, or Mexico.

Insights get humans to share. Again, sharing is a form of gossip. "I found out this thing. Isn't it amazing? Pass it on. It might help you survive." To repeat a paraphrase of Jonah Berger's research on why people share content, people share content that reveals something awe-inspiring about them or about the world around them. Listen to any conversation in a cafe. One person will express a summary of how they feel about themselves or an idea. They will then tell an anecdote as justification. If the conversation seems to peak in a problem, the other person will offer a solution and that solution will often come with an insight and then a recommendation about what to do, a strategy. Listen for conversations about bad dating experiences–"You're too good for him" will often appear with some kind of wisdom about why. On the internet, sharing someone else's insight gives the sharer attention and status. Watch how people post quotes from marketing academics talking at business conferences on social media. Many sharers aim to build this as capital that they can cash in at a later date, whether for money, love, or some kind of rare resource. This doesn't mean generosity is a cynical act. These dynamics have helped humans survive for thousands of years.

Finally, insights cause awe. Humans feel awe in the presence of nature, art, performance, religion, and charismatic leaders. According to psychology researchers Dacher Keltner and Jonathan Haidt, "awe is a sense of vastness that makes you adjust your perceptions of yourself, the world, or even the universe."[20] They suggest that "prototypical awe involves a challenge to or negation of mental structures when they fail to make sense of an experience of something vast." These experiences can feel confusing and scary, they can feel illuminating or like a rebirth. They can also feel like peeing in a winter ocean.

In Australian surfing, there exists a phenomenon known as a wetty warmer. A wetty warmer is this: It's midwinter. A surfer wearing a full-body wetsuit ventures into cold water, scans the

---

[20] *Dacher Keltner, Jonathan Haidt, "Approaching awe, a moral, spiritual, and aesthetic emotion",
Cognition and Emotion 17 (2):297-314 (2003).*

horizon, and paddles. They make peace with the rough tides that surge and rip and with the waves that heave then pummel. They dive under monsters breaking onto them and dash up giants yet to crash. They hope their breath can outlast the ocean and that its depths hold no surprises with sharp teeth, cutting coral, or stubborn rocks. They make their way to where the sets of waves they are hunting tend to appear. Then they wait and, while they're waiting, they might pee a little inside the suit. The pee warms their thighs and lower belly area, but because the surfer is in the ocean the pee can also swim away and the surfer feels relieved, warm, and clean all at the same time. Insights are wetty warmers for the brain. Whether the insight is a Lurker and is naming a hunch or a Surpriser who shoves a door in front of people out of nowhere, it will elicit a feeling of awe down the leg.

Can effective work happen without insights? Yes. But finding insights is one of your most important goals. After you find them, the proper handling of insights includes knowing when to use them and when not to. Like Bruce Lee deciding when to use a punch or a kick.

## HOW INSIGHTS HAPPEN

Insights happen in many ways. Sometimes, a person will make a statement and you'll realize the statement is a Lurker or Surpriser, and in any case hurtling toward an insight. "I haven't achieved enough to go bald" is a Lurker for many men. This sentence is on the verge of insight status. Its verge involves bringing two things together that don't usually belong together, it feels confessional, and it houses raw lifeforce–you'll know this if you giggled at it or your eyes wide-blinked. What it has going against it is that it's a piece of banter–the interviewee might have aimed to shock the interviewer, it needs more substantiating, and it might not be relevant to your brand or product. In your research, these arguments against this phrase don't yet matter. The point is to help insights happen by collecting statements with a similar liveliness and structure, and to collect them from the words people say to you.

Insights don't just happen in talk. An academic might measure an insight into existence, by determining, for example, that couples who argue about how much to donate tend to donate more.[21] This insight may not use stand-up comedy language, but it combines arguments and donations and so the mechanics are the mechanics of an idea and it turns into an insight if it challenges people to change how they behave. And, to apply additional pressure on our insight by putting it through the Four Points framework, we'd want the insight to shed new light on the problem we're trying to solve. But there's still work to do.

For the donation insight, you might decide to stop here or scratch further, like a small puppy dog digging in stiff dirt. "If this is true, why is it true? What makes it happen? What's the opposite? When does the opposite happen?" And you'll see two dynamics at play:

---

[21] *James Andreoni, Eleanor Brown, and Isaac Rischall. 2003. "Charitable Giving by Married Couples: Who Decides and Why Does It Matter?", Journal of Human Resources 38:111– 133.*

1. The couple wants to do something good. They aren't arguing about whether to donate. They're arguing about how much to donate.

2. This is a battle. Someone must win. One partner might make an excessive donation to prove their power or morality or to spite the other partner. What can the other partner say anyway? "I wanted to do good, but not that good."

Our donation insight might even lead to a more powerful reframing of the problem we need to solve: "Our donors aren't arguing enough about how much to donate." And then we'd dig for another insight that pries open this new problem statement. How do we get them arguing more? What does winning a donation battle look and feel like for the winner and the loser? How do they later talk to each other about their behavior? And so on.

*This editorial freedom—that you get to decide when you're done, with which words you're done, and where the words fit in your frameworks— is beautiful yet menacing.* Even with stricter definitions of the word "insight", writing insights isn't the easiest of work. There is always subjectivity in their writing—one person's insight might not be someone else's insight. Insights never sit alone like many strategists do—they need to work in a tight system of other ideas. They're social objects, which is to say they exist within a group of people and the initial group of people they must survive is the group of people working on the project. Problems, insights, and ideas can morph into each other and exchange places in your frameworks in front of your eyes. And, regardless of the inputs used to fetch them and any one person's dogmatic way of fetching them, they can happen in any way that makes them happen.

You might watch an insight happen in real time. In the medical field, the mechanism of the "doorknob conversation" provides insight into how people approach sensitive health concerns. First, a person accrues several symptoms that make a visit to a doctor a worthy and substantial project. The person explains the symptoms to the doctor and they make small talk, appearing to wrap up. Then the person stands, walks to the door, and asks for a drug or referral for an issue that is taboo or awkward. For instance, "Can you prescribe me Viagra?" The person feels they have played along with etiquette— sat in the chair and discussed medical issues, built trust and empathy. That was the baiting. Then comes the switch into a more difficult topic the person wants to avoid discussing officially, but is the real reason for their visit. This conversation could also happen as the doctor gets up to leave and places a hand on the doorknob. It makes you wonder whether any doctor's offices have redesigned themselves to feature doorknobs more prominently and invited patients to start their fifteen minutes of healthcare holding onto one.

Philosophers contemplate insights into existence. The modern world has a strange relationship with philosophy. It can handle it as aspirational quotes on a vision board or words from a rapper or celebrity, but it is suspicious of people who know formal philosophy and the history of thinking. "Oh, you think you're better than me? You aren't. Besides, you think too much."

If Alan Watts, the late Zen author whose work has helped millions of people, came back to life as a strategist and said, "Trying to define yourself is like trying to bite your own teeth,"[22] not only would one colleague respond, "But is that a data-driven insight? Can you prove that?," other colleagues wouldn't pay it attention at all. They'd feel the insight is too foreign and makes for more thinking and, worse, self-reflection, though if they'd open their minds maybe they'd get an idea for a tasty toothpaste campaign.

Artists deploy insights. Not all artists. But many. A painting of a family that is a pleasant reporting of that family at one point in time is not hurrying an insight into the world. A painting of the United States' first family in a White House flying to a warzone flooded by oil yearns to.

Statistics also nudge insights into the world. Although many strategists tire of colleagues holding up statistics and calling them insights, some sentences that use statistics are indeed stepsiblings of insights. For instance, perhaps we've learned that 66 percent of couples who argue about how much to donate will donate more. Or 24.5 percent of men only talk about erectile dysfunction while grabbing a doorknob in a doctor's office. The statistics are invented but perhaps they front insights. Either way, *they are stronger without the statistic, and also stronger when you explore why these statistics exist.* What's happening inside this number? Has it always been like this? Why? Why not? What's new about the number? What's old about it?

---

[22] *Anonymous, "Eager Exponent of Zen," Life 50, April 21, 1961, 88A-B.*

What's really going on here? Can I connect it to something else I read or watched or to a song I know?

And, finally, strategists can feel insights into existence. Keeping a list of observations as you go about your life and then rewriting the observations as insights is a legitimate act of critical and creative thinking, even though some businesspeople are too buttoned-up to respect this. Of course, *the thinking needs a supporting cast of evidence, but this need doesn't delegitimize the thinking.* Over time, you'll develop your go-to techniques for describing observational insights. These techniques will become yoga poses available to you whenever you need them and whenever you are wearing a winter wetsuit in the oceans of the mind.

### QUESTIONS THAT FETCH INSIGHTS

Questions are freeways to insight, but some strategists have funny attitudes to questions.

Some think they don't need to ask them because asking questions is weak and their brilliance has only one sound: answers.

Some start research without thinking about what questions they hope to answer. It can take time to learn what questions to ask, but Just Finding Stuff is usually not the best way to spend all the research time.

And then there are strategists who are very strict with how they conduct research because they've studied how to do it and see research as a pure and academic pursuit and refuse to taint the purity of their expensive research skills by doing it in nonstandard ways. This attitude is not wrong or right. It is admirable on some levels. It's also intimidating to new strategists. Serious, academic, and detached questions are useful. But so are loaded questions that go directly for the inner-world jugular of the research respondents, like these:

What's something nobody other than you knows about this?

What's something that makes you angry that not enough people know about this?

Are there things you do that nobody else knows about?

Do you keep secrets about any of this?

How would you describe other people who do this or don't do this?

How do you talk to yourself when this happens?

What's the strangest story you have heard or seen about this topic?

Do you regret any of this?

And how did you feel about that? In what way? How was it different?

Did you hear yourself say something for the first time today? How do you feel about it?


Questions like these won't work in every interview. Some people won't answer your polite knock at the entrance of their thoughts. But, if you can establish a nonjudgmental rapport with the interviewee, they will often throw open the doors. Sometimes, these doors open because so many of us have so few people in our lives who listen to us. Possibly this is true for most people. But whether the interviewee is shy or forthcoming, there remains a need for you to understand how you're affecting the interview, to not lead but to clarify, to probe with gentle manners, to allow answers to unfurl without opinion, to permit a silence to pose the next question, and to move on when there is little confession.

You can write an insight however you'd like to write an insight. This is because you are an adult, you're in possession of a brain, and you want to take responsibility for your life. You can also define the word "insight" however you would like to define it, for the same three reasons. But there are useful writing techniques. Most of the techniques try to put a twist, a turning point, a tension, or a surprise into a sentence. To think of insights and ideas as surprises can help. Both take something people think they know and then, Surprise! It's not that, it's something else. This is to suggest that insights that are Lurkers are surprises in lurking and insights that are Surprisers are surprises out of nowhere.

> "Look, here's a basketball team. Surprise! It's not a basketball team, it's therapy for angry New Yorkers."

> "Look, here's a bald guy. Surprise! Baldness is a sign of achievement. He's the most successful person here."

> "Look, here's MDMA, yeah that party drug. Surprise! It helps military veterans with PTSD."[23]

The Surprise! is the leap from one known thing to another known thing but in a new reality where the two known things now exist together and do things they were unable to do without each other. This is the opposite of a three-legged race in which two people tie one of their legs to the other person's leg and run. A three-legged race is the opposite of how an insight works because a three-legged race combines two objects that are usually apart in a way that makes them *worse*. The Surprise! in the middle of a three-legged race—the two bound legs—is a handicap, not a boost. But in an insight or idea, the Surprise! helps everyone run faster and get somewhere new.

---

[23] *Mithoefer, M. C., Mithoefer, Mithoefer, A. T., Feduccia, A. A., Jerome, L., Wagner, M., Wymer, J., Holland, J., Hamilton, S., Yazar-Klosinski, B., Emerson, A., Doblin, R. (2018) "3,4-Methylenedioxymethamphetamine (MDMA)-Assisted Psychotherapy for Post-Traumatic Stress Disorder in Military Veterans, Firefighters, and Police Officers: A Randomised, Double-Blind, Dose-Response, Phase 2 Clinical Trial." The Lancet Psychiatry.*

## HOW TO WRITE AN INSIGHT

Here are ten ways to force a surprise into the middle of a sentence and hope an insight will be born.

| | |
|---|---|
| *X is Y* | *Baldness is achievement* |
| *X is not this, X is Y* | *Baldness isn't failure, it's success.* |
| *When* | *When baldness happens, success happens too.* |
| *But* | *People think baldness is failing, but it's a sign of success.* |
| *Despite* | *The height of achievement is succeeding despite baldness.* |
| *Except* | *Everything was working in life except his hair.* |
| *Yet* | *He was succeeding at life, yet his hair was disappearing.* |
| *Even though* | *Success is achieving at life even though your hair is failing.* |
| *Unless* | *Baldness is failure, unless you're rich, then it's just shine.* |
| *However* | *Slow hair loss is failing; however, shaving it off is achieving.* |

Trite or not and well written or not, these insights are starting points and the themes are clear, which is what matters when teammates inherit your brief. Wordplay can continue, but not if it disappears up its own comma.

# INSIGHTS TAKE TURNS

_____ IS _____
_____ ISN'T _____
_____ WHEN _____
_____ BUT _____
_____ DESPITE _____
_____ EXCEPT _____
_____ YET _____
_____ EVEN THOUGH _____
_____ UNLESS _____
_____ HOWEVER _____

@MARKPOLLARD

## HOW TO HELP A WORKSHOP
## WRITE AN INSIGHT

There is a strange pressure in many businesses that makes people want to see work happening, or they'll suspect it isn't happening at all. So they try to make insights happen in public. This is difficult. Public work is often best treated as a way to gather stimuli for a person or small group to take away and edit in private. The private working allows a voice to emerge and other threads of thought and research to sharpen the thinking. Aiming for thoughts that will begin *and* finish in front of people in the same session sets a challenge with a high level of difficulty. It's not impossible, it's just not an honest way to treat brains, because brains typically need time away from other people and away from thinking, time to take a few wrong turns and miss an exit and run out of gas on the freeway to insight.

If working in a group, these are useful techniques to coax people out of their business roleplay.

- You know how?

- You know what's funny?

- The thing is

- It's like

- People believe X, but Y is true

- It's not X, it's Y

- X is Y

- Say it like a comedian

- Say it in a word

- How would your favorite writer put that?

INSIGHTS are
CONFESSIONS
REVELATIONS
ESCAPE ROUTES
TABOOS and IDEAS
DISOBEDIENT
REBELLIOUS
DANGEROUS
ELECTRICITY

@MARKPOLLARD

Some of these techniques are phrases people use in everyday conversation to get a listener's attention and to telegraph that a surprise is coming:

> "You know how you love the New York Knicks but hate how little they win, yet you still go to their games?"

> "You know what's funny? People say I look more successful now that I'm bald."

> "The thing about going bald is, some people say I now look more successful."

> "Watching the New York Knicks is like therapy for my anger issues. I just get it all out."

Some of these techniques reveal the structure of an insight as a template and see if people can fill in the template with sharp words:

> "People believe that you go to the Knicks to watch basketball, but I go there to deal with my anger issues."

> "Shaving your head isn't acknowledging hair loss, it's owning who you are."

> "A bald head is a trophy." Or "A bald husband is a trophy husband."

Some of these techniques, meanwhile, aim to shift a brain into another brain so the first brain can feel and flow.

"Say it like a comedian" can help a brain shift. But the brain might require additional coaching to make a statement like a comedian. Sometimes, a group will start with comedy gibberish such as, "I was walking down the street the other day and I saw this ape and the ape looked at me and then I realized I was standing next to a bald guy and he wasn't the first bald guy I've ever seen but he was the first bald guy I'd seen that day …" Most stand-up comedy features tight phrases even if they sound loose in their delivery. The gibberish needs to land on a short question, premise, or punchline to make comedy gold.

"Say it in a word" can extract a brain from the pages of research it's buried in. "You have one word to spend. What's the theme here?" The brain might then need help to choose a simple word, because the brain spent too long in formal education and is suspicious of short words or usually tries to survive through vagueness:

- **Emotionality.**

- What kind of emotion?

- **Antagonized.**

- So, the New York Knicks antagonize fans? How do the fans feel about it?

- **Angry. They feel anger.**

- Let's work with that—anger.

Nothing will kill this exercise more than a senior job title holder saying, "Let's put these words together. I think the insight territory is High Emotionality-ness." Direct, street-level words make for stronger insights than dried-out word salad.

If empty words mire your workshop, ask your workshoppers to find examples of their favorite writing. Ask them to read a page of this writing and to read it out loud to themselves. Then ask them to write a paragraph of it on paper with their own pens, and to write an insight for your project with similar flare. Ask them to write and rewrite several insights and see if this helps them get where you need to get them. Their favorite writers might become their best teachers.

Groups, like brains, need focus and breathing space. You must put demands on a group and hold group members aloft as they levitate in thought and then allow them to return to earth with better thinking, while creating space in which to write the final insights later. This allows the unspoken in "unspoken human truth" to find words with which to speak.

## INSIGHTS HELP US ESCAPE PROBLEMS

Now, let's return to the Four Points framework and the definition of "insight" as we are using it: *an insight is an unspoken human truth that sheds new light on a problem*. We also need to remember that "human" as an adjective is often odd and that we're defining the word "problem" as "The human problem behind the business problem." We recall we need to embrace our editorial freedom knowing our words could shift between our problem statement and our insight. And we go to work believing we need to define a problem then a way out of the problem.

For example, in your research into male hair-loss, perhaps you feel you can substantiate the interview quote, "I haven't

# INSIGHTS are GLITCHES that REWIRE HOW WE SEE OURSELVES

@MARKPOLLARD

achieved enough to go bald." The quote haunted you and you proved it was not an outlier—many men identified with this. Perhaps, you even adjusted your interview questions to focus on it. You keep alive other quotes and statistics, but you decide to play with this sentence. You realize the quote is a critical problem for your hair-loss product: Buying this product makes men feel like failures so they don't buy it. Denial is easier. Wearing a dad cap or small faux hawk is easier.

You write the problem statement like this: Buying our product makes men feel like failures.

"Failures" is the leading word, so you look at it. You go through your research looking for discussion about failure and success: Why does hair-loss, if it happens to most men, make them feel like failures? Why is failure such a bad thing? Are there times when failure is a good thing? How do their ideas about success change throughout their lives? You search for thoughts that will help you shed new light on the problem so you can help men—and your company—escape it.

You contemplate baldness, failure, and success in the tech start-up world. For the convenience of this exercise, we've decided a large part of our audience works in Silicon Valley. You can't fight off the catchphrase "Fail Fast"–two words on many business park walls near Menlo Park, San Francisco— especially because your product doesn't fight against hair-loss. You write down "Fail Fast" and you stare at it. You ponder, "If the start-up world talks so much about failing its way to success, why don't their employees think of hair-loss in a similar way? Is it because hair-loss is a series of failures but, once it's complete, it's just one big failure—like bankruptcy?"

You write the insight like this: Failing fast is how start-ups succeed but men working in start-ups don't think the same is true of their hair.

You contemplate the stories of start-up founders who wear the same few clothes and live the same habits every day so they can use their brains for important work, and not for making decisions about trivial matters. You recall how many men losing their hair in the start-up world admitted to thinking about hair-loss every day–it's a distraction.

Regardless of the quality of the writing, an escape route from the problem statement is emerging. Yes, it's a convenient escape route for this exercise but it's coming into the light one word at a time. The insight is helping us see the problem in a new way. Knowing you'll aim to write several different problem statements and companion insights, you put these words to the side to consider whether your brand has anything to do with any of this.

07

# Advantage Is *Yours to Give*

CHAPTER SEVEN

# Advantage Is
# *Yours to Give*

## ASK YOUR WAY TO THE EDGE

To discuss strategy is to discuss people. But to discuss people first isn't to discuss strategy at the expense of all discussion about the brand. It's to emphasize that our aim is to see the brand through the eyes of people who'll buy it and to insist that they lead lives perhaps with barely a thought about our brand. It's also to wrestle advertisers out of a myopia–many spend so much time with their own brands they forget to shift their eyes to the people who buy them.

What's a brand? *A brand is how we see something we could buy as different than something else we could buy where we don't just see the product itself–we also look for something about ourselves in the product.* There is a lot of writing about brands–what they are and what they are not. You can explore it and the definitions you stumble upon in it at your leisure.

To develop strategy for a brand is to ask the question, "Based on whom we believe will buy our product, which features, benefits, and use cases are most likely to get them to buy from us?" We're looking to express what makes us better than other products–our advantage. But it's an advantage to our buyers, not just because we made it up in a meeting and it sounds good.

In the Four Points framework, *the advantage is what's unique and motivating about the product in our audience's minds.* As with many thoughts in this book, this isn't new but it does ask you to answer it in one sentence as an idea. This is to encourage audience understanding, bold writing, and strategy as ideas. This is also to stave off lists of bullet-points that exist to avoid difficult questions. One such question is, "What matters most to our audience?"

To edge your way to the advantage, you can lace your interviews with people who've bought the product with questions like these:

- Why did you buy this product instead of another product?

- How do you use the product?

- Do you use this product in the way you intended to when you bought it?

- Did anything about this product surprise you after you bought it?

- What's the best thing about this product?

- Have you spoken with friends about the product and why they haven't bought it? What did they say?

- If you thought a friend would benefit from this product, how would you convince them to buy it?

- Who wouldn't benefit from this product and why?

Trawling through online consumer reviews can yield tens of ways to understand how people thought about the product before they bought it and how they'd recommend–or criticize– the product once it's in hand. Amassing these reviews into word clouds will rarely net anything useful though. Word clouds usually strip chunky phrases of their power.

In articulating the advantage, we are trying to articulate something more powerful than one obvious product trait. We need a sinew between the brand and product. People won't believe how you communicate about your brand if the product has nothing to do with what you're communicating. And, while you might encounter colleagues and clients who bemoan the good old days when "We just worked out what was good about the product and got people's attention with it," a brand idea can help many companies work and communicate more effectively. Besides, a communications plan will help people see they aren't arguing about a single piece of communication. A communications plan will help people determine how much energy needs to be focused on different areas—such as visually displaying the product or service, explaining it, showing people using it, or having experts tout it. And there are a few frameworks that can help you explore it.

## THE PYRAMID OF ADVANTAGE

In the Four Points framework, the term "advantage" brings together a few marketing concepts. There is the "unfair advantage" that lean-canvas business models, often favored by startups, promote: what is something that few companies can

replicate and that makes the company better? A patent is an example of an unfair advantage.

There is also the world of "reasons to believe" or RTBs, which may not express an advantage on their surface but can add up to one. On creative briefs, RTBs are a small set of points that prove a brand's single-minded proposition, i.e., what you are proposing as the brand's most important reason to buy the brand. Here's an example of RTBs supporting a single-minded proposition.

**Single-minded proposition:**

"The New York Knicks will give you a hit of New York rage."

**RTBs:**

1. The owner cares more about money than winning.

2. It's expensive to attend games.

3. The players don't look like they're trying.

4. Coaches come and go with little change.

5. They traded Jeremy Lin.

The RTBs will not always appear in public, though they might. A communications plan will determine that. But the main function of RTBs is to operate in internal documents as points that substantiate the argument of a single-minded proposition. The most common challenges with RTBs are these:

1. Technical jargon—a product marketer stuffs words nobody understands into the RTBs.

2.  Greed and laziness—the RTBs are a long list of any brain
    fart that comes to mind, and they don't all fit within the
    same theme or opinion. For example, the RTBs above
    fit the theme of anger. If the strategy tried to solve a
    different problem–that going to Madison Square Garden
    to watch The New York Knicks wasn't an colossal night
    out any more, you'd deploy different RTBs.

3.  No empathy—the RTBs do not reflect what interests
    a potential purchaser. RTBs are anchors that hope to
    keep a strategy honest, but they are most honest when
    they are few, short, and show an understanding of what
    intrigues people.

It will come as no surprise that you can think of what's
unique in either a linear or lateral way. Perhaps there is new
technology that interests people and it's unique to the company,
and this uniqueness will take time for a competitor to catch up to
or diminish, and this linear, literal advantage is the strongest one
the brand has. It has the fastest flights, the biggest bus, the hottest
sauna, the least sugar, the most protein. *Sometimes, however, what
makes a product unique is a matter of opinion, and a lateral thought can
shift the opinion by combining product attributes into new arguments.*

The Pyramid of Advantage is not from an Indiana Jones
movie, but it would be if it could be. It does require a cinematic
voiceover whenever it is thought of or introduced. Naturally.
You may want to start polishing your megaphone now.

This pyramid attempts to help you work out *what's most
dramatic about the product or service*, and to do so with the business

issue or problem in mind and through the eyes of the audience. There are three parts to it:

1. **Must Have:** "It has to have these things or I wouldn't even consider it"

   Must-have attributes are things a product or service needs for the audience to even think about buying it. A car needs four wheels, a steering wheel, windows, headlights, and turn signals, for example.

2. **Nice to Have:** "It's cool, but not Give You My Money Cool"

   Nice-to-have attributes are things a product or service has that are neither deal breakers nor dealmakers. They elicit a quiet excitement, and, if they are many, the quiet excitement might build, but they are easy for people to argue themselves out of. "I mean, I like that it has these things, but I don't really need them." Some cars have rearview cameras, satellite navigation, and heated seats.

3. **Love to Have:** "This is Give You My Money cool"

   Love-to-have attributes are things a product or service has that make people eager to part with their money because they need them and are excited for them. This is not to overstate the luring power of some products and services, because many only sell best when the discount is good. There is often a difference between "high involvement" categories (categories that require a lot of time and emotion—vacations, cars, houses) and "low involvement" categories (categories that people buy because they have to and in which sometimes they don't even care which brand they buy—chewing gum, laundry detergent, instant noodles). Mix up these categories at your own risk. But in fact, the level of involvement might appear absolute and obvious, yet you'll need to look through the eyes of the purchaser to determine its true state.

If we look at the New York Knicks, they're in the category of basketball. To different people, that category can mean A Night Out, A Weekend in New York, A Reason for a Mega Selfie, A Date Night, Quality Family Time, A Way to Celebrate a Wall Street Bonus, Spoil the Client Night, or Land a New Client Day. These categories are use cases, and while cheeky, they are helpful ways to reconsider why someone is buying something and with what it is competing. The category of Spoil the Client Night might include a dinner, cruise, or training session with a celebrity academic. Even a brief flirtation with this thinking about alternatives to your product can reduce blind spots.

Let's think some more about the category of basketball:

1. **Basketball Must-Haves:** A basketball team that sells tickets needs tickets, halftime entertainment, food and beverage, merchandise, and a respectable amount of winning but apparently not too much if they play at Madison Square Garden. There are certain things basketball teams need to have for people to consider them a professional basketball team to which a person might give money.

2. **Basketball Nice-to-Haves:** The halftime entertainment might be a nice-to-have to one group of people because they don't particularly care about it. Shooting T-shirts out of those massive T-shirt guns—maybe that's amazing to some people while others wouldn't care. The same goes for posters designed for selfie photos and extremely enthusiastic, play-by-play courtside announcements. These things are Nice-to-Haves, perhaps even Must-Haves.

3. **Basketball Love-to-Haves:** People waiting until the New York Knicks start to win before they buy season tickets would love to have a New York Knicks team that is competitive. However, the team ownership has made a decision—based on attendance numbers at Knicks games—that winning is not a Must-Have for attendees, and that the team can make money even if it loses. In other cities the team might need to win to make money.

Sometimes, the attributes shift over time. They can do this because of changing customer needs, the evolution of public opinion, or competitors replicating attributes. Also, thinking about which attributes do *not* exist and how their absence matters to people or would matter if people knew about the absence is useful. Thus we can speak of a flea-control product for dogs that is *not* a registered poison. Plastic cups without BPA. Restaurants without meat. And it's important to think not just of the ingredients or features of the product or service, but also what they do, their functions, and how they benefit people in ways that are unique. To get to those, you'll need to pierce through generic marketing language such as "heritage" and "quality" to the words a real human would use. Finally, *if there is nothing unique and motivating about the product or service, you can do these things:*

1. Risk heavy reliance on short-term tricks such as discounts, cashbacks, and promotions

2. Say the obvious, but say it in a way that isn't horribly obvious and is probably absurd

3. Hope that an insight that's not really connected to the product can make sales happen

4. Change jobs

5. Add something new to the product that makes the product unique and motivating (this does not include lies)

### THE BENEFIT LADDER

The Benefit Ladder helps you contemplate the ultimate point of a product's or service's features. One way to use this ladder is to take the features that purchasers think are Love-to-Haves—features that are unique and compelling to their wallets—and list them in the Features box. Perhaps there will be one of them; perhaps there will be five. Then you think about how those features combine to do something for someone using the product. What do the features do? Some features have obvious functions. For instance, a flying car would help people beat traffic, arrive at their destinations faster, and look cool. The basic features of the New York Knicks combine to help people have a night out together. But that is boring. When you use a more alien eye to examine the features of the New York Knicks, you can characterize a New York Knicks game as a night that will leave people angry or as a night that will cure people of anger.

Then, going up the ladder, you can explore the benefits of the functions. What's the benefit of that to people? How does it help them? And what's the benefit of that? The benefit could be emotional or not. The New York Knicks make people angry. One benefit of this is that *supporting the team makes people real New Yorkers because real New Yorkers are angry.* This is a shallow stereotype, but it makes the ladder work. An alternative benefit is that watching a game will help people release all their anger.

In plain language, here's what happens in your mind as you use the Benefit Ladder: "OK, so these few things are what people want. And this is what these things combine to do. And these are the benefits of that combination." You can make as many rungs on the ladder and as many separate ladders as are useful. The ladders can splay into a mind map. You decide how high to go, how much to rewrite, and, through research, how and where features, functions, and benefits need to appear in communicating any of this to a potential buyer.

To return to the Plaid Pantry example, Plaid Pantry is a chain of convenience stores in the Pacific Northwest region of the US. As a hypothetical exercise, you can pretend Plaid Pantry wants to shift its business focus and get more people in the creative industries to shop there. You can ask, "Why aren't these people shopping there?" And, remembering what some

# The BENEFIT LADDER

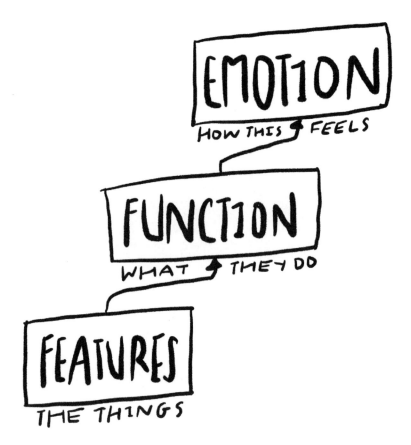

EMOTION
HOW THIS FEELS

FUNCTION
WHAT THEY DO

FEATURES
THE THINGS

@MARKPOLLARD

(hypothetical) research interviewees have told you, you'll muse: "Well, it looks run-down, busted-up, and dirty. Junkies hang out there. Someone would shop there when they have the munchies or when they're making mistakes." So you characterize the problem Plaid Pantry needs to solve as this: "Plaid Pantry is the place people shop when they are up to no good."

If you reimagine Plaid Pantry's problem as its strength and contemplate a possible feature set based on picturing it as a place where *creative folk* can shop when they're up to no good, then its features might include hiding spots, secret entrances, dim lighting, brown or black paper bags, masks for anonymous shopping, art therapy, and so on.

The function of many of these features is to help people buy things in privacy. One benefit of buying things in privacy is feeling less judged. A benefit of feeling less judged is feeling less shame. A benefit of feeling less shame is feeling less distracted. A benefit of feeling less distracted is doing more honest creative work.

A second function of the new store features would be to satisfy creative workers' urge to play. The new store features will let them not only have privacy but let them play with their minds in privacy while they are at it. A benefit of feeling more playful is feeling more relaxed and open to new ideas. A benefit of feeling relaxed and open to new ideas is producing more varied creative work.

You can keep climbing the ladder by asking, "And what's the benefit of that?" The questions behind all these questions are: "What's the point of this to someone who might part with money for it?" and "What argument can I make to make this point?"

**Company:** Plaid Pantry

**Customer:** People who do creative work in Oregon

**Business issue:** Creative workers are shopping elsewhere

**Problem:** Plaid Pantry is where people shop when they're up to no good

**Strategy:** Show that Plaid Pantry is where creative people shop when they're up to no good

**Features:** Hiding spots, secret entrances, dim lighting, brown or black paper bags, masks for anonymous shopping, art therapy

**Function:** Creative workers can buy things in privacy

**Benefit:** Creative workers can shop without shame

The Pyramid of Advantage and the Benefit Ladder help clarify what you find and how it is relevant to your audience. Mess and sprawl are part of the journey and an ally in mess and sprawl is this diagram on a large recycled piece of paper.

## THE PRODUCT WORLD

The Product World seeks to map what you find in the wild without forcing what you find into a structure. It's not

# The PRODUCT WORLD

| FEATURES | FUNCTIONS | BENEFITS |
|---|---|---|
| TRIGGERS | USE CASES | EDGE CASES |

# MAP what you FIND

@MARKPOLLARD

a framework that's fit for presentations. It's unwieldly and busy. It encourages you to capture the following with a writing instrument of your choice:

1.  **Features:** What features do people discuss?

2.  **Functions:** How do people use these features?

3.  **Benefits:** Which benefits do people highlight?

4.  **Triggers:** What prompts a person to search for or buy the product or service?

5.  **Use cases:** How do people typically use the product or service?

6.  **Edge cases:** What are unusual uses of the product or service?

The aim is to keep the language natural and not to rewrite it into vague categories or filter it through business jargon. You'll benefit from keeping it wild and trying to keep a grip on this wild energy as it turns into a report and into a serious document and then into nothing. *The Product World encourages you to see the product or service through the minds of people who use it.* You can choose how specific the audience is and the mind or minds you inhabit can narrow during the hunt. You might first map everything you find in the wild, and then start to focus on what smaller groups of people say. The Product World will help you understand how people view the product and service, how people make decisions about it, how people make comparisons to it, and the stories people tell about it. Then it will help you discover new ways to talk about the product or help you come up with ideas for new products.

A look at the wilderness of New York advertising agencies through the mind of a CEO seeking a new Head of Planning might reveal the following:

1.  **Features:** Forty-five years old, English accent, head of famous British agency, active online

2.  **Functions:** Act as a figurehead, coach strategists, win new business, speak in public

3.  **Benefits:** New projects, bigger projects, prestige, stable clients, less strategist churn

4.  **Triggers:** Last Head of Planning left, big account win, no Head of Planning to help with the account

5.  **Use cases:** Host workshops, run management offsites, save clients, run pitches, speak at Cannes, hire and fire strategists, review strategist utilization, publish think pieces, give company-wide talks, do training, edit strategy case studies, schmooze with senior clients, teach agency why planning is useful

6.  **Edge cases:** Ghostwrite for the CEO, do jazz hands in workshops with unhappy clients, get sent to support struggling offices, help senior clients write their marketing plans or reinvent their internet presences, clean up drunken CEO mess post-Cannes, provide CEO with relationship counseling, host CEO's children as interns, deal with other senior people in the agency network who respond better to an English mind than an American mind

Without judgement and possibly with a delicate slurry of snark and sincerity, you find out what exists before deciding whether it is useful.

Inputs can include anything you can put your own jazz hands on. Keyword research, website and social analytics, customer service logs, consumer reviews, store visits, academic research from the fields of psychology or behavioral economics or sociology, expert interviews with journalists or analysts, stakeholder interviews, surveys, and so on. The point is to look for what happens in the wild and to try to keep it in its natural state, while also keeping an eye out for patterns.

For example, you may find in your wilderness-combing that some New York agency CEOs will use a head of planning who has an empathic, intellectual style to signal that empathy and intellect matter to the CEO, even though the CEO will also continue to allow sociopathic company behaviors to exist and will refuse to take a stand for smart work because dumb work still manages to sell. Is this observation true or false? Is it true enough? Does it need a data point to prove it? If you remove the spice from this and gather the anecdotes that support it into a ball called "Efficacy," a ball that tries to wrangle any and all discussion about whether and how planning works in New York into a ball of verbal shitdust, then it's of no use. And, as it travels, it won't improve. It will worsen. And then you publish a report entitled "The Efficaciousness of Heads of Planning in the New York Advertising Ecosystem," and the report will lead with a word cloud of what you found, even though the only useful thing a word cloud has ever revealed is how useless word clouds are.

The two final diagrams that come in handy here are the Decision Tree—also called a Decision Funnel—and the Path to Purchase.

## THE DECISION FUNNEL

A Decision Funnel takes what you find in research and writes it in the form of the decisions people make before and after they buy the product or service, in an imaginary order. With research in hand, this tree lures empathy into public and doesn't take long, but it requires you to maintain distance from the idea of a perfect and pure decision-making process. People's minds and decisions are jumpy. The Decision Funnel will help you to decide what to say to the audience, knowing that some audience members will make a decision based on one argument and some based on another, and it will help you look for blind spots.

### CEO's Decision Funnel in Finding a New Head of Planning for a New York Agency:

- Oh gosh, we just lost our Head of Planning. Again. We need something different.

- Let's find someone who can play the part, but doesn't have too much to prove.

- I'll collect opinions from the management team.

- I'll share these opinions with our internal recruiters.

# the DECISION FUNNEL

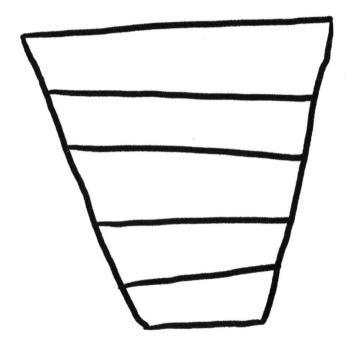

@MARKPOLLARD

- I'll also bring in an external recruiter. Maybe our internal processes are sending bad signals.

- The recruiters will share a shortlist every week for approval.

- They'll try to speak with the possible hire.

- If there's a fit, I'll meet the possible Head of Planning. Not here though. It's ugly.

- If I like the person, I'll get them to meet the rest of the management team.

- I won't get them to meet the strategy team.

- I'll try to convince the rest of the management team to want this. They hate strategists.

- The management team will meet and select the final candidates.

- The internal recruiters will feel them out for more specific information.

- We'll prepare offers and make them via phone, then email.

- Each person will have three days to decide and to sign, or we'll move on.

- If the person signs, we'll prepare for the person's arrival—equipment, meetings.

- We'll speak one final time before the person arrives.

- They'll meet the team that had no say in hiring them.

- Then the person can spend a year trying to get people who don't want strategists to want them, while pretending this isn't the case to the strategy team they never met.

- Then we'll do it all over again.

### PATH TO PURCHASE

A Path to Purchase tries to establish how people go from not knowing about a product to buying it. You can create a Path to Purchase "in general," as in, "How do people generally buy this product?" Or you can create one with a very specific audience in mind, as in, "How do aquarium owners who love basketball decide whether to buy season tickets to the basketball?" You can treat them as maps that report what behavior exists or you can treat them as plans that determine the type of activity you want your budget to pay for.

The difference between using a Path to Purchase as a map or a plan lies in the questions you use to fill it. The version that maps the behavior and talking points that are happening in the wild uses questions like these:

1. **Awareness:** How do people learn about the product or service?

2. **Consideration:** What gets people to add the product or service to their research list, i.e., to consider it?

3. **Intent:** What makes people add the product to their shopping list?

# PATH to PURCHASE

| PHASE | | |
|---|---|---|
| EMOTIONS | | |
| ACTIONS | | |
| CHANNELS | | |
| INSIGHTS | | |
| MENTAL LEAP | | |

\* KEEP IT WIELDY

@MARKPOLLARD

4. **Trial:** How do people try the product?

5. **Purchase:** How do they buy it?

6. **Usage:** How do people use the product?

7. **Repurchase:** What makes people repurchase the product?

The second and more common way to use a Path to Purchase turns the questions into a plan. It asks questions like these:

1. **Awareness:** How will we make people aware of our product or service?

2. **Consideration:** How will we get people to add it to their shopping list?

3. **Intent:** How will we get people to intend to purchase it?

4. **Trial:** How will we get people to try it?

5. **Purchase:** How will we sell it?

6. **Usage:** How will we get people to use it?

7. **Repurchase:** How will we get people to buy it again?


Throughout much advertising history, companies have used surveys to measure how their campaigns were shifting people along the Path to Purchase. Sometimes they'd even decide that the marketing brief for an entire year would focus on one of these three areas —"driving awareness" or "driving consideration" or "driving intent." Such goals evince an attempt at diligence, but excessive belief in these concepts will also create blind spots. Also, some of the concepts can feel fuzzy and duplicative–Consideration and Intent, especially. They often seem to overlap or happen in each other.

As you spin out a detailed plan of action, you can break down each phase along the path further and give recommendations for it, like so:

1. **Phase:** What's a label that characterizes the phase?

2. **Emotions:** How does the person feel about this phase?

3. **Actions:** What do they do in this phase?

4. **Channels:** Where do they do these things?

5. **Insights:** What are unspoken human truths in this phase?

6. **Mental Leap:** What does someone need to think or feel before they move into the next phase?

*Recommendations:*

I. **Content:** Content we recommend for this phase

II. **Channels:** Where we'll put the content

III. **Metrics:** How we'll measure effectiveness

IV. **Goals:** What we'd like to achieve in this phase

Remember, diagrams like the Path to Purchase try to map what exists or could exist, but not in a way that suggests everyone is the same or that everything is linear. There was a time when certain marketers held up such models in disdain, lamenting, "This stuff happens in circles, not lines." So if something seems confusing to you or a client, don't feel obliged to stick to it. None of this is dogma. You can choose and deploy what's useful.

The detail in which you can disappear with various thought models is rich but potentially troublesome. The richness takes the shape of doses of empathy, fewer blind spots, and a more thorough understanding of your product and customer. You might even find a critical brand or business problem by digging in at a deep level of detail, and that problem could inform the company's focus for years to come. Or perhaps some of the problems will reveal information gaps that the company can address.

However, you may have trouble knowing what to do with such a bounty of information. If arriving at this level of detail seems to inhibit your creative faculties, then you need to loosen up. Take a walk and come back to it later. If the amount of detail overwhelms you, you can also back out of it with games. One game is to take a piece of paper and a medium-sized marker and write the ten most important things you found in clearheaded sentences, and then take another piece of paper and rewrite the five most important things, and then take another piece of paper and write the three most important *words*. Fifteen minutes to clarity.

Then there's the question of how much of these explorations to share with other people. Sometimes you'll harbor the finest of intentions and you'll want to share complex details in a pitch, but the people in the room only asked for a television commercial, they want a television commercial, they don't care about the details, and they turn off. Many of these frameworks are not presentation-friendly. Colleagues who want a simple work life might also struggle with an intense level of detail. One trick is to show as little as possible upfront and to put the subtleties in the appendix so people can read them later. This way you can exhibit effort and thoughtfulness, while not trying to kidnap and hold hostage people who do not care for nuance.

08
—

# Strategy Rats Out *Problems*

# CHAPTER EIGHT

# Strategy Rats Out
## *Problems*

### STRATEGY IS IMPORTANT
### BUT WHOSE IS MOST IMPORTANT?

The cold war of the strategy world is the battle to see who's important enough to use the word "strategy" to describe what they do. For some people, the word means "business strategy" and only legitimate businesspeople and management consultants can use it. But they're trying to use one word to say two and this is tricky. Other people will suggest "account planning" is a better label for the work of people who try to make advertising more effective through human understanding. Historically, "account planning" is the name of this work but it's an obtuse name and it requires a system and tradition of people who use it and hire it for it to carry any weight. In places new to the endeavor, it's unclear and, yes, lower in status than a name hugging the word "strategy."

The cold war has also led to the quiet creation of job titles. The job titles are arguments that the types of strategy they do are specialized enough to deserve their own places on project scopes. They are arguments for money. "Digital strategist", "social strategist", "user experience strategist", "content strategist", "communications strategist", "brand strategist", and "creative strategist" are all arguments for money. "Client strategist" is the odd one out because it's usually a title for someone managing an account and seems to exist to say, "I am also capable of critical thought," or, "Please don't see me as a salesperson."

And let's not forget how many strategists exist in companies where colleagues don't want them to do strategy because *that's what I do*. Most strategists will encounter clients and colleagues like this. It leads to a lot of passive-aggressive behavior such as the evasion of meetings and creative briefs, feigning disinterest in conversations, not replying to emails, the appearance of new job titles to snatch back importance, and petitions to remove a strategist from an account.

It's a cold war because it's rarely direct. It's a series of snide skirmishes in which words slide down the corners of people's mouths and under their breath. "That's not strategy. You're not a strategist. I know because I do it and I am it."

This cold war is a war for importance because importance makes more money. If it were a war for clarity we'd hear it more often—"Well, here's what I mean when I use the word 'strategy'. You?"

## A SECULAR START IS A CLEAR START

In its least religious incarnation, strategy is an informed opinion about how to win. You need data to defend it and argue for it, though the argument itself is an opinion. To adopt a strategy to win doesn't make you cutthroat. Strategy can involve compassion, especially if you do it to yourself. But strategy is a struggle or a fight against something. If you only define the word in a way that is specific to your role or industry, you aren't defining "strategy"–you're defining your type of strategy.

The type of strategy in the Four Points framework insists that to win, strategy finds escape routes from problems by mingling insights about people and truths about brands. Its destination is a new way of seeing the brand based on this mingling.

You can apply this type of strategy to any subject matter by switching out the word "brand." Perhaps you replace it with a personality trait ("My Introversion"), a relationship dynamic ("Sunday Night Arguments"), a social issue ("Young Girls Playing Team Sports"), or a life incident ("Redundancy").

However you use The Four Points, it offers you an operating system and a philosophy to apply to a situation. Someone else's type of strategy might hate problems and ideas and empathy, and this is their choice to make. It doesn't make the Four Points incorrect.

Any one person's definition of the word "strategy" rests on many invisible concepts and contexts. An honest way to ply the strategy trade is to acknowledge this, talk about it, and to stay open to other people's definitions but it is not to take part in a futile cold war.

## WHAT STRATEGY IS NOT

There are many things strategy is not. Strategy is not a list of principles. "Be shareable." "Be relevant." "Be different." No. Strategy is not jargon. "Synergistic and holistic innovation to drive competitive growth is our advantage." No. Strategy is not two long words stuck together in a circle. "Brilliantly Vacuous." No. Strategy is not an outcome. "Our strategy is to dominate the market and sell 82 percent of the products in the market." No. Strategy is not merely a list of activities or tactics. "Our strategy is to launch more products on Amazon, create more videos, increase our paid media budget, recruit key opinion leaders, and appear at tradeshows." As a ten-year-old chess player walking down West 96th Street in Manhattan once said, "Tactics are just tricks that people do to distract you when they don't have a strategy." In truth, tactics make strategy happen. They are the actions you undertake to ensure you give the idea in the strategy a shot at winning. Without strategy, however, tactics are actions people do in the short-term that can hurt them in the long-term. This is the chess player's point.

Here are examples of phrases that are not strategy:

"To become relevant to young people."

"To get shared more."

"To increase awareness."

"To empower women."

These are vague outcomes. They're business clichés that atrophy the creative minds in their midst when taken too seriously. They're hot air that would confuse an exhaust fan.

Here's a taxonomy of strategy statements and propositions you'll see if you spend enough years in advertising or marketing:

1. **Vague intention:** "Our strategy is to become relevant to millennials by using Instagram the way they use Instagram."

2. **Grandstanding French- and Latin-based two-word brand essence:** "Empowering Dependability"

3. **Corporate-speak:** "Holistic synergies and value exchanges will drive our innovation to win."

4. **Folksy corporate-speak:** "Better Together"

5. **Territory:** "Authenticity"

6. **Literal marketing value proposition:** "The easiest way for new parents to get their kids to sleep."

7. **Bullet-point list of stuff:** "Positive reviews, new design, long-lasting battery, waterproof."

8. **Lofty tagline:** "A new day every day."

9. **Single-minded proposition:** "Audis are clown-proof."

10. **Purpose:** "To empower dependability."

These statement types have their places, but many people use them interchangeably. This is confusing. Nevertheless, dealing with a lack of clarity about strategy is less difficult than dealing with a lack of desire for strategy.

## HOW OTHER PEOPLE BLOCK STRATEGY

Many strategists will experience internal creative blocks in their lives. This is amusing, because other people also like to block them, and so they may spend years in a vise grip of spiritual constipation. The ambiguity of the discipline, the status of the word "strategy," the threatening nature of insights, and the instability of the human workforce lead to many blocks. Here are some of the sentences that try to block a strategist.

"You're going too far." The benefit of writing the idea of a strategy in one sentence using short words is that this sentence does not pretend it is a campaign idea or tagline. There is still work for other people to do. But some people don't want much work to have happened at *all*. Either through a dogmatic advertising upbringing, years of bad creative briefs, or a fear of the specific, these people will say, "That looks like an idea. You've gone too far." And so you revert to vague notions and territories and other nothingness. Noncommittal words that do not try to solve a specific problem appear. Words like "performance," "durability," and "confidence." This isn't the strategy life.

"I already did the strategy." Many agency strategists work further away from strategy than they realize. With client companies housing increasing numbers of MBAs, consumer insight groups, and product strategists, there are departments of people who do not see a need for any of this from an agency. They build their calendars, promotions, and senses of self around the idea that they are master strategists.

They will not look an agency strategist in the eye. What's more, sometimes a client has briefed one agency before the others, and that agency has a strategist, so they can't fathom why this other strategist is here. This most often happens when media agencies and clients wish to give the advertising agency orders and not hear it talk back.

"What creative brief?" It's incredible how a few days of work after a briefing can make a strategy disappear. Some creative departments hate strategy or don't know what it is or think they are the strategists. Creative departments house wonderful brains and many of them are strategic, and, with experience, many can outdo a strategist. But some creative departments do their work in spite of strategy and in spite of strategists. This is a strange experience. It's as if the strategists don't exist.

"What's a strategist?" A lot of agencies make things for marketers without knowing if those things are successful. As they grow, they decide they need a strategist because other companies use strategists and clients will take them more seriously, and that's how more money will roll in. Then they realize the strategist will need time to research and think and this will slow them down, and, worse still, the company will need to be accountable for their work. Yuck. "Sorry, we don't need this strategy stuff."

"Yes, but that's not a trademarked approach like ours." Some clients need hefty processes to justify how they spend their calendars; some need them to convince people scared of intuition and art that there's a way to know, to really know, to know it all. And sometimes there is a method or technology being applied that really is uncommon and requires an extensive process. But history also gallops with tales of people who had a thought by thinking and then not thinking and then piecing together many half-thoughts into ideas that prospered in the world. "I lived my life. I received the brief. I did some research. I spoke with people. I considered my own life experience. I took a shower. Then one thought came to me. Then another. I raced to a piece of paper and wrote and wrote and wrote. I trademarked this approach as It Just Came To Me™. It will cost you one million dollars."

*It turns out that you need a strategy to be able to do strategy.*

## HOW TO KNOW WHEN STRATEGY HAS HAPPENED

To know when a problem has been usefully stated as a problem, an insight as an insight, an idea as an idea, or a strategy as a strategy, an experienced soul will look for three things: *mechanics, feelings,* and *reactions.* To know if a strategy has appeared, and if it might be a good one, you can look for traces of all of these elements.

First, determine the operating system you are working within, and what "strategy" means in your operating system:

- "What is 'strategy' in my life or in this company or within this project?"

- "What does the word 'strategy' mean'?"

- "Which other words help strategy happen and what do they mean?"

- "What do other people think strategy is?"

- "What do other people need from a strategy
  on this project?"

Then test out the mechanics; a strategy's moving parts
should be in good working order:

- "Does this strategy try to solve a problem?"

- "Who has this problem, and did we do research to find
  it or investigate it?"

- "Is there a strong argument that solving this problem
  will help the business?"

- "Is there at least one insight or revelation in this
  thinking—even if it's the problem?"

- "Is the strategy an idea? Is it a useful combination
  of things that don't usually belong together?"

Then search your feelings:

- "Does this feel right? Not 'right' as in correct, but as in
  a good way to tackle this problem?"

- "Does this tickle my brain? Are there new ways of seeing
  the world here?"

- "Does this feel flat or does it feel explosive? Do I feel
  its energy?"

- "Does this feel familiar? Have I heard it before?"

- "Can I see this? If I drew this strategy as a poster, could I feel my way to something daring?"

Next, look to reactions from other people:

- "Does this strategy feel familiar to them?"

- "Does this strategy confuse them?"

- "Does this strategy go too far into their work?"

- "Do people make primal sounds like snorts, giggles, chortles, or gasps when they hear it?"

- "Do they tell other people about it in good or not-good ways?"

Questions like these do not suggest an algorithm you can follow to arrive at brilliance. These questions are not meant to bully. They are an attempt to document what happens in the strategy brain over time and to shine a light on the unspoken.

In short, a strategy brain might run this gauntlet:

1. "Does this strategy confront the problem?"

2. "Is there an idea at the heart of strategy?"

3. "Does the strategy connect to a powerful theme?"

4. "Is the strategy defendable?"

5. "Can I see it?"

## TEN WAYS TO WRITE A STRATEGY

As a strategy grows into a plan, its expression can sprout tagalong weeds. Other people will add slides and words and noise and hesitation and fear to the deck. They'll water down the strategy while turning the presentation into an overgrown garden. Despite the long presentation, any colleagues who need to work with the strategy will actually need only a handful of words to allow it to enter their working lives and timesheets. As you think about what to give them, the following question can pull your brain back from the infestation: "What's the smallest unit of communication I can use to express this strategy?" Here are eleven techniques:

### 1. STRATEGY STATEMENTS

Strategy statements can take the structure "Show that X is Y" and arrive immediately at the idea in the strategy, and they can do so without trying to act like a tagline or campaign line. Using an imperative verb such as "show" or "make" also acknowledges the statement's audience—an internal team.

**Example:** Show that the New York Knicks are the best anger management in town.

### 2. SINGLE-MINDED PROPOSITIONS

There are many philosophies about the roles of single-minded propositions. Typically, they answer this question: "What's the most important thing we need to communicate?"

They can also merge with the idea of the unique selling proposition (USP), which answers the question: "What can we say that will get someone to try or buy this product or service?" Some people prefer a literal answer to these questions, and some are open to a lateral thought. You need to determine your own stance. A dash of science will help, but so will a spine. You might enjoy first writing a strategy statement to ensure the language keeps its feet on ground. Then you can shorten it to create a single-minded proposition.

There is an idea contained or implied in most propositions:

- X is Y

- X does Y

- X isn't Y

- X does not do Y

- X is the best at Y

- X is the worst at Y

- X is the most Y

- X is the least Y

- X is the opposite of Y

- X is the same as Y

- It's not X, it's Y

- X is for Y

It is worth your time to experiment with nouns and verbs more than adjectives, because there is something blunt and direct about rubbing two nouns against each other with the help of a take-no-prisoners verb. Many strategists' hopes can evaporate in debates about corporate-speak adjectives that nobody uses in the real world: "Are we delicious or nutritious? We are delicious and nutritious! Yay!" A brutal focus on simple verbs can strengthen the writing while preventing the disappearance of meaning.

**Example:** The New York Knicks cure New York anger.

(nouns: Knicks, anger | verb: cure)

On the other hand, debates about highfalutin adjectives and verbs, debates that match one nonsense word with another and refuse to take the thinking to the ground are nauseating:

- **We celebrate and empower the synergistic delivery of nutritious and delicious health outcomes via edible means to the receptors of the human condition.**

- *I think we 'elevate' and 'instigate' it.*

- **No, we are definitely going to celebrate and empower.**

- *I hear you. But 'synergistic' instead of 'holistic,' surely?*

- **Yes, you're right. Let's change that.**

- *Excellent. We'll get better work now.*

### 3. *BRAND ESSENCES*

Brand essences sit in the middle or top of a strategy shape and try to anchor all the thoughts that flow around them. Like any tool, they are useful until they aren't. They are less useful when they whisper words you can hear in aftershave and perfume advertising at Christmas. Below are brand essences that fall on the cringeworthy side:

- Hidden Captivation

- Passionate Irreverence

- Man-Made Masculinity

- Exceptionally Exceptional

- Nutritiously Delicious

A stoned royal from the 1800s might have uttered language like this while slumped in a throne, gown open at the thighs, goblet of red wine propping up the chin, crown close to falling off, soiled underpants visible to all. Issuing decree after decree after decree. It's total adjective abuse. And, worse, confusing. A brand essence won't be heard in public and will have other words near it in a presentation to deflect its ickiness, but that doesn't mean you should show an utter disrespect for the language and your teammates when writing one.

**Example:** New York Anger Management

### 4. CEO ANNOUNCEMENTS

CEOs of publicly traded companies are worth watching. They might signal a shift in strategy with a sneaky lateral thought. They've been known to say things like:

"We aren't in the business of building blocks, we're in the business of creativity."

"We aren't in the gaming business, we're in the entertainment business."

"We aren't in the sports business, we're in the therapy business."

"We aren't in the business of basketball, we're in the business of anger management."

"We aren't a yogurt brand, we're a lifestyle brand."

"We don't sell motorcycles, we sell a way of living."

"We don't sell shoes, we sell an attitude."

Most corporate-speak tries to signal broadly rather than specify an exact strategy, but the structure of announcements like these is a useful tool.

### 5. PURPOSE STATEMENTS

If a brand's purpose answers the question, "How do we serve humanity?," where the answer to the question does not have to please a majority of humanity, or even seem noble to a majority of people, and if the purpose sits at the heart of a business model and not in a department or CSR initiative or hashtag on social media, then the purpose statement can plow its way into being a powerful idea. Some purpose statements:

"We exist to help middle-aged couples re-establish intimacy."

"We exist to help New York deal with its anger issues."

"We exist to give every strategist a gang."

"We exist to help people face their fears."

Each of these statements contains an idea. There is a hint of corporate poetry about them, but the words are simple enough. The language doesn't try to whisk people into the heavens of angelic brand language that makes no sense outside of the clouds.

Whether you are thinking about a brand purpose or business purpose or deep-down life purpose, the format and goals of a purpose remain the same. This tool is even helpful if you inherit vague or useless strategy from another agency. You can throw an adjective such as "digital" in front of the word "purpose" to ensure various swim lanes feel respected and to ensure that there is thinking that resembles strategy.

Brand essence: Nutritiously Delicious (weak)

Proposition: Nutritious meals that taste great too. (weak)

Digital purpose: To give divorce-ready parents a night off from arguments.

These gymnastics are tricky, but sometimes a strategist's sanity requires magic.

### 6. VISION AND MISSION STATEMENTS

The problem with most vision and mission statements is that they are meconium. Meconium is the first and darkest of dark poos a newborn baby shares with their parents. It's the archetypal poo before the rest of life's poos. Most vision and mission statements are meconium because they are primal and naive crap. The one bonus is that because "meconium" sounds like a rare, expensive rock and few people know its definition, you can praise vision and mission statements as meconium and many will nod in satisfied agreement. What's less thrilling is the number of committees and offsite meetings that go into making this meconium. Businesspeople smear it onto walls in business parks everywhere. They don't care how much it stinks as longs as it dries. "Look, Ma, I just shat on the wall. Quick, let's take a selfie in front of this. It won't happen again in my lifetime."

And so business parks blush with phrases like "To empower the betterment of the healthcare and ecology system using our technologically advanced advancements to march forward with humanity's dignity and proximity." Sometimes the word "vision" will sit in front of these words. Or "mission." It's as if nobody cares what it's called or if it's called anything at all. But you do, because strategy is words.

Here is how a strategist can think of these words:

- *A vision is how the world will be different because of the company's work.*

   "How will the world change because of us?"

- *A mission is how the company will do this.*

   "What's our way of trying to make this change happen?"

Answers to these questions can take many structures and stretch into pages. However, single sentences and short phrases will help them live and not baffle their readers. Here's another way to state what visions and missions are, and some examples:

**Vision:**   **A world in which ... something is different for someone else.**

**Mission:** **Our mission is to ... tackle a task to bring the vision closer to reality.**

Vision:     A world in which people can enjoy touch even as they age.

Mission:     To help middle-aged couples re-establish intimacy.

Vision:     A world in which people who think for a living aren't their own worst enemies.

Mission:     To give strategists a gang.

Vision:     A New York which is less angry.

Mission:   To help New York deal with its anger issues through basketball.

## 7. STRATEGY STORIES

Strategists often disappear into presentations and briefing templates before doing any thinking. This isn't wrong, but there are other ways to think and there may appear periods in your career where you would like to think outside of a template. Choosing a free format such as a blank piece of paper, some way to put down thoughts (pen, paper, paint), and a question are all you need. A strategy story is not a thing. It's not a technical term. It does not seek to become a thing in the way that a concept like "Path to Purchase" is a thing. All it wants you to do is take one piece of blank paper and words from your brain, and ask the question, "Well, how could I explain this strategy in one page where I capture the most important twists and turns?"

You might write one or three or ten strategy stories on the same topic. *You might even sell these stories, and not your time.*

You can write a strategy story in the first person or third person, in a silly voice, in the voice of a client, or in the voice of a research interviewee. You can add challenges such as writing with words that have one or two syllables only, starting every sentence with the same letter, writing with dialogue only, or using ten quotes from research. These are your decisions. And these decisions encourage you to treat all acts of strategy as acts of creativity, to explore new ways of working, to allow streams of words to fall out because you know that the work starts after the words are out, and to commit to coherent ideas that survive by captivating teammates.

### DRAMBUIE

Drambuie is a Scotch whisky blessed with honey, herbs, and spices. We need to get younger people to drink it but young people don't drink it because old people drink it. That's what the research says.*

A fool's errand would be to try to make Drambuie the drink most drunk by young adults who drink. Drambuie won't hit their palettes how they want it to hit and it isn't cheap–in New York, a bottle sits on the shelf with a price tag of $40-$55.

Just as well not all young adults are the same. Some young adults are actually old. You know the kind–you went to high school with them, didn't see them for a few years, and now they're twenty five years old going on sixty nine. They dress old, smoke cigars, talk about property prices and golf and yachts, play cards always cards, and they bemoan modern etiquette because, in the modern world, they are called sexist if they hold the door open for a woman, or, if they are a woman, they don't like how young women sometimes wear pants and not gowns to special events. They're old at heart.

They believe that youth is wasted on the young but they also believe that old age is wasted on the old. The old have all the money, dominate the free world's elections, live on cruise ships, own all the houses, and own all the holiday homes. Drambuie drinkers believe that acting old can make old-people things happen … while they're young.

All the other fancy drink brands try to tell their histories in a young way–"Look, we were once young, too." But, at Drambuie, well we're going to act our age. After all, our founder Prince Charles Stuart Edward was old when he was young. At 26, he fled battle and holed up with the MacKinnon clan to whom he gave the Drambuie recipe. And guess what people called him? The "Young Pretender" and the "Young Chevalier."

Drambuie doesn't need to act young to get young people to drink it. It needs to find the young people who like acting old and show them that acting old can bring forward all those things others will need to wait decades for. Drambuie can make the best of aging happen sooner.

* This is a hypothetical strategy in response to a make-believe marketing brief made by hosts of the *Son of a Pitch* podcast Vincent Usher and Max Learmont.

**In short**

Problem

Drambuie is what old people drink

Audience

The Old At Heart - for people who've aged young

Insight

Drambuie drinkers believe that acting old makes good old-people things happen young

Advantage

Drambuie has been old since it was young

(the recipe came from a man who was too old too young)

Strategy

We'll show that Drambuie makes the best of aging happen sooner

Campaign Idea

**Act Their Age**

A campaign that shows people how a Drambuie lifestyle is a fast track to the life they think
they'll never have or, if they get it, they'll be too old to enjoy it.

Communications Idea

We'll turn up where young people admire what's old - museums, art galleries, libraries,

opera, golf courses, cruises, Florida, retirement homes, obituaries, cemeteries, morgues,

memorials, heritage sites and ruins, the old towns of popular cities.

One common structure for a strategy story is this:

1. "Here is the situation as we first encountered it and why it was this way."

2. "But we researched it and the reasons for the situation were not what they seemed."

3. "At first, the difference murmured to us when we found this thing."

4. "Then we found other things in interviews and research papers, and it grew."

5. "And it made us wonder: what if there is another way to look at this?"

6. "So we did. And here's what we think."

7. "And here's why we think this."

The aim is to use as little business-speak as possible and to avoid making commentary on the strategy or strategy process. A strategy story can take thirty minutes or half a day to write. If you write the same story from different perspectives, you can pay attention to which of the stories takes the longest and why. Was the story hard to make sense of? Was it the most captivating and deserved the most toil? With a story in hand, you can also surprise trusting clients by asking them to close their eyes and then reading the story to them, and doing this before any additional work happens. Even selecting a strategy story to read is a major strategic decision, because a confident client will know the right story when they hear it.

The final benefit of developing a strategy story is that, once you know your client and team are entranced by the initial tale, you'll have a presentation structure to guide the full pitch down the line. The power of strategy stories is almost too good to be true, but that's only because many ways of working are too bad to be true.

### 8. CREATIVE BRIEFS

Creative briefs are important, but they are not sacred. They capture your strategy on a page but they don't absolve you of speaking with your team. They provide structure but they aren't inflexible. They make bold statements but they don't fend off questions. In the wrong hands, they are a false climax. Even if they are the culmination of weeks of work, they don't stop thinking. They start it.

The question "How do I write an inspiring creative brief?" isn't one question—it's tens of questions. To answer it, you need to understand the agency's philosophy, how the agency uses language, what the strategy department does, what projects and teams need from creative briefs and whether each project or team has different needs, as well as how creative briefs interface with clients' marketing briefs. You might also prefer to write a haunting creative brief or a creative brief that traps the brains of a creative team with thoughts they can't fight off because they're so charismatic. All of this means the only reasonable answer to the original question is this: "With words."

Trying to find the perfect creative brief template is like trying to find the perfect plot for a movie. Screenwriters are

**Creative Brief**

# Drambuie

**Problem**

Drambuie is what old people drink

**Insight**

Old-at-heart Drambuie drinkers believe that acting old makes old-people things happen young

**Advantage**

Drambuie has been old since it was young

**Strategy**

We'll show that Drambuie makes the best of aging happen sooner

| Briefing date | Version | Project name | |
|---|---|---|---|
| 22 April, 2020 | 1 | Drambuie relaunch | |
| Launch date | Marketing lead | Creative lead | Production budget |
| 21 May, 2020 | NAME | NAME | $XXX,000 |

**Creative Brief**

# Drambuie

| | |
|---|---|
| **Audience** | The Old at Heart. They're in their twenties but they act much older. They don't fear adulthood; they think childhood is for kids. They love a country club, a slow drive through wine country in an old prestigious car, history museums and watching opera. They like a cigar, ocean cruises, and owning homes years before their peers. They like steak houses. And they like Scotch. |
| **Insight** | Old-at-heart Drambuie drinkers believe that acting old makes old-people things happen young |
| **Strategy** | We'll show that Drambuie makes the best of aging happen sooner |
| **Proposition** | Drambuie helps you act beyond your age |
| **Proof** | The recipe came from a man known as the "Young Pretender" and the "Young Chevalier" who, at 26, was leading battles. What's more, the taste of Drambuie takes a knowing palette to appreciate it. And the price needs you to be successful and to want to spend your success on fine things. |
| **Tone** | A modern Great Gatsby - dripping in splendor, going places, astute, traditional but not stuffy |
| **Success** | Increase awareness among this audience by 15% |
| **Mandatories** | Logo. Bottle. Fancy glass. Ice. Brand guidelines. |
| **Deliverables** | Initially, a campaign idea that can stretch from television into online video, pre-rolls, social posts, out of home, a stunt, PR, and into the trade. Communications plan to come. |

usually aware of story structures that have worked before but if there were a perfect structure and one way to build it, every movie would be a success. And the same.

The availability of a lone creative brief template–perfect or otherwise–can even cause problems. One author's good intentions may detour into a savage series of workarounds as they try to write a brief for an email newsletter in a brief template intended for a campaign idea. A triage of creative brief templates may need to appear.

Each template would do its job, no more. And you'd choose a template depending on your answer to these questions:

1. Do we need a new brand or campaign idea?

2. Are we working an existing brand idea into a new campaign?

3. Do we just need to churn this thing out for one particular channel?

If you work with marketing clients, you'll need to consider the difference between a marketing brief and a creative brief. Each brief has a different set of audiences and roles. The marketing brief aims to unlock budget from businesspeople and give the external or internal agencies an understanding about the situation the brand faces, what needs to change, who the audience is and why, metrics, budgets, timings, and decision-making processes. Perhaps there's a hint of research and media channel selection too. The creative brief's audience is the agency and, especially, the teams coming up with the campaign ideas.

Should an agency help the marketing team write their marketing brief?

Should an agency accept a verbal brief from a client?

Must a marketing team approve an agency's creative brief?

You can answer these questions yourself. What's important is to remember the audiences and roles of each brief and to stand up for them.

Marketing briefs cause tension when there's nothing in them. Many long marketing briefs contain very little so this isn't a matter of long or short. It's more a matter of excessively broad audience definitions, traces of copy-and-paste from the last marketing brief, a desire to do and measure everything so nobody can poke holes in the brief, treating the brief like a dumping ground for product specifications, and jargon.

Marketing briefs also cause tension when marketers intend them as creative briefs. Most strategists have seen a client's eyes say, "What do you mean, 'Here's our creative brief'? I don't need your strategy messing with my strategy. I did the strategy. I wrote the brief. Now you're just being difficult." This kind of marketer sees agencies not as thinkers but as executioners of someone else's thinking.

Creative briefs comprise both logistics and thinking. Logistics can include the name of the creative brief author, the client's brand name, a project name, a job number, the document version, the budget for production and media, names of key team members and approvers, project timings, and deliverables.

Most creative briefs offer answers to these kinds of questions:

What are we trying to achieve?

How will we measure success?

Who's the audience?

What do we need to convince them of?

How can we support our argument?

How and where will this campaign appear?

And they label their answers in conventional ways like this: objectives, audience, insight, single-minded proposition, reasons to believe, channels, brand tone, project considerations, and mandatories.

Most of your favorite work will turn on a handful of phrases and ideas—fewer than you'd have expected before you made enough work that some of it could be called your favorite. But creative briefs are political beasts and many strategists want to display as much of their work as possible to show they're diligent people, in the hope something sticks, or because they aren't sure what they're doing. You can apply techniques similar to those used in strategy stories to writing a creative brief—different voices, short words, and short phrases. Dare to use no marketing language. Say your strategy out loud. See if it makes sense. Take it for a walk and whittle it. In a capable operating system, you always need less than you think.

### 9. STRATEGY SHAPES

Just because a strategy exists in a triangle, keyhole, onion, donut, or house does not mean it is good. Shapes are fun. Shapes pretend things are simple and official. But when the shapes contain vague, overlong words, then they aren't worth much more than the printed paper upon which they stand.

On the following page, you'll find one potential shape based on the concepts in this book.

### 10. PRESS RELEASE HEADLINES

The agency Crispin Porter + Bogusky made press release headlines popular in creative departments. "We won't see the idea until you write it as a press release." Writing a concept as a press release headline forces an interlocking set of useful consequences:

1. A press release headline is short

2. Shortness can lead to clarity

3. If the idea is confused, that will immediately be apparent

4. A press release exists to excite other people in the hope they'll share it

5. A press release headline might encourage people to drop business-speak

**Example:** The New York Knicks Take Basketball To New York's Angriest Street Corners

**PERCEPTUAL TARGET**

Target Name

A short synopsis
describing key beliefs
and behaviours of
the audience

**PLATFORM**

A short phrase

that brings to life

the strategy

**COMPANY BELIEF**

The belief at the heart
of the company

**VISION**

"A world in
which... " – How
the world will
change when
the company
succeeds

**BRAND PROMISE**

A short

statement that

anchors all

**MISSION**

How the
company executes
the vision

**THE PROBLEM WE SOLVE**

The problem the company exists
to solve – possibly a lateral thought
or insight (i.e. not obvious)

**LOGO**

Tagline

**TONE**

We choose 4
phrases to describe
how the brand talks

**BEHAVIORS**

We choose 4
phrases to describe
how the brand
behaves

**VALUES**

We choose 5 values
that drive all
company decisions
(not corporatespeak)

**ENEMIES**

We identify 4 things
that are the opposite
of what we stand for

@MARKPOLLARD

The challenge with this method will pierce the face of most public relations practitioners when you mention it. Advertising agencies might cite the method in the hope that their campaign idea becomes famous and that the idea's fame will make the client's brand famous. A lot of PR work happens the other way around or it might see a campaign idea from an advertising agency as inconsequential. PR's work is to manage the reputation of the client and their brand more than it is to manage the reputation of the client's advertising campaigns. It's a form of aikido where the advertising agency risks doing aikido to the breeze.

## COMMUNICATIONS FRAMEWORKS – A SHORT WORD

A communications framework usually happens after a campaign idea has sprung into a project. It exists to help the campaign idea appear in a way where the idea and how it appears play with each other and create more energy in their play based on an understanding of the audience they will interact with and the resources at the campaign's disposal.

If a campaign idea deals with anger, are there angry places the idea could appear? If a campaign idea deals with intimacy, are there intimate places or places that could use intimacy in which the idea could appear? If a campaign idea deals with forgetfulness, are there places people go to remember or to find things they've forgotten or to improve their memories that make sense for the campaign to play with?

Communications plans try to solve these problems:

1.  Mindless media plans that focus only on efficiency, not effectiveness,

2.  Campaign ideas that are just TV or video scripts but not ideas, and

3.  Trying to get one piece of communication to say everything.

The main tweak in process you need to insist on is simple: get a shortlist of media channels the audience uses and that your budget is considering before you write the creative brief then allow the campaign idea to lead the final decision about which media channels are best suited to the idea. Use up-to-date marketing science plus what you've learned from the brand's previous campaigns to inform all of this but allow space for the idea, the art, and the intuition to shape the final plan in unexpected ways.

Let's say you're looking for love and you locate a block in the Upper West Side of New York where you think you have good chances of finding the kind of lover you need in your life. You could walk the block, stick your head into every door and say, "I'm looking for love." Or you could stick your head into the doors of places where you might find other people looking for love–bars, libraries, and supermarkets–and say, "I'm looking for love." Or you could go to the same couple of bars every week and randomly approach people and say, "I'm looking for love." These three scenarios seem sensible because most creative briefs and media plans read like this. However, after years of trying these techniques, you might decide to think about what you need and what you have to offer and then appear at specific times in specific ways.

Let's say you'd like to try the love of someone who uses their brain for fun, but you also want a lover who's interested in your brain. You might choose to turn up to trivia nights and work out how to appear intelligent in front of the right people and talk about the most challenging questions and answers of the evening. Let's say you want more rhythm in your life, but you'd like someone else to make the important decisions. You might choose to turn up to salsa evenings, show enthusiasm, but feign the need for someone else to lead your moves. Let's say you like people who drink until the night ends. You might choose to become a bar tender and listen without saying anything.

Your love life knows its own communications plan. It asks questions like these:

What do I want?

What do the people I want want?

Where do they go to get it?

What will I say to get it?

How will I behave to get it?

How will I know if I'm getting it?

How do I keep getting it?

The bits about libraries, supermarkets, and your love life knowing what it wants were made up. People don't know what they want but they think they'll find it on the internet. This seems like a chain of non-commitment, doesn't it?

There are a few common ways to build a basic communications plan. We'll use our Hello Hallow campaign idea "Play with Death" from earlier for this exercise. The campaign features adults with toddler faces playing with what scares them in a sandbox. And remember–the goals of a communications plan are to ensure the message and the medium work with each other, and to help apportion money and time to all the activity.

The first way is to deploy a generic three-act structure such as Tease, Launch, Sustain. The Tease phase asks, "How and where can we get people's attention in a sneaky way?" The Launch phases asks, "How and where can we make this feel epic?" The Sustain phase asks, "How and where can we keep the campaign going?"

The second way deploys language more closely connected to the campaign idea: 1. Scare – "We're going to scare the crap out of people." 2. Sandbox – "We're going to invite people to play with what scares them." 3. Sell – "We'll ask them to buy the product."

The third way leads with how the brand wants to persuade people, with what it wants to say. For example, 1. When you play with what scares you, it will scare you less. 2. Many other people love playing with what scares them and this is how it has helped them. 3. You can buy the product here.

# HELLO HALLOW

## PLAY WITH DEATH

| TEASE | SCARE |
|---|---|
| LAUNCH | SANDBOX |
| SUSTAIN | SELL |

| MESSAGE 1 | BARRIER 1 |
|---|---|
| MESSAGE 2 | BARRIER 2 |
| MESSAGE 3 | BARRIER 3 |

| CHANNELS | | | |
|---|---|---|---|
| TACTICS | | | |

@MARKPOLLARD

The fourth way leads with the objections people might have expressed toward the product. For example, 1. "I don't want to think about death," 2. "I don't like playing games," 3. "I don't have friends to play with." The messages, tactics, and channels would then answer back to these objections like this, 1. "Here's why it's useful to think about death," 2. "Yes, you do. Remember that one time? Come play. See?" 3. "Come on, now. Just ask them over or make new friends here."

You could choose channels based on where people go to experience fear or to avoid fear. You could add channels based on where people go to play or to avoid play. You could add channels based on where people go when death is near, when friends and family are dying, when death has happened, or near memorial situations. The more extreme and tone-deaf of these options aren't yours to discard until you've explored them. You never know what you'll come up with.

Communications frameworks like these—and there are as many as there are people who do communications planning—help ideas stand a better chance of getting attention and traction. They intend to make budgets work smarter and they have the secret bonus of helping creative teams make more justifiable work, not just zany work for zany's sake. Although sometimes zany needs love in the Upper West Side of Manhattan, too.

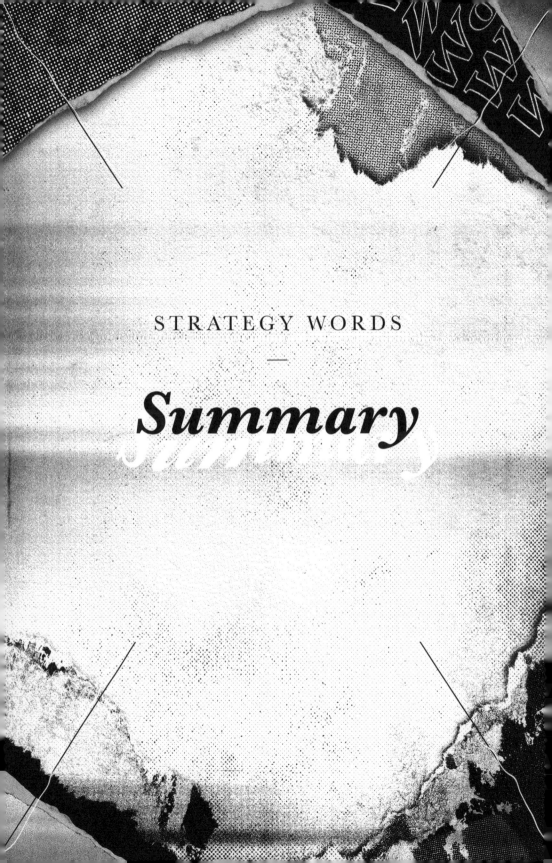

STRATEGY WORDS

—

*Summary*

# *Summary*

S trategy isn't meant to hurt. It's not torture, it's not a divorce, and it's not an abusive relationship. It can feel like these three things all at once though. Throw in a strategist's fear of being found out, add a dash of constant confusion, and words that make no sense, and it's a profession that hurts itself more than it hurts other people. If words hurt, strategy words can hurt the most.

Its pain rumbles in the clash between two continental plates that pretend the other continent doesn't exist: 1. Strategy is important work and to do it makes you important and to do it well requires expensive words. 2. The ideas we all spend time with hit us in the gut and we can explain them in a short series of simple words.

So, gather your frameworks and gather your words and head for Flero. Andrea Pirlo might not be there waiting for you but the echo of his words will be: less running, more play.

Keep on you at all times a handful of questions:

Where am I trying to go?

What do I think is the best way to try to get there?

Which words will best help me make my way there?

Then frolic with your frameworks and practice how you think and put your ideas into public with good people at your back. Life will come and go but when you stare death in the face, what words will you say to it?

# Final *Words*

# Final *Words*

Here's how to get good at strategy: words. Start with words, continue with words, and finish with words. You have one job—get good at words.

Why? At some point, everything is words. If you can see it, it's words. If you can think it, it's words. If you can feel it, it's words.

You live in a world of your own making and you use words to sustain it because you see the world through the words you've used to create it. Like everyone else, you choose the meaning of these words because their meaning keeps your world's meaning alive. Words are your world's life support. And a word you use every day means something else to someone else somewhere else, because that's how that someone keeps his or her world alive.

Yes, words make worlds. A novel's words can take us into a stranger's life. Two words can seal a promise. Words can start and end marriages, deals, and wars. One word can forever follow a newborn. A magic word can help a child get what she needs. Final words can give peace to a life as it ends.

You can use words as maps, torches, and breadcrumbs.
You can use words as fireworks, tickles, and palliatives.
You can locate yourself with words, stand a career on words,
and expose ideas good and bad with words.

If your words can, you can.

When you do strategy, you make meaning from mess, and
words do this for you. Research is a hunt for words—you can
watch and count for a long time, but at some point, you'll use
words to guide and later explain your counting. An insight
updates how you see the world—it gives you words that
introduce you to something magnificent that you never knew
existed, or it gives you new words for something you knew existed
but that you now understand with magnified meaning. A creative
brief is a brave attempt to capture only the most important
words. A presentation is a long set of words that gets you to the
creative brief. An idea happens in words. Job titles, too, otherwise
you wouldn't keep asking for that promotion. Words can do
almost anything and they excel at seeing through chaos.

But words aren't easy. Words will stumble through you and
plop into the world, hoping you can teach them to walk. Many
words will need to take that walk to draw you to the one word
that can run a marathon. And, on some days, words will not
stumble out at all.

At their worst, words make everything hard. If you think
word length impresses people, if you think education earns you
more syllables, if you think presentations are better with more
slides, understand this: big words are hiding places, and good

strategy doesn't hide. Good strategy wants to be seen and it uses words with bite to reveal itself. So, you have a choice— either do the hard work of finding words that work hard, or use words that make hard work for everyone else.

There are ways to dismiss words. You can say actions speak louder than words. But here's the thing: words act louder than actions. Words lead to actions and they tell the stories of those actions. Words are the brains and memories of actions.

You can try to spurn words. You can say words don't matter at all. Yet you'd be using words to make that point.

In strategy, words are all that matters.

Strategy is your words.

*Word*

# *Word*

A lot of people are in this book. If you squint your eyes at the right parts of the right pages, you'll see them. I'd like to thank these people whose specific whispers are here:

Todd Sampson, Julian Cole, Tony Clement, Clare La Palombara, Ilona Levchenko, Rob Grundel, Rob Estreitinho, Miguel D'Souza, Lauren Joyce, Vincent McSweeney, Heather LeFevre, Adam Pierno, Lucy Cochran, Faris Yakob, Rosie Yakob, Scott Davis, Rachel Mercer, Kieran Ots, Justine Bloome, Sophie Hauptfuhrer, Harry Bee, Brian Dolan, Mark Cripps, Nayantara Dutta, Kieran Antill, Suzy Batiz, Hugh Munro, Marie-Claire Dean, Elizabeth Lukas, Becky Wang, Natalie Tran, Sam Hammington, Tim Levinson, Jerrold McGrath, Matthew Kentmann, Tom Donald, Mo Seetubtim, Jonathan Colmenares, Edwin Rager, Vikki Ross, Deborah Morrison, Eaon Pritchard, Ryan Wallman, and Andrea Pirlo.

Also, thank you to Lauren Wilson for editing the book, as well as Nerrida Funnell and Ben Funnell for designing the book.

# About the *Author*

Mark Pollard is a strategist, speaker, and writer bred in Sydney and alive in New York. He once published *Stealth*, Australia's first full color hip hop magazine with a CD-Rom, and hosted Sydney's longest running hip hop radio show *The Mothership Connection*. Now, he focuses his life on helping people who think for a living live.

At Mighty Jungle, Mark has worked with The Economist, Poo-Pourri, Facebook, Twitter, the Wall Street Journal, Jabra, La Colombe, Mozilla, and Euronews.

He's spoken at the *Cannes Lions International Festival of Creativity*, he's trained strategists on nearly every continent, he pairs with Julian Cole to dispense the strategy binge session *The Strategy Megaclass*, and he runs the community and podcast *Sweathead*.

He's contributed to tens of publications around the world including Vice, Quartz, Wharton's *Future of Advertising*, and the Society of Digital Agencies Report.

You can find him @markpollard and at www.markpollard.net

You can email him here: mark.pollard@mightyjungle.co

# Bibliography

# Bibliography

Alain de Botton, "How Romanticism Ruined Love", *ABC*, July 19, 2016 https://www.abc.net.au/religion/how-romanticism-ruined-love/10096750.

Anonymous, "Eager Exponent of Zen," *Life 50*, April 21, 1961, 88A-B.

Bob Gill, *Logo Mania*, Rockport Publishers, 2006.

Brent Adamson, Matthew Dixon, Nicholas Toman, "The End of Solution Sales", *Harvard Business Review*, July-August 2012.

Bruce Lee, Gilbert Johnson (Introduction), *Tao of Jeet Kune Do*, Black Belt Communications, 1975.

Dacher Keltner, Jonathan Haidt, "Approaching awe, a moral, spiritual, and aesthetic emotion", *Cognition and Emotion* 17 (2):297-314 (2003).

Daniel H. Pink, *Drive: The Surprising Truth About What Motivates Us*, Riverhead Books, 2011.

Ed Spielman, Jerry Thorpe, Herman Miller, *Kung Fu*, Warner Bros. Television, 1972-1975.

Edward de Bono, *The Use of Lateral Thinking*, International Center for Creative Thinking, 1967.

Edward L. Bernays, *Crystallizing Public Opinion*, Kessinger Publishing, 2004 (first published 1923).

Ephrat Livni, "Keyboards Are Overrated. Cursive Is Back and It's Making Us Smarter," *Quartz*, July 25, 2017, https://qz.com/1037057/keyboards-are-overrated-cursive-is-back-and-its-making-us-smarter.

Erin Meyer, *The Culture Map: Breaking Through the Invisible Boundaries of Global Business*, PublicAffairs, 2014.

Ernest Tupes, Raymond Christal,"Recurrent personality factors based on trait ratings," *USAF ASD Technical Report* (61–97), 1961.

Gary Chapman, *The Five Love Languages*, Northfield Publishing, 1992 (Later printing edition 1995)

Henry Engler, "MLS making gains to bridge 'cultural void': Pirlo," *Reuters*, May 20, 2016, https://www.reuters.com/article/us-soccer-mls-pirlo-idUSKCN0YB23Y.

James Andreoni, Eleanor Brown, and Isaac Rischall. 2003. "Charitable Giving by Married Couples: Who Decides and Why Does It Matter?", *Journal of Human Resources* 38:111–133.

Jane Onyanga-Omara, "Mystery of London Fog That Killed 12,000 Finally Solved." *USA Today*, December 23, 2016, https://www.usatoday.com/story/news/world/2016/12/13/scientists-say-theyve-solved-mystery-1952-london-killer-fog/95375738.

John Kay, *Obliquity: Why Our Goals Are Best Achieved Indirectly*, Penguin Books; Reprint edition, 2012.

John Tierney, "Will You Be E-Mailing This Column? It's Awesome", *The New York Times*, February 8, 2010, https://www.nytimes.com/2010/02/09/science/09tier.html.

Johnny Cash, *I Walk the Line*, Sun Studio, 1956.

Julia Cameron, *The Artist's Way: 25th Anniversary Edition Paperback*, TarcherPerigee, 2016.

K. Anders Ericsson, Ralf Th. Krampe, and Clemens Tesch-Romer, "The Role of Deliberate Practice in the Acquisition of Expert Performance," *Psychological Review* 1993, Vol. 100. No. 3, 363-406.

Kim Kauffman, "Leo's Cannes Contenders: Always '#LikeAGirl'", *LeoBurnett.com* https://leoburnett.com/articles/work/what-it-means-to-be-likeagirl/.

Kyle Mahowald, Phillip Isola, Evelina Fedorenko, E. L. Gibson, Aude Oliva, "Memorable Words Are Monogamous: The Role of Synonymy and Homonymy in Word Recognition Memory," 2018/02/05, https://psyarxiv.com/p6kv9/.

Leslie A. Perlow, Constance Noonan Hadley, Eunice Eun, "Stop the Meeting Madness," *Harvard Business Review*, July-August 2017, https://hbr.org/2017/07/stop-the-meeting-madness.

Maria K. Kronfeldner, "Creativity Naturalized", *The Philosophical Quarterly*, Vol. 59, No. 237, October 2009.

Michel Foucault, A.M. Sheridan-Smith (Translator), *Discipline and Punish: The Birth of the Prison*, Vintage, 1995 (first published 1975).

Mithoefer, M. C., Mithoefer, Mithoefer, A. T., Feduccia,
A. A., Jerome, L., Wagner, M., Wymer, J., Holland, J.,
Hamilton, S., Yazar-Klosinski, B., Emerson, A., Doblin, R.
(2018) "3,4-Methylenedioxymethamphetamine (MDMA)-
Assisted Psychotherapy for Post-Traumatic Stress Disorder
in Military Veterans, Firefighters, and Police Officers: A
Randomised, Double-Blind, Dose-Response, Phase 2 Clinical
Trial." *The Lancet Psychiatry*.

Pauline Rose Clance and Suzanne Ament Imes, "The Imposter
Phenomenon in High Achieving Women: Dynamics and
Therapeutic Intervention," *Psychotherapy: Theory, Research and
Practice* 15, no. 3 (Fall 1978).

Richard D. Lewis, *When Cultures Collide: Leading Across Culture*,
Nicholas Brealey International, 2006 (Originally published 1996).

Rob Reiner, Cary Elwes, Mandy Patinkin, Chris Sarandon,
Christopher Guest, Wallace Shawn, Andre, et al. 1987.
*The Princess Bride*. Burbank, CA: Princess Bride Ltd.

Terence McKenna, *Food of the Gods*, Bantam Books, 1993
(first published 1992).

Tom Monahan, "The Hard Evidence: Business Is Slowing
Down", *Fortune.com*, January 28, 2016, https://fortune.
com/2016/01/28/business-decision-making-project-
management/.

Victor Frankl, Harold S. Kushner (Foreword), William J.
Winslade (Afterword), Isle Lasch (Translator), *Man's Search for
Meaning*, Beacon Press, 2006 (first published 1946).

Will Dahlgreen, "Why are Nobel Prize winners getting older?", *BBC News*, October 7, 2016, https://www.bbc.com/news/science-environment-37578899.

William Goldman, *The Princess Bride*, Ballantine Books, 2003 (first published 1973).

Wu-Tang Clan, *Enter the Wu-Tang (36 Chambers)*, Loud, 1993.

# STRATEGY is YOUR WORDS

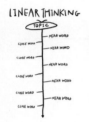

LINEAR THINKING

TOPIC

CLOSE WORD — NEAR WORD
CLOSE WORD — NEAR WORD
— NEAR WORD
CLOSE WORD — NEAR WORD
— NEAR WORD
CLOSE WORD — NEAR WORD

IDEAS are
THOUGHTS,
but not all
THOUGHTS
are IDEAS.

YOUR MISSION:
PLAY
MORE THAN YOU
RUN

LATERAL THINKING

TOPIC A { IDEA } TOPIC B

WHEN YOU SAY
ONE THING,
IT IS NEVER
ONE THING.

---

PROBLEM
└ THIS PROBLEM IS CAUSING EVERYTHING
PROBLEM

PROBLEM

PROBLEM
└ YOU THINK THIS IS THE PROBLEM

INSIGHT
NOVEL IDEA
TAGLINE AND
MANIFESTO
ALL THE THINGS
CLICHÉ
WINNING HAPPENS HIGH

DUMP-A-PROBLEM
1 _____
2 _____
3 _____
4 _____
5 _____
6 _____
7 _____

S.W.O.T.

STRENGTHS | WEAKNESSES

OPPORTUNITIES | THREATS
↑ or ↓ | ↑ or ↓

• INTERNAL • EXTERNAL

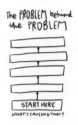

The PROBLEM behind
the PROBLEM

START HERE
WHAT'S CAUSING THAT?

---

INSIGHTS
are GLITCHES
that REWIRE
HOW WE SEE
OURSELVES

The PYRAMID of
ADVANTAGE

LOVE
to HAVE
LIKE to HAVE
HAVE to HAVE

The BENEFIT LADDER

EMOTION
HOW THIS FEELS

FUNCTION
WHAT THEY DO

FEATURES
THE THINGS

The PRODUCT WORLD

| FEATURES | FUNCTIONS | BENEFITS |
| --- | --- | --- |
| | | |

| TRIGGERS | USE CASES | EDGE CASES |
| --- | --- | --- |
| | | |

MAP what you FIND

The DECISION FUNNEL

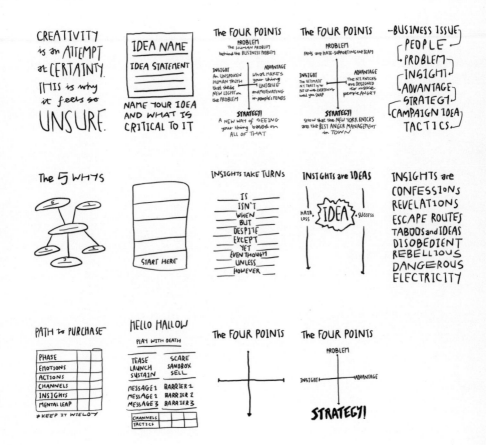

CREATIVITY is an ATTEMPT at CERTAINTY. THIS is why it feels so UNSURE.

IDEA NAME
IDEA STATEMENT
NAME YOUR IDEA AND WHAT IS CRITICAL TO IT

The FOUR POINTS
PROBLEM
The HUMAN PROBLEM behind the BUSINESS PROBLEM
INSIGHT
An UNSPOKEN HUMAN TRUTH that sheds NEW LIGHT on the PROBLEM
ADVANTAGE
What MAKES your thing UNIQUE and MOTIVATING in people's MINDS
STRATEGY!
A NEW WAY of SEEING your thing based on ALL OF THAT

The FOUR POINTS
PROBLEM
FANS are HATE-SUPPORTING the TEAM
INSIGHT
The ULTIMATE NY TRAIT is to PUT UP with EVERYTHING until you SNAP
ADVANTAGE
The NY KNICKS are DESIGNED to make people ANGRY
STRATEGY!
Show that the NEW YORK KNICKS are the BEST ANGER MANAGEMENT in TOWN

—BUSINESS ISSUE
PEOPLE
PROBLEM
INSIGHT
ADVANTAGE
STRATEGY
CAMPAIGN IDEA
TACTICS

The 5 WHYS

START HERE

INSIGHTS TAKE TURNS
IS
ISN'T
WHEN
BUT
DESPITE
EXCEPT
YET
EVEN THOUGH
UNLESS
HOWEVER

INSIGHTS are IDEAS
HAIR LOSS     IDEA     SUCCESS

INSIGHTS are
CONFESSIONS
REVELATIONS
ESCAPE ROUTES
TABOOS and IDEAS
DISOBEDIENT
REBELLIOUS
DANGEROUS
ELECTRICITY

PATH to PURCHASE

| PHASE | |
| EMOTIONS | |
| ACTIONS | |
| CHANNELS | |
| INSIGHTS | |
| MENTAL LEAP | |

* KEEP IT WIELDY

HELLO HALLOW
PLAY WITH DEATH

| TEASE LAUNCH SUSTAIN | SCARE SANDBOX SELL |
| MESSAGE 1 | BARRIER 1 |
| MESSAGE 2 | BARRIER 2 |
| MESSAGE 3 | BARRIER 3 |

| CHANNELS | |
| TACTICS | |

The FOUR POINTS

The FOUR POINTS
PROBLEM
INSIGHT     ADVANTAGE
STRATEGY!

@MARKPOLLARD